STUDIES IN THE ROMANCE VERB

Studies in the Romance Verb

Essays Offered to Joe Cremona on the Occasion
of His 60th Birthday

Edited by
Nigel Vincent and Martin Harris

CROOM HELM
London & Canberra

© 1982 Nigel Vincent and Martin Harris
Croom Helm Ltd, 2-10 St John's Road, London SW11

British Library Cataloguing in Publication Data

Studies in the Romance verb.
  1. Cremona, Joe 2. Romance languages — Verbs
  — Addresses, essays, lectures
  I. Vincent, Nigel   II. Harris, Martin
  III. Cremona, Joe
  448.2   RC119

  ISBN 0-7099-2602-2

Printed and bound in Great Britain by
Biddles Ltd, Guildford and King's Lynn

CONTENTS

DEDICATION

Thematic and organisational unity is something we
hope the reader will find in this book; it is certainly something we believe to be there for the
finding. But a historically earlier and perhaps
intellectually more deepseated unity, and one which
inspires the overall coherence of content, is to be
found in the biographical fact that each of the
contributors to this volume studied Romance languages
and general linguistics in the University of Cambridge
and took Part II of the Modern and Mediaeval Languages Tripos at some stage during the period of
Joe Cremona's tenure, more than a quarter-century
long and still uncompleted, of that University's
Lectureship in Romance Philology.
    Joe's cosmopolitan background, upbringing and
studies served to provide him not only with an
enviously broad and deep knowledge of languages, but
also an appreciation of the need to discipline and
organise our knowledge about languages. Born in
Rome in 1922 of Maltese parents, his schooldays were
spent, and the French Baccalauréat passed, at that
city's celebrated Lycée Chateaubriand. After some
years of medical training and then war service in
the Royal Navy, he graduated in French and Spanish
from University College, London in 1948. There
followed a period of research and lecturing at
Westfield College, London, as first student and then
colleague of W. D. Elcock, leading eventually in
1956 to the award of the Ph.D. for a dissertation
entitled 'The dialect of the Vallée d'Aure (Haute
Pyrénées)'.
    In 1955, Joe moved to Cambridge, since which
time he has exercised his own peculiar blend of
intellectual vigour and personal charm on successive
generations of students, to whom he has always in-
sisted on the importance of combining traditional

standards of philological care and accuracy with the
insights and theoretical understanding yielded by
work in general linguistics. The significance, and
in British Romance studies in the 1950's the novelty,
of this second ingredient is perhaps most clearly
reflected in the fact that none of the eight contributors to this volume is currently attached to a
traditional British 'language-and-literature'
department.

   To be a pupil of Joe's, then, has always led to
a keen awareness that languages require linguistics
and linguistics requires languages. We hope that
he will find this same spirit pervading the pages
of the essays which have been assembled here and
which we affectionately dedicate to him on the
occasion of his sixtieth birthday.

ACKNOWLEDGMENTS

The editors would like to thank most warmly all the
contributors to this volume, who have without exception kept to the very tight schedule needed to
ensure its production on time. They would like to
thank Croom Helm, and in particular Tim Hardwick,
for encouraging and supporting the project from its
inception. The camera-ready copy was prepared in,
and at the expense of, the Department of Modern
Languages of the University of Salford, and the
editors are particularly grateful for the enthusiastic help they have received in this onerous task
from Claire Robinson and Stella Walker.

University of Salford   Martin Harris

University of Cambridge   Nigel Vincent

INTRODUCTION

Why, it might be asked, compile a volume entitled
Studies in the Romance Verb? Why not 'Studies in the
Romance Noun', or 'Adjective', or 'Preposition'?
Why Romance rather than Germanic or Malayo-
Polynesian? Why only 'Studies' and not a complete
survey? A simple and uncompromising answer suggests
itself: because that is what the authors of the
papers included here are interested in; because that
is what they wanted to write about; because that is
all we had time and space for. Such a reply, though
undoubtedly valid on one level, begs other and more
profound questions, to which this introduction will
serve as a partial answer.

   To return, then, to our first query: Why select
the verb rather than any other grammatical category?
The answer lies in the traditional view that the
verb is the nucleus of the sentence (cf. Matthews
1981, esp. Ch.5): the verb is the one category that a
sentence must have. Thus, although it is common
enough to talk about subjectless sentences, or verbs
without objects, converse locutions - e.g. verbless
sentences or objects without verbs - do not make
sense. Of course, there are plenty of verbless
utterances - e.g. unaccompanied vocatives or explet-
ives - but they are marginal to a full account of
the grammar of a language. A more forceful object-
ion might be thought to come from the so-called
'phrases nominales' (Ernout & Thomas 1951: para 171,
Benveniste 1960: 188) such as Latin *omnia praeclara
rara* 'everything which is outstanding is rare'.
Even here, however, the sentence without a verb is
only possible in the present indicative: as soon as
the tense or mood varies, even the verb 'to be'
becomes obligatory. Herein we see another reason
for treating the verb as the central element of the
sentence. It is the form of the verb which typically

gives realisation to such sentence categories as
mood, tense, voice, etc., categories which, as many
of the studies in this volume will make clear, have
traditionally and justly been the focus of diachronic Romance syntax. A third line of reasoning sees
the verb as central because it is *par excellence*
the part of speech which expresses the predicate,
which in turn is the core of the semantic structure
of the proposition expressed by the sentence. Such
an approach is to be found in case grammars and
studies of thematic relations exploited here in the
contributions of Vincent and Lyons in particular.

As has already been hinted, if the verb is the
pivot of the sentence, changes in verb morphology
and syntax will be among the natural foci of attention in historical syntax, thus prompting the obvious
and traditional answer to the question 'Why Romance?'.
These languages and dialects offer an unparallelled
testing-ground for research into the historical
development of language: there is almost continuous
attestation of a better or worse kind over more than
two millennia; there is an ancestor language about
which more is known than about any other dead language; there is a wealth of structural diversity in
the daughter languages; and there is a wide range of
socio-historical contexts against which to view the
changes. This, of course, is not to suggest that
there are no problems in these areas - attendance at
the first of Joe Cremona's lectures on the concept
of Vulgar Latin would suffice to dispel any linger-
ing naiveties in that regard! Nor, as Posner rightly reminds us in her introduction to Posner & Green
(1980-2), should we think of Romanists solely as the
technical assistants of general linguists, carrying
out tests on behalf of the latter in their specially
equipped diachronic laboratories. But the fact
nevertheless remains that if one wishes to examine
the complex interplay of factors at work in the
development of a verb system, then the Romance languages offer extensive and unique facilities for
such research.

In that case, our persistent questioner might
urge, why limit yourselves to 'Studies', why not
profit from the special benefits attending a conjunction of Romance and general linguists and construct a full-scale theory of the evolution of the
Romance verb? Here our response must be: because
the time is not yet right, although we hope the
contents of this volume will help to make it so.
Theory and data must go hand-in-hand, the one illum-
inating and informing the other in a reciprocal

relationship. Traditionalists and structuralists
have worked long and hard on the Romance verb
system: were this book to seek to synthesise what
they have had to say, an all-encompassing survey
would be feasible, though it would have precious
little in the way of originality. On the other hand,
transformational grammar has been relatively silent
concerning the theoretical problems which impinge
most directly on the archetypally Romance issues of
verbal morphosyntax and grammatical meaning. We
have then a situation where the data has yielded
just about all it can by way of answer to the old
questions, but the new theories have not yet succe-
eded in framing fresh questions with which to probe
anew the old data.

The reason for this impasse is not hard to find.
Traditional approaches have been indicted, often
without much justice and usually without much understanding, by structuralists and generative grammarians alike on various counts of atomism, notionalism,
prescriptivism, etc. Structuralists have found
their remedy for these defects in a concentration on
the patterns of opposition between, for example,
past simple and present perfect, or the indicative
and the subjunctive. Their questions have been essentially paradigmatic ones involving the relation
between *habeo factum* as a single unit versus *feci*,
or *facere habeo* as a replacement for *faciam*, rather
than on the nature of the syntagmatic links between
the two parts of the periphrases. To put it epig-
rammatically, syntax has been reduced to morphology.
By contrast, generative grammarians, when they have
broached the question at all, have normally tried to
assimilate morphology to syntax, analysing for example Romance futures as still synchronically consisting of the infinitive followed by a form of *avoir/*
avere/etc. (cf. Matthews, this volume, for some
discussion, and also our remarks below pp. xxiii-xxiv.
Now, of course, the principal lesson of Romance in
this regard is not that syntax can be analysed as
morphology or vice versa, but that from a diachronic
perspective syntax can change - and can be seen to
change - into morphology. The problem then is,
ultimately, to construct models which allow naturally
for a gradual transition from the syntactic component to the morphological component, and, as we shall
see, from the lexicon to the grammar. Such is the
context of ideas, explicit or otherwise, against
which the papers in Part II of this work have in
their various ways been conceived. They offer a
mixture of data and theory, with more emphasis on the

former as is only proper at the present stage of the
enquiry, from which it will - we hope - be possible
to go on to develop a more adequate and theoretical-
ly richer account of the patterns of breakdown and
regeneration within the verbal system of the Romance
languages. The two contributions in Part I are concerned with similar issues which arise in the relation between morphology and phonology. More of this,
however, anon: in the meantime back to morphosyntax
and theories thereof.

One of the reasons why a structuralist interpretation of the history of the verb in Romance is
so attractive and intuitively plausible is that it
departs relatively little from the traditional
understanding of the verbal paradigm in Latin.
According to the schoolroom grammars, a Latin finite
verb is inflected for six tenses, two moods (three
if the imperative is included here), and two voices
(the categories of person and number will not enter
into these discussions). It is only a short step
from this to the linguistically more informed analysis such as that of Meillet (summarised and tabul-
ated in Matthews, 1972: Appendix 1) in which the
six tenses are reorganised into two aspects
(*infectum* and *perfectum*) and three intersecting
tenses (past, present and future), thus:

	Past	Present	Future
Infectum	FACIEBAM	FACIO	FACIAM
Perfectum	FECERAM	FECI	FECERO

Allowing for the neutralisation of the present/
future opposition in the subjunctive, we have therefore ten groups of forms in the active voice, and an
equal number in the passive, or twenty sets of
person-number inflections in all, which taken together constitute the Latin verb paradigm. We have
deliberately approached the question of the paradigm
in this arithmetical fashion, for it brings out
clearly the way one may then proceed to deduce the
existence of combinations of properties. One can
ask, for example, 'What is the past indicative
infectum passive form of the verb *facere*?', and be
answered: *faciebar*. But what if one had substituted
perfectum for infectum in the foregoing request?
The answer then would have been: *factus eram*: in
other words, a periphrasis. The warrant for including this periphrasis within the so-called conjugation
but excluding, say, *faciendum est*, would be that the

former but not the latter has an inflectional or
synthetic congener elsewhere in the paradigm. A
historical variant of the same argument permits the
contrastive discussion of *habeo factum* and *feci*,
since the former is treated as the diachronic congener of the latter. For a fuller and more nuanced
account of the evolution of the Romance verb system
along these lines, see Harris (1978: Ch.6, and this
volume).

In fact,discussions on the temporal and aspectual systems within Romance divide broadly into two
main groups: those which Heger (1963) terms
'onomasiological' and those which he terms 'semasiological'. The former approach seeks to establish
logical or notional systems independent of any particular language and then to examine the ways in
which a particular language 'codifies' the logical
or notional categories so identified: Heger himself
adopts such an approach in his discussion of French
and Spanish, as does the seminal work of Bull (1960)
on Spanish and, following him, Klum (1961) on French.
The 'semasiological' approach starts from the linguistic unit - in this case, a verbal paradigm in the
sense defined above - and seeks to establish its
'valeurs' or, ideally, its 'valeur', its quintess-
ential or core meaning, sometimes within a particular language and sometimes contrastively with
respect to the 'equivalent' unit in some other related language. The literature on the Romance verb,
and in particular on the verb in French, abounds
with works within this second tradition, some of
them of outstanding quality: Imbs (1960) may perhaps
be taken to exemplify the success which this method
can attain. Certain Romanists would argue, following Guillaume, for a third approach in a sense midway between the two, where a conceptual system peculiar to one particular language, its specific
'psycho-system', is identified by virtue of a close
study of the linguistic units available in that language, the linguistic system and the system of
thought it embodies thus serving to illuminate each
other reciprocally.

Studies of the uses of indicative verbal paradigms in Romance may in turn be classified into two
main groups: those which are concerned, often historically, with the morpho-syntax of a particular set
of forms, taking for granted - or sometimes ignoring
- the system of which the forms in question are an
integral part; and those which explicitly recognise
that the changing use - or contrastive synchronic
use - of particular forms can only be studied

meaningfully within the tense/aspect system as a whole, or at least a significant sub-part of it. Deserving of special mention in the latter category, in addition to the 'onomasiological' works noted earlier, are the studies of French by T.B.W. Reid (1955, 1970). As we have already noted, a broadly similar approach is followed by Harris, at first (1971) in respect of French and later (1978) more generally across Romance. Two main areas which have attracted particular attention within the indicative sub-system are first the inter-relationship between the 'past simple' and the 'perfect', (cf. Harris this volume) and second the question of the marking of future time, in Vulgar Latin and now again in contemporary Romance (see below pp. xxiii-xxiv.)

Another recurrent theme within studies of the indicative verb in Romance is the nature and extent of the role of verbal aspect. Firstly, the distinction is clearly drawn between lexical and grammatical aspect, often known respectively as *Aktionsarten* and *Aspekten*. This question is well surveyed in Christmann (1959); lexical aspect in French is examined in some detail in Ducháček (1966). Within the domain of grammatical (verbal) aspect, the principal themes have been the evolving values of the 'compound perfect' paradigms, generally taken to be from aspectual to temporal in the period between Vulgar Latin and the emergence of the standard languages, the creation of new markers of perfectivity - the double compound tense - in much of the Romance-speaking area, and, less controversially, the nature of the opposition between the preterite and imperfect and, to a lesser extent, the past anterior and the pluperfect.

In regard to mood, now, Romanists have long shared with Latinists a preoccupation with the syntax and semantics of the subjunctive. As far as its syntax is concerned, almost all are agreed that this mood already and increasingly in Latin showed signs of being taken as a marker of subordination. This development is now virtually complete in French but significantly less so in Spanish and Italian, where certain main-clause uses are still attested (particularly in apodoses). The syntactic differences between French on the one hand and Spanish and Italian on the other hand are parallelled by clear - though by no means absolute - semantic differences. Whereas indicative/subjunctive minimal pairs (and hence meaningful oppositions) are reasonably common in Spanish and Italian - an indication that the subjunctive mood is still a significant marker of

modality in those languages - such pairs are residual in French, suggesting to many scholars that the
subjunctive in that language is now largely a (lexically conditioned) marker of subordination rather
than a marker of modality in its own right. We
might note in passing that to those who, like
Guillaume and his disciples, hold that a formal distinction must necessarily indicate also a distinction of meaning, such a view is of course unacceptable. In sum, the subjunctive mood survives throughout the Romance standards as a formal category predominantly, and in French almost exlusively, found
in subordinate clauses. Its semantic status as a
marker of modality seems secure in Spanish and
Italian, but at best marginal in the case of French.
      An obvious corollary of the picture just given
of the regression of the subjunctive as a *meaningful*
category, particularly in main clauses, is that
other markers of modality, whether from within the
verbal system or without, would be likely to develop.
Modal verbs and various indicative paradigms, such
as the future and the imperfect, were pressed into
service in this respect. Two indicative paradigms,
however, - the 'conditional' and 'conditional perfect' - are now so frequently used with a primarily
modal rather than temporal value that the question
has often arisen as to whether these forms are not
best regarded (with or without the 'future' and
'future perfect') as a mood in their own right.
This issue is discussed at length in Harris (1981);
here we will simply make the traditional observation
that indicative paradigms marking times other than
the here and now - and in particular those marking
posteriority (Hahn 1953) - potentially contain a
degree of uncertainty within their total semantic
specification, and as such are readily amenable to
carry modal nuances. The conditional paradigm -
marking as it does posterior time on the past time
axis - is thus particularly liable to develop modal
uses as well as, and possibly ultimately instead of,
its original temporal values with the indicative
mood. Certainly, whatever its current theoretical
status, the conditional paradigm is now used in many
main clause contexts where the subjunctive was at
one stage appropriate, a process which is already
being extended in French to subordinate clauses also.
      Although the preceding paragraphs have follow-
ed a time-honoured tradition in treating tense, aspect and mood as three distinct categories, it will
have been apparent from the discussion that in practice these categories are not as discrete as

traditional nomenclature suggests. Tense and aspect overlap in particular in an area central to the Romance verbal system, namely perfectivity, a general phenomenon noted by Comrie (1976) and alluded to more fully elsewhere in this volume; in essence, this overlap arises from the simple fact that events seen as completed (aspect) at any given moment clearly took place at an earlier time (tense). Equally, we have seen that tense and mood overlap considerably, in that paradigms whose temporal value is non-present may be used as markers of modality, to the point that rigid distinctions between 'tenses' and 'moods' often seem rather artificial.

The final major category relevant to an analysis of the verbal system (apart from person and number, which do not concern us here) is voice. The most widely accepted current view of voice sees the morphological passive (that is, verbal paradigms consisting, *inter alia* of the auxiliary verb *être, ser* etc. and the past participle form of the main verb (cf. Green, this volume)) as one of a number of strategies available in different languages to indicate subject demotion (the 'full' passive) or subject deletion (the 'reduced' passive), the surface subject position then being filled by a 'promoted' direct object. The need for such a strategy arises from the fact that there are times when what would be the subject of a transitive verb in the unmarked instance is not in fact realised as the subject, whether for intra-linguistic reasons (such as anaphora, emphasis etc.) or extra-linguistic ones (tact, prudence and the like). Such nominals may then reappear in the guise of prepositional phrases (subject demotion) or disappear entirely from the utterance (subject deletion), and the morphological passive is one strategy which permits both outcomes in all the Romance languages. A construction having the same general function and of at least equal importance, particularly in Spanish and Italian, is the pseudo-reflexive (e.g. Sp. *se alquilan cuartos* , lit. 'rooms rent themselves'), discussed at some length in this volume. Interestingly, in such cases subject deletion does not always entail object promotion: hence structures such as *se alquila cuartos*, where the absence of concord shows that the original object has not become the surface structure subject. For a detailed survey of these constructions in one language, cf. Green (1975); for some of the theoretical issues involved, cf. Lyons and Green (this volume) and Harris (1978a), together with the references cited there.

Introduction

Once again, one must conclude by observing that linguistic reality is not as clear-cut as the above remarks might suggest, since the functional differences between the constructions are often blurred. For instance, can pseudo-reflexives take an overt agentive phrase, like a passive, or not? (For Spanish, cf. Green 1975: 356). Even worse, the distinctions between reflexives, reciprocals, 'inherent' reflexives and pseudo-reflexives are by no means easy to draw definitively, although each of these categories is clearly of relevance to a full understanding of this area of Romance grammar, whether the perspective be synchronic or diachronic.

Mention of passives and reflexives brings us conveniently back to the recurrent problem of the relation between inflections and periphrastic constructions. Within the orthodox view, as we have stated, the categories of mood, tense, etc. define a series of 'slots' for which there are then exponents in the shape of inflectional endings. The almost perfect symmetry of one form per slot which Latin exhibits when seen in this way can be disrupted in one or more of at least three directions:

(i) A given form can be associated with two slots or combinations of morphosyntactic properties. Harris (1978: 132ff and this volume) diagnoses just such a situation in Latin where *feci* in addition to its role as exponent of the present-perfectum slot is also used as a marker of past punctual aspect. We can regard such a state of affairs as structural ambiguity, alleviated then by *habeo factum* inheriting the present perfect role, and with a consequent reorganisation of the other terms in the system.

(ii) For a given slot there might be two competing forms - a case of structural synonymy to go with the ambiguity already identified. Such is a possible interpretation of the situation - presumably real at some point in the evolution of Romance - where *feci* and *habeo factum* can both be used to mark present perfect.

(iii) For a given slot there are no available forms - a gap in the system, or *case vide* in Martinet's French terminology. This logical possibility has aroused a number of theoretical doubts. How does one know there even is a slot, the argument goes, if there are no forms to fill it? At the level of individual lexical items there seems relatively little difficulty. The traditional class of

'defective verbs' are precisely those which do not
have all their expected forms, or, in another Latin
example, verbs like *sonare, fervere, tremere, bibere*
etc. are usually said not to have a past participle.
   In another instance the answer is not so clear.
If there are no exponents of the combination future
plus subjunctive in Latin, can we say that this is
an unrealised gap, or is the combination to be ruled
out in advance on general semantic grounds? Compare
here the case of the English verbs *contain, own,*
etc., which are often said to lack the construction
with *be + ing*. An alternative approach, however,
would be to say that the *be + ing* form conveys a
meaning of impermanence or incompleteness, and that
this is incompatible with the meaning of the verbs
in question. A container either contains its contents or it doesn't: a house or a car either is or is
not my property - *tertium non datur*. On this view,
is containing, is owning etc. are then semantically
deviant in the same way as *drink the bed* or *sleep
furiously* are. We will not pursue this line of
argument further in the present context, but it does
suggest an interesting alternative to or companion
of the empty slot view.
   In some ways the papers in this volume which
investigate paths of grammaticalisation (notably
those by Green, Pountain and Vincent) can be seen as
initiating the semantic approach we have alluded to.
If it is true to say that a periphrasis such as
habeo/volo/debeo facere or *habeo factum* takes on a
grammatical role, it does not do so overnight. In
the first place, an independent lexical item like
habeo, volo etc. will have semantic restrictions of
its own which will mean that it combines more naturally with some verbs than others. The hallmark of a
grammatical item, on the other hand, is that it goes
with all the members of the class it signals. Hence,
there will have to be a period of distributional extension and concomitant semantic 'bleaching' as a lexical item gets incorporated into a closed system of
grammatical oppositions. This in turn suggests a
period of variation, when a moribund form such as
the Latin inflectional future exists side by side
with one or more periphrases. The dilema of the
empty slot is thus neatly removed, but at the expense
of requiring a fuller - and as yet unavailable -
account of the second of the abovementioned possibilities: structural synonymy. Of course, what the
foregoing discussion really succeeds in demonstrat-
ing is the well-known difficulty inherent in comparing terms across systems. Yet, if we do not make

the comparison, how are we to explain the continuity
and gradual developments which are so typical of
linguistic change (*pace* Lightfoot 1979, and cf.
Vincent 1982, Harris, forthcoming a, b)?

Such continuity emerges from the study of the
morphology and syntax of the verb in Romance in the
guise of two very general tendencies in the history
of this language family: firstly, a move from synthetic (ie. morphological) to analytic (ie. syntactic) structures and then (at least partly and particularly in French) back towards synthetic structures,
and secondly the progressive replacement of syntagms
involving postposed grammatical information with
those involving pre-position. The increased use of
auxiliaries and their placement, together with the
progressive cliticisation of many personal pronouns,
both clearly illustrate these long-term changes, and
demonstrate the important intermediate role played
in change by such categories as clitics and auxiliaries.

In Latin, the typical verb form consisted of a
stem followed by a series of morphological suffixes,
the only significant compound structure being, as we
have noted, the exponents of certain perfective passive values - e.g. *laudatus est* : '(he) was praised'
- in which the relative ordering of the main verb
and the auxiliary was, as usual in Classical Latin,
not rigidly fixed. Two important new paradigms
arose in Vulgar Latin, *facere habet* (the etymon of
the modern 'future simple') and *facere habebat/
habuit* (the etyma of the modern 'conditional'),
which are interesting in that, while analytic in
structure ('he has/had (it) to do'), they reflect the
last clear instantiation of the original stem + grammatical information order and thereby contrast
clearly with other late Latin and Romance creations.

This is not the place to discuss in detail the
creation of a wholly analytic passive structure (the
uses of which are alluded to briefly elsewhere), and
of a set of analytic markers of 'perfectivity', (*habeo
factum* etc.), the subsequent evolution of which is
discussed in Harris' paper herein. Suffice it to
say that in each case the auxiliary + main verb word
order was preferred, and has survived to the present
day. Modal verbs too, a frequent alternative to the
subjunctive as a marker of modality, usually precede
their attendant infinitives, as do the increasingly
frequent analytic markers of posterior time, *va
faire, va a hacer, sta per fare* etc.. The move towards analysis and pre-position is thus widely attested at many points in the Romance verbal system.

Introduction

It is in respect of the marking of person and number that there is greater divergence between French on the one hand and Spanish and Italian on the other (cf. Harris 1980). The two latter languages still mark the person and number of the (surface) subject of finite verbs by means of suffixed morphemes, albeit imperfectly and with some neutralisation. In these languages, subject pronouns remain optional, being used essentially for disambiguation or emphasis. In many registers of spoken French, however, subject pronouns are now almost mandatory concomitants of a finite verb, being cliticised to main verb or auxiliary as appropriate, and are best seen as bound prefixes marking the grammatical person of the subject, exactly as did suffixes in Latin. Thus, in standard French, clitic subject pronouns may be omitted if the subject position is filled by a noun - *Jean part* - whereas this tends not to be the case in informal spoken registers - *Jean il-part*; equally, the only element (*ne*) which may occur between clitic and finite verb in the standard language tends strongly to be omitted in popular speech: see Ashby (1977) for a full discussion.

Whereas the use of preposed clitics to mark the grammatical person of the subject is peculiar to French, all the Romance languages make some use of what are traditionally called pleonastic pronouns to serve as pre-verbal markers of oblique nominals: cf. Sp. *le he visto a Juan*. Given a relatively flexible word order, particularly in Spanish (cf. Green 1976), a clear method of identifying unambiguously the syntactic function of a particular nominal can obviously be of advantage. Such an arrangement is taken furthest in popular registers of French, where a structure such as *je le lui* (or *je l'y*) *ai donné moi le livre à Pierre* shows a sequence clitic + clitic + clitic + finite verb, with the clitics marking clearly the function of the associated nominals and thus permitting the ordering of these vis-à-vis the verb as a whole and vis-à-vis each other to be in effect syntactically free (though subject of course to heavy contextual and stylistic constraints).

What emerges clearly from the foregoing paragraphs is a shared tendency for analytic structures to replace synthetic ones, and for pre-position to replace post-position with the verbal unit. The development of auxiliary verbs illustrates both these developments, and is a pan-Romance phenomenon. Equally, all the principal languages show some inclination to use pre-verbal clitic pronouns to

disambiguate nominal groups, particularly in contexts
where some flexibility in word order is permissible.
In this instance, however, one should distinguish
clearly between Spanish and Italian, where the process is not fully systematised and is limited to the
oblique cases, and French, where, in popular registers at least, a full system of pre-verbal affixed
morphology marking the syntactic function of associated nominals is apparently developing from the
earlier conjunctive pronouns, leading to the emergence once again of synthetic structures.

An example which has cropped up at several
places in these introductory remarks, precisely
because it encapsulates most of the problems and
issues we have been discussing, is the evolution of
Romance future markers. By cataloguing here the
various stages of this development - not treated
elsewhere in this volume - and by listing some of
the main questions which then arise, we can conveniently recapitulate the points that have been made
so far about the areas and questions of theoretical
interest in the history of the Romance verb. We
note therefore that:

(i) there is an inflectional marking of the
future in Latin;

(ii) this marking has interesting formal and
semantic overlaps with the subjunctive;

(iii) most of the modern Romance languages have
futures which are superficially at least inflectional;

(iv) the Romance future desinences require us to
assume as etyma Late Latin periphrases.

Thus, in turn, a number of questions suggest themselves:

(i) what was the structural relationship of
these periphrases to the Latin inflection at the
time of the rise of the former and the decline of
the latter?

(ii) why these periphrases rather than any
others, and what are the stages of their semantic
development?

(iii) can we justifiably compare futures in Latin
and Romance given that both their etymological

origins and structural roles are so different, especially once the Romance development of conditionals
is brought into the picture?

(iv) what are the morphosyntactic stages in the
move to a new synthetic pattern? Note particularly
the relation here to clitics, and the interesting
evidence of Portuguese, where clitics may still
separate verb stems from the bound morphemes marking
future and conditional.

(v) what are the relations between the new
inflections and a second generation of periphrases
such as *va faire* etc.? Is there evidence here for
a cyclic pattern of change from synthesis to analysis and back again?

(vi) why did the periphrases not give rise to
new synthetic structures in Sardinian, Southern
Italian and Sicilian dialects, and Rumanian, to name
but three well-known cases?

Answers, in their turn not always uncontroversial,
are to be found to some of these questions, together
with very interesting general discussion and full
references, in Suzanne Fleischman's recent monograph
(1982). *Mutatis mutandis* similar questions could
be raised for other categories in the evolution of
the Romance verb, and indeed they are raised, and
we hope in part answered, in contributions to this
volume.

What goes for syntax has a habit of also going
for phonology, and such is indeed the present case.
Just as the paradigm has proved a central construct
in morphosyntax, and orthodox generative grammar
has had to be indicted for ignoring its significance,
so too in phonology the role of the paradigm in
morphophonemic statement is often fundamental. This
is emphasised in Matthews' paper in relation to two
classic problems, and investigated in newer areas
in Parkinson's study of the acceptance of sound
change into morphological structure in Portuguese,
both Brazilian and peninsular. The theoretical
debates between Chomsky and Halle (1968), with its
diachronic wing reinforced by Kiparsky - see now
his collected papers, Kiparsky (1982) - and the
Natural Generative Phonology of Hooper (1976) again
receive crucial input from Romance.

Basically, however, we hope to have offered
here a set of *Studies in the Romance Verb* to stimul-
ate and interest general linguist and Romanist alike,

Introduction

and thereby to honour the intellectual debt we all
owe to Joe Cremona's influence on and interest in
our several abilities to contribute to the further-
ance of Romance and general linguistic scholarship.
As always, the reader will be the judge of our, and
thus of his, success.

Nigel Vincent   Martin Harris

Cambridge   Salford

Chapter 1

TWO PROBLEMS IN ITALIAN AND SPANISH VERBAL INFLECTION

Peter Matthews

I am not a Romance philologist, or even (pace Posner, 1970: 424, n.6) a lapsed Romance philologist, but a classicist turned general linguist who, at a crucial point in his transition, read two papers for Part II of the Cambridge Mediaeval and Modern Languages Tripos under Joe Cremona's supervision, before being directed, partly by him, into my true field of research. I therefore owe him a great deal, and it is a pleasure as well as an honour to contribute to this volume. But I do so as an outsider, or as a student of inflection systems generally, not as an authority on either of the major languages referred to.

An outsider may, however, comment on the accounts that respective specialists have given. I propose to look, from a critical viewpoint, at two problems. The first concerns the treatment of the future and conditional, whether as simple or, as their history might at first be thought to suggest, as covertly compound formations. In Spanish the latter account is plausible and relatively economical, but in Italian it may reasonably be asked whether, if the history were unknown, it would ever have been suggested in a synchronic description. The second problem concerns the role of stress and the degree to which it can or should be seen as phonologically determined. In neither language can a single rule be devised, even if the future and conditional are compound, even if underlying short and long vowels are distinguished, even if certain morphological forms are excluded, and so on. But in Spanish it is at least tempting to try and write one, whereas in Italian the obstacles, even to this very sophisticated treatment, are more obvious. These differences are brought out, in particular, by an examination of the generative descriptions that appeared

in the late 1960s and early 1970s. But to anyone
who is not a morphological analyst the languages are
strikingly similar. In both cases we must ask if we
want to preserve the similarity, and if so at what
level.

FUTURES AND CONDITIONALS

As Harris points out in one of the earliest and best
generative studies, Spanish cantaré is formally like
an unstressed form of the infinitive (cantar not
cantár) plus the corresponding present indicative of
'haber' (orthographically he). Similarly in four
other persons: cantar + has = cantarás, cantar + ha
= cantará, cantar + hemos = cantaremos, cantar + han
= cantarán. The exception, as he remarks in a footnote, is the second plural (cantaréis, not simply
cantar + habéis); but since that person is not in
general use among his Mexican subjects, he ignores
it throughout, in this tense as in others. He then
points to a parallel between the epistemic Estará
aquí ahora 'He is probably here now' and the similarly epistemic Ha de estar aquí ahora, though noting
cases where such forms are not 'entirely synonymous'
(Ha de cantar mañana versus Cantará mañana). Putting
these separate parallels together, he argues that
the apparently simple cantaré should be seen as a
transformation of he de cantar, which is then
dominated by a single V node $(_V[\text{cantar} + \text{he}]_V)$,
stressed at first on both parts $(_V[\text{cantár} + \text{hé}]_V)$
and finally subject to a special rule by which the
first accent is suppressed $(_V[\text{cantar} + \text{hé}]_V)$. The
alternative, he claims, is to propose 'ad hoc
phonological rules' for the endings, an 'ad hoc
device' for the final accents, and so on (Harris,
1969: §3.9.1).

Harris gives no explicit rules for the conditional, merely remarking, in a footnote, that 'the
entire discussion ... carries over with only minor
modifications' to it (1969: 91, n. 24). But in
Italian the details are spelled out for both tenses
by Costabile (1973: 197ff.; earlier, 1969: 237ff.).
In the future canterò derives from cantare ho by
elision of the final vowel of the infinitive
(cantar- (h)o), with a further rule by which the
conjugation vowel is changed to e (canter- (h)o);
an accent is then added to what has become a
termination (canter-ò). Of the other persons
canterai derives similarly from cantare hai, canterà
from cantare ha, and canteranno from cantare hanno.
In the first plural the -e of the infinitive is

retained, and <u>cantare abbiamo</u> reduced by the
'elision', as <u>it is again described</u> , of <u>abbia-</u>; the
accent is then put on the last vowel of the stem
(<u>cantaré-mo</u>). Similarly, <u>canterete</u> is from <u>cantare</u>
<u>avete</u> with elision of <u>ave-</u> to yield (again with
change of conjugation vowel) <u>cantaré-te</u>. In the
conditional <u>canterei</u> derives <u>from cantare ebbi</u>, with
elision first <u>of the</u> -e of the infinitive and then
of -<u>bb</u>-, and the third persons <u>canterebbe</u> and
<u>canterebbero</u> from <u>cantare ebbe</u> and <u>cantare ebbero</u>,
in both cases with -<u>bb</u>- retained. The first plural
again retains the -<u>e</u> of the infinitive, with <u>cantare</u>
<u>avemmo</u> reduced, as <u>in</u> the second plural of the
<u>future</u>, by the elision of <u>ave-</u>. Likewise <u>cantereste</u>
is derived by the elision <u>of ave-</u> in <u>cantare aveste</u>
(<u>cantaré-ste</u>). But the singular <u>canteresti</u> shows
the elision first of -<u>e</u>, as in the other singular
persons, and then simply of <u>av-</u> (<u>canter-ésti</u>). In
short, two rules are proposed for the accent, one to
put it on the stem in the first and second plurals
and the other to put it on the termination everywhere else, and the same forms, in particular the
-e of the infinitive and the -bb- of <u>ebbi</u>, <u>ebbe</u> and
<u>ebbero</u>, are variously either 'elided' or not
'elided', in not dissimilar circumstances.

It takes little thought to appreciate that a
compound treatment of Italian, at least in the form
given by Costabile, is inflectionally less attractive than a similar account of Spanish, especially
when made explicit for only five persons of the
future. But for a fairer assessment we need both to
spell out the alternatives in Spanish and to see how
far Costabile's rules might be improved. We must
also take into consideration the semantic oppositions
into which these tenses enter, and the form of the
proposed syntactic derivation, as well as the morphophonemics.

So far as the syntax is concerned, there seems
no way of avoiding an anomaly. For the basic construction Harris proposes that of a main verb governing a preposition and an infinitive: first singular
<u>he de cantar</u> and, implicitly, <u>había de cantar</u>. But
the subsequent transformation is unique and these
are the only forms which would undergo it. In particular, if <u>he de cantar</u> can be realised by <u>cantar-hé</u>,
why cannot <u>voy a cantar</u>, which also enters clearly
into the system of tense oppositions, be realised
as <u>cantar-vóy</u>? Costabile does not discuss the
syntax; but clearly one asks why, in this construction alone, the auxiliary should follow the lexical
verb: if <u>cantare ho</u>, why not <u>cantato ho</u> or, with

another auxiliary, <u>cantando sto</u>, and so on? Among
other treatments of Italian, that of Saltarelli
simply acknowledges that the case is exceptional:
the basic forms are those of 'avere' followed by the
infinitive but 'unlike traditional compounds ...
these undergo a change of sentential order', with
'special morphophonemics' to follow (1970: 69).
Again there is no synchronic account of why the
order should be aberrant. Stockwell, Bowen and
Martin had earlier proposed a treatment of Spanish
in which <u>habría</u>, which they give as their illustration, derives from a form which they represent as
'Past + <u>-haber</u> + <u>haber</u>': transformations switch the
Past Tense affix and <u>-haber</u> (so '<u>-haber</u> + Past +
<u>haber</u>'), then reduce '<u>-haber</u> + Past' to -ía, and
finally switch -ía and '<u>haber</u>' (1965: 147). But the
two '<u>haber</u>'s plainly represent two different things.
The first ('<u>-haber</u>') must be a representation either
of the lexeme or of the root (hab-): similarly, for
example, in the derivation of <u>había</u> from 'Imperfv +
Past + <u>haber</u>' (143). But the second must be the
infinitive specifically (or, to be precise, <u>habr</u>-).
Alternatively, as Harris points out (1969: 94), the
-r- is not accounted for. Nor is it clear quite
what the hyphen means in '<u>-haber</u>': in effect, '<u>-haber</u>
+ Past' is first derived as a word - so at that
point the hyphen is irrelevant - and then altered
into an affix. Other treatments add nothing of importance: for Spanish, Cressey (1978) simply assumes
Harris's and Wheeler (1979: 69-71), for Catalan,
also follows him in essentials.

In semantics the first problem concerns the collocation of 'to have' and the infinitive. If it
were transparent it could readily be seen as idiomatic: just as the meaning of <u>ho cantato</u>/<u>he cantado</u>
need not derive literally from individual meanings
of <u>ho</u>/<u>he</u> and the past participle, so that of whatever might then be the form of <u>canterò</u>/<u>cantaré</u> -
whether Auxiliary + Preposition + Infinitive, or
Auxiliary + Infinitive, or simply Infinitive + Auxiliary - would not have to relate straightforwardly
to individual meanings of <u>ho</u>/<u>he</u> and the infinitive.
But even in Spanish the collocation is as at least
partly opaque (<u>cantaréis</u> not <u>cantar(h)abéis</u>, and so
on). We must therefore ask if, for both tenses together or in either tense individually, there are
good semantic reasons for positing it.

A second problem concerns the opposition between
the tenses. If we accept the hypothesis, then in
Spanish <u>cantaré</u> stands formally to <u>cantaría</u> precisely
as the present indicative <u>canto</u> stands to the

4

imperfect indicative <u>cantaba</u>. Similarly, in Italian, <u>canterò</u> and <u>canterei</u> are placed in the same formal relationship as the present indicative <u>canto</u> (same tense as the posited auxiliary <u>ho</u>) and <u>the past def</u>-inite <u>cantai</u> (same tense as <u>ebbi</u>). But is there also a semantic regularity? If the forms were transparent we might again resign ourselves to a discrepancy: in English, for example, we continue to describe <u>should sing</u> as the past tense of <u>shall sing</u>, despite the separate semantic statements which, at least in many uses, they now need. But since they are not transparent we must again ask whether the analysis has real semantic value.

In the case of Spanish it is clear what arguments will be offered. If I interpret Harris correctly, <u>he de cantar</u> might be represented as a base form of which <u>cantaré</u> is an allegro variant: compare English <u>cannot</u> and <u>can't</u> or, again with a change of order, <u>am I not?</u> and <u>aren't I?</u> The base form is itself formally transparent; so, if the relation is of that sort, our first problem can be set aside. As to the second, <u>cantaré</u> will be represented as a present future (future in relation to the moment of speaking) and <u>cantaría</u> as a future in the past (future in relation to some earlier moment). This is the analysis of Stockwell et al. (1965: 144-6), who assign both tenses to a category of 'subsequence'. It is also that of Alarcos (1949, 1959), who presents a matrix in which <u>cantaré</u> and <u>cantaría</u> share the feature 'prospectivo' (opposed to the non-prospective <u>canto</u> and <u>canté/cantaba</u>), while <u>cantaría</u> and <u>canté/cantaba</u> share a feature 'irremotoprospectivo' (opposed to the 'unremote-prospective' <u>cantaré</u> and <u>canto</u>). The opposition of <u>canté</u> and <u>cantaba</u> is then subsidiary within the category of past non-future. Alternatively, it is neutralised in the past future (thus Stockwell et al.) where, in our postulated base form, it is the form of the imperfect (<u>cantar (hab)ía</u> or <u>había de cantar</u>) rather than the past definite (<u>hube de cantar</u>) that serves as a common realisation.

In the case of Italian it is not clear that such arguments can be found. Costabile and Saltarelli say nothing: she deals just with the inflections and his remarks are, in any case, very brief. But, firstly, we cannot speak of an allegro form, or of a phonological reduction generally, if there is no full or lento form (<u>ho</u> and <u>ebbi cantare</u>, <u>ho</u> and <u>ebbi di cantare</u>, or whatever) that we can point to as a source. Where such a form does not exist it can be established only as a syntactic base structure;

in that case we require that it should contribute
to the semantic description, or at least represent an
analysis, into separate elements, of an observed
semantic value. Secondly, it is not obvious that
the future and conditional do form a single category.
The former is again basically a 'future with respect
to the moment of speaking'; we may add that it is
the only such form, with no periphrastic competitor
(such as a Spanish-like vado a cantare) which might
usurp this temporal role. But the conditional is
more problematic. In an article based on Alarcos's
account of Spanish, Tekavčić begins with the statement that both canterei and cantaría have 'two essentially distinct functions': one as a 'combinatory
variant of the future', the other as a mood of contingency, independent of the time dimension (1970:
7f.). That, of course, reflects their origin in
Late Latin (as set out in Tekavčić, 1972: 308ff.).
But in present-day Italian the first function belongs
more to the compound conditional: in particular,
whereas in Spanish the simple form still corresponds
to the future in the sequence of tenses (present
digo que vendrá; past Dije que vendría), in Italian
Dico che verrà now has as its past equivalent -
standardly according to the handbooks, if not obligatorily - not Dissi che verrebbe (with verrebbe in
the role of future in the past), but Dissi che
sarebbe venuto, with anteriority marked by the construction of past participle and auxiliary.
Tekavčić acknowledges this in a footnote (1970: 7,
n. 19) and in his actual description rejects a
matrix like that of Alarcos, in favour of one in
which canterei and avrei cantato share just the
feature '+ Eventualità'; the other tenses are all
'- Eventualità', including canterò and avrò cantato,
which alone are classed as '+ Futuro'.
     The uses of the conditional are summarised by
Lepschy and Lepschy (1977: 233-5; 1981: 208-10); if
we try to include all of them, the postulation of a
single feature of contingency - or, for that matter,
a single feature '+ Conditional' - may well prove
simplistic. But it seems more accurate than simply
calling the Italian conditional a past future, as
in Hall's classification (table in Hall, 1948: 25,
1971: 85). It is also legitimate to wonder why the
past compound should be formed with ebbi rather than
avevo. In Spanish Alarcos sees the imperfect as the
unmarked aspect ('unbounded' in opposition to the
'bounded' past definite). Similarly Tekavčić (1970)
for Italian; indeed the arguments seem decidedly
stronger in a language where the role of the

preterite (cantai) is increasingly taken over by the
present perfect (ho cantato). In the base form of
the conditional the opposition of 'past bounded' and
'past unbounded' might again be seen as neutralised.
But why should 'past' on its own have its marked
realisation?

In this light let us return to the inflectional
paradigms of Italian, and try to consider the problems as a field linguist, without our own extensive
philological knowledge, might confront them. He
will, of course, be struck by the similarity between
the future and conditional stems, especially where
they are irregular: forms like avrò and avrei or
verrò and verrei, let alone sarò and sarei, would be
common in his records. Let us assume that his subjects retain the full use of the past definite: in
that case he will also be struck by the similarity
between its endings and those of the conditional.
Cantasti and cantaste match canteresti and cantereste, both with -s(t)- inserted before the usual
-i or -te; cantai and cantammo also match canterei
and canteremmo, with first singular -i (elsewhere
only in the past subjunctive) and doubling of m in
first plural -mo; even the -ro of canterebbero
recurs in irregular past definites. He will thus
establish a formal matrix in which both the future
and the conditional have stems in -r-, in contrast
to the present and past definite, and both the conditional and the past definite have a marked set of
terminations, in contrast to the present and future.
He will also look for correspondences in meaning;
but, if he is careful, he will have to admit that
he cannot quite find them.

Would he then go on to consider a deeper analysis? He might certainly toy with a connection
between the -r- stems and the infinitive. But
homonymous formatives are not unknown, and since
canterò does not have the same thematic vowel as
cantare, and there are other discrepancies where
the future and conditional are irregular (avrò but
avere, verrò but venire, and so on) he has no strong
formal reason to pursue it. A connection with
'avere' surely would not occur to him. Of its four
root alternants (av-, (h)- and abb(i)- in the
present; av- and ebb- in the past), the regular av-
does not appear at all in either the future or the
conditional; nor does abb(i)-; (h)- is , in any case,
null; ebb- appears in only two of the three forms in
which, if it were indeed derived from the paradigm
of 'avere', it should appear. Nor, in general, will
his dissatisfaction be of the sort that the

postulation of an underlying structure might be
expected to remedy. The aim of such structures is
to reconstruct a formal parallel in cases where the
semantic parallel is clear but the surface form is
obscured. But the problem here is precisely that
the surface form is clear (stems with and without
-r-, terminations with and without -s(t)-, and so
on) and the semantics obscured.

The compound analysis is therefore justified
only to the extent that it can achieve a formal
simplification. If we do not adopt it then in both
tenses we will establish a stem ending in r and a
stressed vowel: thus canteré- in canteremo and
canterete. In canteranno we must recognise a different vowel, and one which in addition doubles a
following consonant: thus, if we may borrow Hall's
notation, canterá*-no (asterisk = superscript x in
Hall, 1971: 101 et passim). Doubtless hanno would
be represented similarly (há*-no), as would vanno
or sanno (vá*-no, sá*-no) and other forms at least
with internal doubling (trarre = trá*-re; traggo,
with the alternant in -g- of colgo or scelgo, =
trá*-g-o). But that does not require us to say that
canteranno has hanno within it. The same stem may
be posited in canterai and canterà (canterá*-i, with
no consonant to double; canterá*-∅, with no termination); also in canterò (canterá*-o, with a plus o,
which is excluded as a diphthong, fused, as also
in cantò = cantá-o or cantá-u, to o). The endings
of the future (-o, -i, -∅, -mo, -te, -no) are then
the same as those of the present and imperfect indicative, which are the other least marked tenses:
canto = cánta-o, cantavo = cantáva-o; canti =
cánta-i (with a plus i monophthongised in an unstressed syllable) and so on.

In the conditional the stem would be constant,
except to the extent that -r[e]- and -r[ɛ]-
alternate (paradigms as in, for instance, Reynolds,
1962: 885ff.). Canteremmo might suggest canteré*-:
thus canteré*-mo. In that case canteresti =
canteré*-sti, where canteressti, with distinctive
doubling of the first consonant in the cluster, is
not possible. Likewise cantereste = canteré*-ste;
canterei might be canteré*-i, and canterebbe(ro)
either canteré*-be(ro) or simply canteré*-bbe(ro).
Alternatively, -mmo is a morphological mark of both
the past definite and the conditional: thus cantá-
mmo and canteré-mmo. In that case the other forms
are simply canteré-i, canteré-sti, canteré-bbe,
canteré-ste and canteré-bbero. Of the terminations,
first singular -i again matches that of the past

Italian and Spanish Verbal Inflection

definite and past subjunctive; -sti can be said to
consist of a second person marker -st-, characteristic again of both the past definite and the
conditional, followed by second singular -i, again
corresponding to the -i of the unmarked tenses;
likewise -ste = -st-te-, where -stt- would be
another impossible cluster; finally, -bbe and -bbero
= -bbe-∅ and -bbe-ro, with -bbe- as a special marker
of third person. Now -bbe- is, of course, an oddity
and requires a rule peculiar to it. So too is the
vowel alternation in the stem, especially in the
future: it is not usual for a stem suffix, as opposed to the thematic or conjugation vowel or its
positional equivalent, to vary in that way. But
otherwise the idiosyncrasies are no more than in
other tenses.
    If we accept the compound analysis our first
problem is to formulate the rule by which, in six
of the twelve forms, the root of 'avere' is deleted.
We could say 'delete av- and abb(i)-': thus cantere
⟨av⟩ete, cantere ⟨av⟩esti, cantere ⟨av⟩emmo, cantere
⟨av⟩este and cantere ⟨abb⟩iamo. But that is not
sufficient, since ebb- is also deleted in cantere
⟨ebb⟩i. But then we cannot say 'delete av-, abb(i)-
and ebb-', since ebb- is retained in canterebbe and
canterebbero. We must therefore refer to specific
persons: for example, we might say 'delete av-,
abb(i)- and ebb-, but the last only in the first
person'. Alternatively, we might say 'delete av-,
abb(i)- and ebb-' (or, if we like, 'delete any root
alternant that is not null'), 'except in the third
person'. In either case, the forms in -bb- of
canterebbe and canterebbero are as exceptional in
this treatment as they are in the other.
    A second problem is the penultimate e in
canteremo. In, for example, canterà and canterete
our first treatment forces us to recognise two separate stems: canterà*-, canteré-. In the compound
treatment these could be seen as simply canter⟨e⟩
(h)a and canter⟨e⟩ ⟨av⟩ete. But by the same rule
canteremo ought to be canter⟨e⟩ ⟨abbi⟩amo or
canter⟨e⟩ ⟨abb⟩iamo. Costabile's solution was to
say that, in this case, it is the -e of the infinitive that is preserved: so, canteré ⟨abbia⟩mo.
For good measure she said that this always happens
in the first and second plurals: so, cantere ⟨ave⟩te
and not, as we just thought, canter⟨e⟩⟨av⟩ete;
similarly, conditional cantere ⟨ave⟩mmo and cantere
⟨ave⟩ste (though still canter⟨e⟩ ⟨av⟩esti in the
second singular). In her formulation this required
both a morphological limitation of the rule deleting

9

-e in the infinitive (Costabile, 1973: 197, rule 1)
and separate deletions of av- in one form and ave- in
others. Alternatively, having first deleted the root of
the auxiliary, we could say that the following vowel is
also deleted in the first and second plurals: so, for
example, cantere <abbi>(i)amo would be further reduced to cantere <abbi><(i)a>mo. The -e of the
infinitive would then fail to elide, simply because
it is followed by a consonant. Alternatively, we
could say that the following vowel is deleted in
just the first plural of the future; still other
options are to say that, in the first plural of the
future, -(i)a- is exceptionally changed to -e-, or
simply (to tackle the problem at its root) that in a
compound formation with the infinitive abbiamo has an
exceptional variant emo. But whatever we say, the
alternation of vowels again requires at least one
special rule.

In short, the compound treatment offers no
simplification, and for the same reasons which suggest that, in the history of Italian, the connection
with 'avere' has been lost. These are, in particular,
the Tuscan substitution of abbiamo for avemo (Rohlfs,
1968: §541), without repercussion on canteremo; and
the ousting of canterebbi by canterei, matching the
regular past definite (cantasti:canteresti = cantai:
canterei) and not that of 'avere' specifically. The
inflectional obstacles may well be worse in dialects
whose conditional forms have derived from both
infinitive + preterite and infinitive + imperfect
(Rohlfs, 1968: §599). But where the case in Italian
falls the case in Spanish remains impregnable. If
we accept the compound analysis there is again a
special rule for the syntactic transformation (he
de cantar → cantar 'he) and for the collapse of two
words into one. But we can state a general rule for
the deletion of hab- (cantar <hab>ía, and so on),
the terminations which are left require no tinkering,
and the only irregularities are in the morphophonemics of a dozen or so infinitives: those of 'querer'
and four others, whose future and conditional simply
lack a thematic vowel (quer-r-); of 'salir' and five
others, with no thematic vowel (sal-r-) and epenthetic -d- to regularise the cluster (saldr-); of
'hacer', with har- arguably a reduction under sandhi
of ha[θ]/[s]-r-; of 'decir', for which we must add
the vowel change (dir-). In Spanish there is also
more of a semantic case, as we saw earlier. Then
are the forms simple in one language and compound
in the other? That could, in principle, be argued:
in Italian we can point to evidence that the paradigm

has been restructured, whereas in Spanish, apart
perhaps from the replacement of héis as an independent second plural of 'haber' (Menéndez Pidal, 1952:
§116, (2)), there is no positive change which would
confirm that their source has been lost sight of.
Nevertheless it might be hard to persuade speakers
of either language that the structures are basically
different. Or should the Italian forms be treated
on the model of Harris's analysis of Spanish, to
preserve a parallel? Or, despite his arguments,
should the Spanish forms be seen as simple?

The last alternative is at least worth considering; and perhaps, since I write here even more as
an outsider, I may again put myself in the position
of our imaginary field linguist. In both tenses I
would, of course, encounter forms of all conjugations, not just that of 'cantar'. In the conditional, therefore, I might well be struck not, at first,
by a specific connection between cantaría and había
but rather by the general resemblance, in the -e-
and -i- conjugations, between the conditional and
imperfect of the same paradigm. Thus I would analyse temía as tem-ía, with suffix -ía, and temería
as teme-r-ía, with the same morpheme preceded by an
intermediate suffix -r-. My only problem, in that
light, is why canta-ba, in the -a- conjugation, does
not match canta-r-ía. But in canta-ba versus tem-ía
I am forced to recognise allomorphy. Therefore, in
default of other evidence, I would simply say that
the forms of what I would tentatively call the
imperfect morpheme are: -ba- when directly following a stem in -a- (canta-ba); in all other environments, -ía- (tem-ía or tem(e)-ía, following a stem in
-e-; part-ía or part(i)-ía, following a stem in -i-;
canta-r-ía, and so on, following -r-).

The -r- of cantaría would then be compared with
that of cantaré; the most obvious reason is that in
both of them the accent follows. We would therefore
look for a common meaning and might decide, tentatively, that this was a future morpheme. But what
of the r's elsewhere in the paradigm? One is in the
first imperfect subjunctive: cantara. This too
follows the thematic vowel (canta-ra); are cantaría
and cantaré perhaps canta-r(a)-ía and canta-r(a)-é?
That casts no semantic light and I am sure it would
be rejected very quickly. But is there any better
reason - again, for a field linguist who does not
know the history - to connect -r- with the infinitive? We have already identified a future stem
(cantar-, also querr- and the like) common to both
tenses. We have also identified -ía with the

11

imperfect; the -é of cantaré is then left as a corresponding ending of the present. There is nothing
self-evidently 'future' about forms such as cantar
or querer. As in Italian, we may toy with the
connection but there is nothing to gain by establishing it. To extend further the discussion of this point,
it is worth adding that in Catalan, where the -r of
the infinitive exists only in the spelling and as a
generative phonologist's construct (Wheeler, 1979:
275ff.), it could be mooted only after a sophisticated analysis.

But the compound structure does deal very neatly
with the endings of the future. If we do not accept
it, the -é of canteré is like that of canté; in
Harris's account of the past definite - 'ingenious
and convincing' according to a useful review by
Craddock (1973: 101) - canté derives from, in effect,
cantá-i (Harris, 1969: 85f.); similarly, cantaré
could be canta-r-á-i. But why a past ending in a
tense already characterised as present? Cantarás
would be canta-r-á-s, with the regular non-preterite
ending of canta-s; likewise cantará and cantarán
would be canta-r-á-∅ and canta-r-á-n (compare
canta-∅ and canta-n). But according to Harris the
accent would be anomalous, since there are no other
forms, in his analysis, in which it would fall on
the last syllable of an underlying representation.
Cantaremos and cantaréis would have to be
canta-r-e-mos and canta-r-e-is (compare canta-mos
and cantá-is); but why do they show -e- in place of
-a-? The compound treatment removes all the snags:
first singular -é is also found in he; has, ha and han
are naturally accented as monosyllables; the -e- of
-éis is simply the thematic vowel of habéis; the
irregularity of -emos is referred to that of hemos.

The accent will be our topic in the second
section of this paper. But the choice is, in general,
clear. If the forms are compound we must posit
rules by which they are made simple. These apply to
all futures and conditionals, but nowhere else in
the language. If they are simple we require perhaps
three morphologically restricted rules for their
inflections. Now to a generative linguist one sweep-
ing adjustment is always likely to appeal more than
a series of little ones, and this preference was
enshrined in the now defunct proposals for a phonological evaluation measure, which when Harris's book
was written were in full vigour. But in the light
of our earlier findings for Italian I am not entirely sure that it is, in this case, right.

Italian and Spanish Verbal Inflection

STRESS

Our second problem can be dealt with more briefly.
In Italian, in the view of most scholars, the accent is in part lexically and in part morphologically
determined. Thus, in the verb, it is a lexical
matter that, in present forms of, for example,
'evitare' and 'derivare', it should fall in one case
on the first and in the other on the second syllable
of the root (évito-o, derív-o). Still in the present, it is by a morphological rule that it remains
on the root before the -CV termination of the third
plural, but shifts to the position of the thematic
vowel in the first plural and second plural (cántono,
but cantiámo, cantáte). The lexical evidence is
reinterpreted by Saltarelli, who tries to predict
the differences, by a rule very like the familiar
one in Latin, from a distinction of underlying long
and short vowels (1970: 29, rule 6). For example,
évito might be évĭt-o, with light penultimate
('light' is Saltarelli's own term) and stress on the
syllable preceding, while derivo is derív-o. But
even he does not deny that there is morphological
conditioning. In the derivational morphology of the
noun, the diminutive suffixes -ett- and -ell- must
have short vowels, since it is because the vowel is
short and stressed that, in his account, the following consonant is double (29, rule 7); but the stress
in turn is then unpredictable, and must be specially
marked (76f.). As for the verbs, 'the formulation
of rules assigning the feature stress to Italian
verbs can only be achieved by recourse to syntactic
information' (38). His own statements are given
hand in hand with other individual rules for their
inflections (69 - 74).
    In Spanish the generative phonologist is again
on a much easier wicket. For the verbs there is no
lexical conditioning, except (at first sight) in the
types envío/sitúo versus cambio/fraguo (cámbio and
fráguo). In Harris's account, this is simply a
difference between a disyllabic root (envi-, situ-)
and one whose underlying form ends in a glide
(camby-, fragw-)(1969: 122ff.). In nouns like
corazón, where the accent seems to be final, Harris
posits a deleted -e: corazon(e). The stress is then
as in, for instance, teme; but there the -e is not
deleted because, he argues, it is marked as '+ Tense'
('final e deletion' in Harris, 1969: 177ff.; discussion by Craddock, 1973: 103f.). In a noun like
número it is on the antepenultimate; in Harris's
account, which at this point matches Saltarelli's,

that is because the penultimate is '-Tense', whereas
in, for example, romero it is '+ Tense' (roméro).
In the verb morphology, the infinitive ends in a
deleted -e: cantár(e). There are also apparent
final accents in the past definite: canté, cantó.
But, as we said earlier, the former is seen as
canta-i; let us now add that the -i is '-Tense'.
Similarly, cantó is canta- plus a '-Tense' -u (Harris,
1969: 83). In both forms the accent then falls regularly on the underlying penultimate (cantá-i,
cantá-u) before the syllables are fused. In the
third singulars of the other conjugations (temió,
partió), it is first placed on the thematic vowel
(temé-u, partí-u) but switched to the second member
of the diphthong, to avoid tautosyllabic [ew] and
[iw] (I paraphrase somewhat Harris, 1969: 83f.).
Harris has then disposed of every anomaly, except
for the first and second plurals of the imperfects.
If cantamos and cantáis are cantá-mos and cantá-is,
one cannot explain phonologically why cantábamos and
cantabais are not canta-bá-mos and canta-bá-is, or
cantáramos not canta-rá-mos, and so on. But it is
only in these forms that morphological conditioning
is unavoidable.

When we turn to his actual rules there is perhaps a mild disappointment, in that, instead of
simply treating the imperfects as exceptions, and
then applying one rule to all other cases, he divides
a general rule into two parts. The first is called
the 'Latin Stress Rule' (118ff.), but is valid only
for nouns and adjectives. It therefore handles
corazón(e) but not cantár(e); planta (plánta) but
not canta (cánta); still less cantaba and the other
persons of the imperfects generally which, unlike
the first and second plurals, are not anomalous.
The second part applies just to verbs and places the
stress on the penultimate vowel of the underlying
representation - as, among others, in cantár(e),
cantá-u, cánta and so on - except that it always
precedes an imperfect morpheme. In that way, both
cantábamos and cantaba are presented as exceptions
to a general rule which deals with forms like canta,
even though cantaba could be brought within it; in
turn, that rule is presented as distinct from the
'Latin Stress Rule', even though both canta and
cantaba (the latter if it had a '+ Tense' vowel in
the penultimate) might also obey it. But the general picture is clear. In both Spanish and Italian,
nouns and adjectives can be accented as in Latin;
but only if we are willing to have underlying long
and short vowels - or vowels which are underlyingly

14

'+ Tense' and '- Tense' - which subsequently, as a generativist puts it, undergo 'absolute neutralisation'. But in Italian verbs the accent must be assigned morphologically; whereas in Spanish verbs the only problem springs from the apparent levelling of the imperfect paradigms (Menéndez Pidal, 1952: §106, (4)) in cantábamos and so on. Otherwise, if we set aside the future and accept Harris's account of the past definite, they are regular.

The accent of nouns and adjectives does not immediately concern us. If we accept generativist devices in one language we will accept them in the other; if we reject them we will reject them. In either event our descriptions will remain parallel. Nor need we bother with a further hypothesis, advanced by Harris (1969) but abandoned in a later article (compare Cressey, 1978: 99f.), by which '+ Tense' was identified with a feature of diphthongisation. But our findings for the verb are worrying. Once more the paradigms appear, to most students and to Spanish and Italian speakers generally, very similar. Yet, when a linguist studies them closely or perhaps too closely, he proposes rules that are largely if not radically different. If the difference is not real, which view is illusory?

I doubt whether this essay will find a generativist reader, if they are still to be found. If it did he might demand a re-examination of Italian, to see if the accent of the verb can, after all, be made predictable. But let us take the opposite line, and try to spell out the morphological factors. In Italian generally, the accent is associated both with the root, where most scholars would say that it is subject to lexical conditioning, and with specific suffixes, which can then attract it. For example, in camera the stress is lexically on the first syllable (cámer-a), but in camerino it is attracted to a position on the derivational suffix (camer-ín-o); in derivo it is lexically on the second syllable (derív-o), but in deriviamo it is attracted to a position before the first plural termination (deriv-iá-mo). Alternatively, we can follow Garde (1968: 124-7) and say that in camerino there are basic accents on both camer- and -in- (so cámer-ín-o) but the later cancels the earlier. Similarly, there are basic accents on deriv- and immediately before -mo (let us therefore write this as ´-mo). So, derív-ia-´-mo = derív-iá-mo → deriv-iá-mo.

The verbal patterning is then as follows. Of the terminations in the present, -o does not attract the accent; nor -i; nor third plural -no: thus

cánt(a)-o, cánt(a)-i, cánt-o-no. In that respect
they are like the derivational suffix in, for example, donnola (dónn-ol-a). But the first plural has
⁻-mo, as we have seen (cant-ia-⁻-mo = cant-iá-mo),
and the second plural has ⁻-te (canta-⁻-te =
cantá-te). This is part of a larger pattern of
marked and unmarked oppositions, which I have explo-
red in another Festschrift (Matthews, 1981). In the
imperfect indicative we have the same endings, preceded by a formative which, in the same notation,
we may write as ⁻-va-. Thus, in the singular,
cantavo and cantavi are canta-⁻-v(a)-o and canta-⁻-
v(a)-i, and cantava simply canta-⁻-va (or canta-⁻-
va-Ø). In the plural, cantavano is canta-⁻-va-no.
But in cantavamo and cantavate, the accent is attracted twice: first to the conjugation vowel, because
it is followed by ⁻-va-; then to the next vowel,
because it is followed by ⁻-mo or ⁻-te. Thus, by
Garde's rule, cánta-⁻-va-⁻-mo → canta-vá-mo;
cánta-⁻-va-⁻-te → canta-vá-te. In that respect the
forms are like Garde's own example fusellato, with
successive attraction by two derivational formatives:
fús-éll-át-o → fus-ell-át-o. In the future and
conditional the accent is attracted to the suffix
itself: canteró = cante-rá*-o (with -á-o fused to
-ó); canterei = cante-ré-i, and so on. In, for
example, canteremo the accent is already on the
vowel preceding ⁻-mo (cante-ré-⁻-mo) and the termination has no further effect. Similarly, perhaps, in
the past definite, but with no overt formative:
first singular canta-⁻- plus -i; first plural canta-
⁻- plus ⁻-mmo (or conceivably canta-⁻*-i, canta-⁻*-
⁻-mo). Alternatively, the accent is attracted by
the whole set of endings: cantai = canta- plus ⁻-i;
cantasti = canta- plus ⁻-st-i; likewise, in the
conditional, canterei = canteré- plus ⁻-i. In the
past subjunctive the basic formative is ⁻-sse
(third singular canta-⁻-sse); but why not cantassímo,
or indeed cantassémo, in the first plural? It is
tempting to say that in both the first and second
plurals the stem has, anomalously, no final vowel:
canta-⁻-ss-. Then canta-⁻-ss-⁻-te → cantaste, with
reduction of -sst- to -st-; canta-⁻-ss-⁻-mo, so far
as the accent goes, would be cantá-ss-mo, and -i-
is epenthetic. Finally, cantare would be canta-⁻-re
(but a non-attracting -re in vendere); cantando and
cantato would be canta-⁻-ndo and canta-⁻-t-o.
   This account differs variously from those of
Hall (1970), Saltarelli (1971) and Costabile (1969,
1973), and may be too much influenced by Garde's
formulation. But its interest in this context is

that, if the accent in Spanish were not to be seen
as phonologically predictable, a similar treatment
would require only one crucial modification. In
Spanish, as in Italian, there are stems in which the
accent remains on the root (present indicative
cánta- and subjunctive cánti-). In others it moves;
but at that point it cannot be moved again by a
termination. For example, in cantamos we can posit
a termination ⁻-mos: cánta-⁻-mos → cantá-mos. But
in the corresponding imperfect the accent is already
attracted once by the stem formative: cánta-⁻-ba-
→ cantá-ba. When ⁻-mos is added it moves no further:
canta-⁻-ba-⁻-mos → cantá-ba-mos not, on the Italian
model, canta-bá-mos. Similarly, cánta-⁻-is →
cantá-is but cánta-⁻-ba-⁻-is → cantá-ba-is; and, in
the subjunctives, cánta-⁻-ra-⁻-mos, cánta-⁻-ra-⁻-is,
cánta-⁻-se-⁻-mos, cánta-⁻-se-⁻-is → cantá-ra-mos,
cantá-ra-is, cantá-se-mos, cantá-se-is. Otherwise
the languages would not diverge. In the preterite
the accent would be attracted to the end of the stem,
however canté and cantó were resolved (Harris's
cantá-i, cantá-u). Similarly in the future, if it
is not compound. In the conditional, the accent of
cantaría would be that either of (hab)ía or of the
-e- and -i- conjugation imperfects generally; in
cantaríamos and cantaríais it again moves no further.
     I am not sure that I would wish to argue, on
the basis of Spanish alone, that this treatment is
right. But if we take both languages together,
these are the alternatives. In Spanish, we can say
that the accent is fixed morphologically in one
group of tenses, but phonologically in the rest.
That is Harris's solution and is undoubtedly neat.
But in Italian we cannot say this, in the light
particularly of oppositions like canta-vá-mo and
cantá-va-no, where, with the same syllabic structure
and ineluctably the same penultimate vowel, the accents differ. We must therefore conclude that the
languages have developed differently. In Italian,
the accent was not levelled, as in Spanish, in the
imperfect indicative. Furthermore, third plural
-NT developed, problematically, into -no (survey of
explanations in Tekavčić, 1972: 359ff.). The implication or the consequence, we have to say, is that
the Latin rule of phonological conditioning has been
lost. In Spanish, -NT developed unproblematically
into -n. In addition, the accent was levelled in
both the imperfect subjunctives and the imperfect
indicative. Now the levelling is itself confirmation
that, at that time, the Latin rule of phonological
conditioning had been lost. But the result, we say,

is that a rule not unlike it, by which the accent simply falls on the penultimate, is restored elsewhere in the paradigm.

It would be rash for someone who is not a specialist to discuss the history too confidently. But a plainer man's view is that the languages have developed similarly but differ in detail. One detail is that Italian levelled the accent only in the imperfect subjunctive: the result is that, in any set of rules devised to cover the other tenses, _cantassimo_ and _cantaste_ will be exceptional, if not accentually at least in their stem formative. In Spanish the levelling was general, but 'general' with respect to what factor? The usual answer is: with respect to the morphosyntactic feature 'Imperfect'. But arguably that reads too much into the terminology for the modern tenses. Another answer is: in all forms with a stem formative. But this has precisely the effect that, when the accent has been moved once by such a formative, it cannot move again.

Chapter 2

PHONOLOGY VERSUS MORPHOLOGY IN THE PORTUGUESE VERB

Stephen Parkinson

The Romance languages generally display a rich pattern of morphophonemics[1] closely linked with inflectional and derivational morphology. The relationship between the phonological rules proper and the
morphological rules can be seen as the interplay of
two different patterns, rather than the strict separation envisaged by American Structuralism, and
latterly Natural Generative Phonology, or the total
integration found in Generative Phonology. The
complex vowel phonology of Portuguese provides a
case in point.
    The two main dialects of Portuguese, European
Portuguese (EP) and Brazilian Portuguese (BP)[2], have
closely corresponding patterns of vowel alternation
in verbal paradigms. In each dialect a basic seven-
vowel system is subject to neutralisation rules of
phonological and morphological conditioning, which
conflict in that the operation of one creates exceptions to the other, so that both cannot represent
true generalisations. This conflict is resolved in
favour of phonology in BP, where the phonological and
morphological patterns are clearly distinct; in EP
the morphological pattern has prevailed in some cases, by the absorption of a phonological rule of BP
into the morphological rules of EP. In both dialects, however, there is a separation of morphological
and phonological rules not only in terms of their
order of application but also in the distinctive
features used in them.
    The analysis will use the formal apparatus of
Generative Phonology, with the rules formulated in
terms of segments rather than features, so as not
to prejudice subsequent discussion of the appropri-
ateness of rival feature systems. To do this, I
have to brush the dust off the old notational device

19

Phonology versus Morphology

of long square brackets (cf. Harms 1968:59; also
Brasington 1971) which are used to combine several
rules sharing the same context, in advance of (or
in the absence of) a distinctive feature analysis
showing them to be a unified process. By this device a set of rules such as (1):

1)   a $\rightarrow$ x / __Q

      b $\rightarrow$ y / __Q

      c $\rightarrow$ z / __Q

are combined as (2):

2) $\begin{bmatrix} a \\ b \\ c \end{bmatrix} \rightarrow \begin{bmatrix} x \\ y \\ z \end{bmatrix} / \_\_Q$

1. MORPHOLOGY: METAPHONY

In the Present Tense forms of regular 2nd and 3rd
conjugation verbs there is a pattern of root-vowel[3]
alternations, which is illustrated in (3)[4].
      The basic pattern is as follows: an underlying
mid (high- or low-mid) root vowel is low-mid in all
root-stressed Indicative forms except the 1st person
singular; in this form and in all root-stressed Subjunctive forms it is high-mid in a 2nd conjugation
verb and high in a 3rd conjugation verb. The quality of unstressed root vowels is determined in part
by the rules of atonic vowel quality (see sect. 2a);
taking these into account we find that the unstressed root vowel is high in 3rd conjugation Subjunctive forms, and mid elsewhere.
      The 1st conjugation has no alternations inside
its paradigm, a mid root vowel being realised as
low-mid when stressed.
      In this way, mid vowel distinctions in verb
roots are always neutralised. The only means of
establishing the underlying quality of root vowels
is by comparison with cognate nouns, where the vowel
distinctions remain (e.g. selar 'to seal', selo
['selu] 'seal, stamp'; cegar 'to blind', cego
['sɛgu] 'blind man').
      Most generative phonologies analyse Metaphony
as the interaction of two general rules of verb
morphophonemics: a rule of vowel Harmony by which
the root vowel is assimilated to the Theme vowel
(see note 3) in forms where the Theme vowel itself
is deleted, and a rule of Lowering by which all

Phonology versus Morphology

3)

	meter 'to put' (2nd conjugation)		ferir 'to wound' (3rd conjugation)	
Indicative				
1st pers. sg.	meto	['metu]	firo	['firu]
2nd pers. sg.	metes	['mɛtəʃ]	feres	['fɛrəʃ]
3rd pers. sg.	mete	['mɛtə]	fere	['fɛrə]
1st pers. pl.	metemos	[mə'temuʃ]	ferimos	[fə'rimuʃ]
		[me'temuʃ](BP)		[fe'rimuʃ](BP)
2nd pers. pl.	meteis	[mə'tɐiʃ]	feris	[fə'riʃ]
3rd pers. pl.	metem	['mɛtẽĩ]	ferem	['fɛrẽĩ]
Subjunctive				
1st pers. sg.	meta	['metɐ]	fira	['firɐ]
2nd pers. sg.	metas	['metɐʃ]	firas	['firɐʃ]
3rd pers. sg.	meta	['metɐ]	fira	['firɐ]
1st pers. pl.	metamos	[mə'tɐmuʃ]	firamos	[fi'rɐmuʃ]
		[me'tɐmuʃ](BP)		
2nd pers. pl.	metais	[mə'tais]	firais	[fi'raiʃ]
3rd pers. pl.	metam	['metẽũ]	firam	['firẽũ]

	correr 'to run' (2nd conjugation)		dormir 'to sleep' (3rd conjugation)	
Indicative				
1st pers. sg.	corro	['koRu]	durmo	['durmu]
2nd pers. sg.	corres	['kɔRəʃ]	dormes	['dɔrməʃ]
3rd pers. sg.	corre	['kɔRə]	dorme	['dɔrmə]
1st pers. pl.	corremos	[ku'Remuʃ]	dormimos	[dur'mimuʃ]
		[ko'Remuʃ](BP)		[dor'mimuʃ](BP)
2nd pers. pl.	correis	[ku'Rɐiʃ]	dormis	[dur'miʃ]
3rd pers. pl.	correm	['kɔRẽĩ]	dormem	['dɔrmẽĩ]
Subjunctive				
1st pers. sg.	corra	['koRɐ]	durma	['durmɐ]
2nd pers. sg.	corras	['koRɐʃ]	durmas	['durməʃ]
3rd pers. sg.	corra	['koRɐ]	durma	['durmɐ]
1st pers. pl.	corramos	[ku'Rɐmuʃ]	durmamos	[dur'mɐmuʃ]
		[ko'Rɐmuʃ](BP)		
2nd pers. pl.	corrais	[ku'Raiʃ]	durmais	[dur'maiʃ]
3rd pers. pl.	corram	['koRẽũ]	durmam	['durmẽũ]

Note: 2nd person verb forms are not a regular feature of BP verb paradigms, all functions of the 2nd person being taken over by 3rd person forms allied to distinctive address pronouns (see Pontes 1972, Wilhelm 1979).

other root vowels are realised as low-mid. Harmony
explains the difference between the conjugations,
as it produces high-mid vowels (assimilated to
Theme /e/) in the 2nd conjugation and high vowels
(assimilated to Theme /i/) in the 3rd conjugation.
The lack of alternations in the 1st conjugation is
also explained, as assimilation to the Theme vowel
/a/ will produce the same result as Lowering, namely
a low-mid vowel.

The rules of Harmony and Lowering are given
below, following Redenbarger 1978:

4) Harmony[5] $\left\{\begin{matrix} e \\ \varepsilon \\ o \\ \mathfrak{o} \end{matrix}\right\}$ $C_o \underset{[\alpha F]}{+ V}$ $+ V$ $\begin{bmatrix} vb \end{bmatrix}$

$\qquad\qquad$ STEM

$\qquad [\overset{}{\alpha}F] \qquad\qquad \phi$

5) Lowering[6] $\begin{bmatrix} e \\ o \end{bmatrix} \rightarrow \begin{bmatrix} \varepsilon \\ \mathfrak{o} \end{bmatrix} / \underline{\quad} C_o$ ROOT $\begin{bmatrix} vb \end{bmatrix}$

There is also a small but significant class of
3rd conjugation verbs such as fugir 'to flee',
frigir 'to fry', which have high root vowels but
show the same alternations as verbs with mid root
vowels, except that the root vowel is always high
in unstressed positions (e.g. frigimos [fri'ʒimuʃ]
'we fry'). These verbs require an extension of
Lowering discussed in sect. 10.

2. PHONOLOGY

a) Atonic Vowel Quality

In atonic syllables the number of oral vowel contrasts is very much reduced.[7] In pretonic syllables
EP has four contrasting units and BP has five:

6)   EP   BP

  /i/ /ə/ /u/   /i/   /u/

       /a/ [ɐ]   /e/   /o/

                          /a/ [a] ~ [ɐ]

while in atonic final position each system has only
three units:

7)   EP   BP
                  /ə/   /u/   /i/   /u/
                  /a/   /a/ [ɐ]

In each case the principal mechanism is neutralisation rules affecting the mid vowels. The contrast
of /e o/ - /ɛ ɔ/ is always lost (EP [ə] representing the neutralisation of /e ɛ/) and in many cases
the contrast of mid and high vowels is also lost.
The patterning accounts for the quality of unstressed root vowels in the verb forms of (3), and also
for the differences of realisation between EP and
BP forms. It can be formalised with the following
rules:

8)   Neutralisation[8]

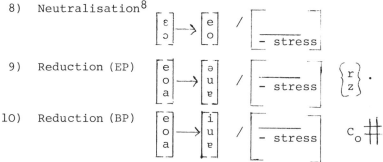

9)   Reduction (EP)

10) Reduction (BP)

b)   N-vowel Quality

There is a general rule of Portuguese phonology by
which the low-mid vowels /ɛɔ/ do not appear before
nasal consonants (Viana 1883:40). Vowels appearing
in this context are phonetically nasalised (strongly
in BP, weakly in EP) and have traditionally been
called nasalised vowels (Lacerda and Strevens 1954:
16) to distinguish them from the nasal vowels which
are in phonemic contrast with oral vowels. (Phonologically, nasal vowels are homosyllabic /VN/ sequences,[9] while nasalised vowels are those followed by
heterosyllabic /N/, that is, in /V.N/ sequences.)
For phonological purposes the nasality of nasalised
vowels is not the determinant of vowel quality, but
a secondary effect of consonantal context:[10] these
vowels will accordingly be labelled N-vowels, and
the rule specifying their quality is N-vowel Quality (NVQ):

11) NVQ $\begin{bmatrix} \varepsilon \\ \mathfrak{o} \end{bmatrix} \rightarrow \begin{bmatrix} e \\ o \end{bmatrix} / \underline{} \begin{bmatrix} C \\ \text{nasal} \end{bmatrix}$

3. INTERACTION OF MORPHOLOGY AND PHONOLOGY

The rules so far discussed act on contexts which are not mutually exclusive. There will thus be forms to which more than one of the rules can apply. However, the phonological rules are essentially raising rules, while Lowering and some cases of Harmony are lowering rules; they cannot both be true of derived forms, so one rule must override the other.

Harmony and Lowering provide no surface exceptions to the rules of Atonic Vowel Quality (AVQ), since regular verb paradigms have only /iueə (BP e)/ in atonic open syllables. This does not mean, however, that AVQ blocks Harmony and Lowering, or that Harmony and Lowering do not operate in atonic open syllables. Forms such as ferimos and firamos (Figure 3) show that AVQ operates on the output of Harmony/Lowering. Where the output of Harmony/Lowering does not conform to AVQ, as in ferimos (/ɛer+i+muʃ/—→*/fɛ'rimuʃ/) it is modified by AVQ (/fɛ'rimuʃ/—→[fə'rimuʃ]); where the output of Harmony/Lowering already conforms to AVQ (firamos /fer+i+a+mus/—→[fi'ɾemuʃ], it is unmodified. If AVQ operated on the underlying root vowel, of firamos, the incorrect form */fə'remuʃ/ would result. The interaction of Metaphony and NVQ is a major point of divergence between EP and BP. In BP we find that NVQ is exceptionless, overriding Metaphony in all cases where it would produce a low-mid vowel. In EP, Metaphony operates unconstrained by NVQ, so that metaphonic vowels are a significant class of exceptions to NVQ.

The contrast between EP and BP phonology can be illustrated by the relevant forms of the verbs comer 'to eat' and sumir 'to sink':

12)

EP	comer	BP	EP	sumir	BP
['komu]	como	['komu]	['sumu]	sumo	['sumu]
['kɔmə]	come	['komi]	['sɔmə]	some	['somi]
['kɔmẽ ̃]	comem	['komẽĩ]	['sɔmẽ ̃]	somem	['somẽĩ]

(NB: <u>sumir</u> has root /u/, so that the root vowel of
<u>sumo</u> is underlying, not harmonised. There are app-
arently no cases of metaphonic 3rd conjugation verbs
with a mid N-vowel as root vowel.)

4. MORE MORPHOLOGY: IRREGULAR PRETERITES

Many Portuguese irregular verbs form the Preterite
with a suppletive stem formation which replaces the
regular segmented Root+Theme structure.[11] Stress
falls (regularly) on the final or penultimate vowel
of this stem. The final vowel of the stem is usually realised as /ɛ/ when stressed, and as /ə/ (EP)
or /i/ (BP) when unstressed (in accordance with the
rules for atonic final syllables, sect. 2a).
    In the 1st person plural form the stem is
followed by the Person/number suffix /muʃ/, making
it an N-vowel; this gives us another case of conflict between NVQ and a morphological rule, resolved in the same way as the preceding case. In EP
the stem vowel remains /ɛ/, so that the process of
Special Stem Formation (SSF)[12] overrides NVQ; in BP
the stem vowel becomes /e/, showing that NVQ overrides SSF.
    The forms of the verb <u>dizer</u> 'to say' illustrate
these points.

13) <u>dizer</u> regular stem /diz+e/ special stem /disɛ/

Preterite		EP	BP
1st pers. sg.	<u>disse</u>	[ˈdisə]	[ˈdisi]
3rd pers. sg.	<u>disse</u>	[ˈdisə]	[ˈdisi]
1st pers. pl.	<u>dissemos</u>	[diˈsɛmuʃ]	[diˈsemuʃ]
3rd pers. pl.	<u>disseram</u>	[diˈsɛrẽũ]	[diˈsɛrẽũ]

The situation in EP is not an isolated fact, but
can be related to a well-known phonological peculiarity of EP, the surface contrast of /a/ and /ɐ/.

5. MORE PHONOLOGY: /a/ VERSUS /ɐ/ IN EUROPEAN PORTUGUESE

In both EP and BP the phoneme /a/ has amongst its
allophones a raised vowel [ɐ] or [ɑ] found in N-
vowels and nasal vowels.[13] Most phonologists view
this allophonic rule /a/→[ɐ] as an extension of
NVQ, whose full formulation becomes:

14)   NVQ (extended)

$$\begin{bmatrix} \varepsilon \\ \mathfrak{o} \\ a \end{bmatrix} \rightarrow \begin{bmatrix} e \\ o \\ \mathfrak{v} \end{bmatrix} \quad / \underline{\hspace{1cm}} \begin{bmatrix} C \\ + \text{ nasal} \end{bmatrix}$$

The interaction of NVQ and Metaphony is not affected by this change as root /a/ is not subject to
Metaphony.
    In EP, however, the situation is complicated
by the fact that /a/⟶[ɐ] is not a simple allophonic rule. It is blocked in one single grammatical
form, namely the 1st person plural of regular 1st
conjugation Preterites, with the result that there
is a contrast between /a/ and /ɐ/ in corresponding
Present Indicative and Preterite forms:

15)   <u>falar</u> 'to speak'

        1st pers. pl., Pres. Ind. <u>falamos</u> [fɐ'lɐmuʃ]
            (NVQ operates)

        1st pers. pl., Preterite   <u>falámos</u> [fɐ'lamuʃ]
            (NVQ blocked)

    Traditional phonemicists (e.g. Sten 1944;
Barbosa 1965:67) maintained that there was no alternative -hélas- to recognising /ɐ/ as a distinct
phoneme, the opposition between /a/ and /ɐ/ being
neutralised (by NVQ) everywhere except in this cor-
ner of verb inflection.
    Generative phonology has a different way of
showing quite how marginal the contrast is. The
inventory of underlying phonemes does not contain
/ɐ/; the contrast of /a/ and /ɐ/ is derived, by a
grammatically conditioned blocking of NVQ.
    The blocking of NVQ in this case, and its non-
application in irregular Preterites can be seen as
a more general regularity: the rule of NVQ, in EP,
<u>never</u> affects stem-final vowels in Preterites.
We have seen that irregular verbs and regular 1st
conjugation verbs behave in this way; the remaining
cases, that is regular 2nd and 3rd conjugation verbs,
do not undergo NVQ at all (except vacuously) since
the stem-final vowels of their Preterite forms are
the Theme vowels /e/ and /i/ respectively. We can
in fact extend this restriction, and formulate NVQ
as (16) so that it never operates in Preterite forms:
apart from the cases mentioned, all N-vowels in
Preterite forms will be atonic, and their quality
is fully accounted for by AVQ (rules 8-9) which effects the same changes as NVQ.

16) NVQ (EP) $\begin{bmatrix} \varepsilon \\ \mathfrak{o} \\ a \end{bmatrix} \rightarrow \begin{bmatrix} e \\ o \\ \mathfrak{e} \end{bmatrix}$ / ___ $\begin{bmatrix} C \\ + \text{ nasal} \end{bmatrix}$ $\begin{bmatrix} \text{-preterite} \end{bmatrix}$

6. MORE PHONOLOGY: NASAL VOWEL QUALITY

Nasal vowels show a restricted range of contrasts
which matches the N-vowel system in that the standard forms of EP and BP have no low-mid nasal vowels,[14] and the nasal counterpart of /a/ is /ẽ/.
We can account for this by a rule of Nasal Vowel
Quality (NasVQ) of the form:

17) $\begin{bmatrix} \varepsilon \\ \mathfrak{o} \\ a \end{bmatrix} \longrightarrow \begin{bmatrix} e \\ o \\ \mathfrak{e} \end{bmatrix}$ / $\begin{bmatrix} \rule{1.5cm}{0.4pt} \\ + \text{ nasal} \end{bmatrix}$

There is such similarity between NasVQ and NVQ that
generality demands that we attempt to conflate them
(cf. Mateus 1975:46-62). In BP, where the phonetic
nasality of N-vowels is as strong as that of nasal
vowels, the rule of NasVQ will do the work of NVQ
as well, as can be illustrated by the derivations
of cama 'bed' ['kẽme] and campo 'field' ['kẽpu]:

18)

	cama	campo
	/kama/	/kaNpu/
Nasalisation	kãma	kãpu
NasVQ	kẽma	kẽpu
Other rules	['kẽme]	['kẽpu]

In EP this conflation is impossible,for all its plausibility, because NVQ and NasVQ interact with Metaphony in crucially different ways. NVQ, we have
seen, is overridden by Metaphony; NasVQ, on the
other hand, is an exceptionless rule, in EP as well
as in BP. Verbs with nasal mid root vowels show
only the raising effects of Harmony, and none of the
lowering effects of Harmony and Lowering, as is shown by the verbs mandar 'to order' vender 'to sell'
and sentir 'to feel'.

27

19) Present
     Indicative <u>mandar</u>

1st	pers.	sg.	<u>mando</u>	['mẽdu]
3rd	pers.	sg.	<u>manda</u>	['mẽdɐ]
1st	pers.	pl.	<u>mandamos</u>	[mẽ'dɐmuʃ]
3rd	pers.	pl.	<u>mandam</u>	['mẽdẽũ]

<u>vender</u>

1st	pers.	sg.	<u>vendo</u>	['vẽdu]
3rd	pers.	sg.	<u>vende</u>	['vẽdə]
1st	pers.	pl.	<u>vendemos</u>	[vẽ'demuʃ]
3rd	pers.	pl.	<u>vendem</u>	['vẽdẽĩ]

<u>sentir</u>

1st	pers.	sg.	<u>sinto</u>	['sĩtu]
3rd	pers.	sg.	<u>sente</u>	['sẽtə]
1st	pers.	pl.	<u>sentimos</u>	[sẽ'timuʃ]
3rd	pers.	pl.	<u>sentem</u>	['sẽtẽĩ]

In EP, then, we require separate rules of NVQ and NasVQ, the former blocked by Metaphony and the latter operating freely after it; in BP we have a single rule of N(as)VQ operating freely after Metaphony. NasVQ does not block Metaphony, since like AVQ it overrides the lowering subcases without affecting the raising subcases; it must thus be seen as operating on the output of Metaphony.

The 1st person plural forms of (19) illustrate the general rule that nasal vowels are not subject to atonic vowel reduction. This is not a question of rule interaction, however, but an instance of the more general rule that reduction does not affect the class of strong syllables comprising diphthongs, nasal vowels and syllables closed by /l/, (see note 8).

The EP rule of NasVQ will be the simpler form (20):

20)
$$
\begin{bmatrix} \varepsilon \\ \mathrm{ɔ} \end{bmatrix} \rightarrow \begin{bmatrix} e \\ o \end{bmatrix} \ / \ \overline{\begin{bmatrix} + \text{ nasal} \end{bmatrix}}
$$

It will not require a subcase converting /a/ to [ɐ], since the underlying form /aN/ will already have been converted to /ɐN/ by NVQ.

7. MORE MORPHOLOGY: 1ST CONJUGATION VERBS IN EP

In BP the 1st conjugation patterns with the other conjugations in the sense that the quality of root vowels is determined by the same combination of Harmony, Laxing, AVQ and NVQ. There is room for discussion as to the precise interaction of the rules (compare Harris 1974, Redenbarger 1978) but there is no doubt that the rules of Metaphony affect all conjugations.

In EP, however, the situation is often different. According to the classic accounts of Goncalves Viana (1883:53-6; 1903:76) the 1st conjugation differs from the others in that it does not provide a regular source of exceptions to NVQ. A regular verb such as <u>remar</u> 'to row', has root /e/, not /ɛ/, in the root-stressed forms:

21) Present   <u>remar</u>
     Indicative

1st pers. sg.	<u>remo</u>	['ʀ emu]
2nd pers. sg.	<u>remas</u>	['ʀ emɐʃ]
3rd pers. sg.	<u>rema</u>	['ʀ emɐ]
3rd pers. pl.	<u>remam</u>	['ʀ emẽũ] (Viana 1883:55)

Only in a small number of 1st conjugation verbs do we find low-mid root N-vowels. Viana 1883 names only <u>tomar</u> 'to take', with <u>somar</u> 'to add' and <u>domar</u> 'to tame' added in Viana 1903.

To account for this situation, we must follow Viana in taking Metaphony to affect 2nd and 3rd conjugation verbs only, with a separate rule of Root Vowel Quality affecting 1st conjugation verbs. Irregular verbs such as <u>tomar</u> will be marked either as exceptions to NVQ (this constituting a third constraint on it) or as irregularly subject to Metaphony (presumably using the same diacritic that will be applied to 3rd conjugation verbs such as <u>fugir</u> (sect. 1)).

Modern Lisbon dialects have developed beyond this situation. Mateus (1975:93) claims that all 1st conjugation verbs are subject to Metaphony, and are thus exceptions to NVQ, and I have been able to confirm this from Lisbon informants; it is not clear to what extent other dialects of EP have followed Lisbon.[15]

8. SUMMARY OF RULES

The rules so far formulated,with others referred to
but not formulated, are listed below, with a summary
of their interaction and sample derivations.

22)   Root Vowel Quality   (conservative EP) sect. 7
                            Precedes NVQ or blocked by it.

    Special Stem Formation   sect.4
                            Precedes NasVQ (BP)
                            Precedes Neutralisation and
                            Reduction

    N-Vowel Quality (EP) (16)
                            Blocked by Harmony and
                            Lowering

    Lowering (5)   disjunctive rules
    Harmony   (4)
                            Precede NasVQ, Neutralisa-
                            tion, Reduction. Block NVQ

    Stress (stress is placed on antepenultimate
            syllables containing a Theme Vowel; on
            final strong syllables (diphthongs or
            syllables closed by a non-inflectional
            consonant); otherwise on penultimate
            syllables.)[16]
                            Follows Harmony
                            Feeds Neutralisation, Reduc-
                            tion

    Neutralisation (8)   Fed by Stress
                            Follows Lowering, Harmony

    Nasalisation sect.6 (vowels are nasalised when
                            followed by a nasal conson-
                            ant (in the same syllable
                            in EP))

$$V \longrightarrow \begin{bmatrix} + \text{ nas} \end{bmatrix} \quad / \underline{\quad} \begin{bmatrix} C \\ + \text{ nas} \end{bmatrix} \quad \begin{Bmatrix} \\ \cdot \end{Bmatrix} \quad \begin{matrix} \text{BP} \\ \\ \text{EP} \end{matrix}$$

                            Feeds NasVQ

Nasal Vowel Quality (17 (BP);20 (EP))
                    Fed by Nasalisation
                    Follows Lowering, Harmony

Reduction (9 (EP); 10 (BP))
                    Fed by Neutralisation
                    Follows Lowering, Harmony

9.   RULE APPLICATION

If the rules of (22)were to be applied in a single ordered sequence, the order would be:

24)   i.   Root Vowel Quality
                 Special Stem Formation

           ii.   NVQ

          iii.   Lowering

           iv.   Harmony

            v.   Stress

           vi.   Neutralisation
                 Nasalisation

          vii.   Reduction
                 NasVQ

Where the relative order of two rules is indeterminate, they have been grouped together. The main indeterminacy remaining is the position of the rule of Nasalisation, which depends on the overall analysis of nasal vowels and diphthongs.[17]
     The rule order given in (24)shows that the morphological rules (RVQ,SSF, Lowering, Harmony, Stress) precede the phonological rules (Neutralisation, Nasalisation, Reduction, NasVQ). NVQ, which at first seemed to be a phonological rule, has shown itself to be morphologised by the grammatical constraints upon it and now by its position in the middle of the morphological rules. However, many of the ordering relationships of (24) are unnecessary (e.g. feeding relationships such as Nasalisation-NasVQ) and nearly all of the remainder are cases of morphological rules preceding phonological rules. They are thus consistent with a simpler scheme in which the main ordering relation is one of a block of morphological rules preceding a block of phonological rules, with

31

23) Sample derivations

	como /kom+e+u/	come /kom+e/	come (BP) /kom+e/
NVQ	kom e u	kom e	–
Harmony/Lowering	kom u	kɔm e	kɔm e
Stress	'komu	'kɔme	'kɔme
Neutralisation	('komu)	('kɔme)	('kɔme)
Nasalisation	–	–	'kõme
NasVQ	–	–	'kõme
Reduction	('komu)	'kɔmə	'kõmi
	['komu]	['kɔmə]	['kõmi]

	sinto /sent+i+u/	sente /sent+i/	sentimos /sent+i+muʃ/
NVQ	(sent i u)	(sent i)	(sent i muʃ)
Harmony/Lowering	sint u	sɛnt i	sɛnt i muʃ
Stress	'sintu	'sɛnti	sɛn'timuʃ
Neutralisation	–	'sɛnte	sen'timuʃ
Nasalisation	'sĩtu	'sẽte	sẽ'timuʃ
NasVQ	–	'sẽte	(sẽ'timuʃ)
Reduction	('sĩtu)	'sẽtə	(sẽ'timuʃ)
	['sĩtu]	['sẽtə]	[sẽ'timuʃ]

	sintamos /sent+i+a+muʃ/	tomamos (EP) /tɔm+a+muʃ/	tomamos (BP) /tom+a+muʃ/
NVQ	sent i ɐ muʃ	tom ɐ muʃ	–
Harmony/Lowering	sint ɐmuʃ	tom ɐmuʃ	tom amuʃ
Stress	sin'tɐmuʃ	tɔ'mɐmuʃ	tɔ'mamuʃ
Neutralisation	–	to'mɐmuʃ	to'mamuʃ
Nasalisation	sĩ'tɐmuʃ	–	to'mãmuʃ
NasVQ	–	–	to'mẽmuʃ
Reduction	(sĩ'tɐmuʃ)	tu'mɐmuʃ	–
	[sĩ'tɐmuʃ]	[tu'mɐmuʃ]	[to'mẽmuʃ]

	tomámos (EP) /tɔm+a+muʃ/	dissemos (BP) /diz+e+muʃ/
Special Stem Formation	–	disɛ muʃ
NVQ	–	–
Harmony/Lowering	tom a muʃ	–
Stress	tɔ'mamuʃ	di'sɛmuʃ
Neutralisation	to'mamuʃ	–
Nasalisation	–	di'sẽmuʃ
NasVQ	–	di'sẽmuʃ
Reduction	tu'mamuʃ	(di'sẽmuʃ)
	[tu'mamuʃ]	[di'sẽmuʃ]

Phonology versus Morphology

the rules unordered inside the blocks.

25)   block I   Root Vowel Quality
                            Special Stem Formation
                            Lowering
                            Harmony
                            NVQ (blocked by Lowering/Harmony)
                            Stress

       block II   Neutralisation
                            Nasalisation
                            Reduction
                            NasVQ

Universal conditions of application such as Stifling[18]
will take care of any remaining precedence relationships inside the blocks, such as the relationship
between Lowering and Harmony. It has always been
claimed that Stress must follow Harmony, since a
stress rule operating before or simultaneously with
Harmony would stress precisely the vowel which is
deleted by Harmony. In fact the incompatibility of
the two rules means that Stifling can be invoked to
give Harmony precedence over Stress.

10. DISTINCTIVE FEATURES FOR PHONOLOGY AND MORPHOL-
OGY

In most generative analyses (e.g. Harris 1974,
Mateus 1975) the vowels of Portuguese are analysed
as a system distinguishing three degrees of aperture
(represented by the combinations of the features
[±high] [±low]) and three combinations of the features [±back] [±round], as diagrammed in (26):

26)   + high
      - low   i   ə   u

      - high
      - low   e   ɐ   o

      - high
      + low   ɛ   a   ɔ

                  - back   + back   + back
                 (- round)   - round   + round

Redenbarger 1978 has shown that this framework does not allow an adequate formulation of Harmony, and creates problems in the formulation and application of Lowering.

Harmony requires that the mid vowels /e o ɛ ɔ/ excluding /a/ form a natural class, which is only possible in the above framework if one makes use of variables, which has been shown to be suspect (Wheeler 1972):

27) $\qquad$ /e o ɛ ɔ/ = $\begin{bmatrix} - \text{ high} \\ \alpha \text{ back} \\ \alpha \text{ round} \end{bmatrix}$

For the assimilation process of Harmony it is /ɛ ɔ a/ which must have common features, since /ɛ ɔ/ are mid vowels assimilated to /a/. To cover both these groupings of sounds, we require the arrangement of (28):

28)

+ high − Y	i		− X				u
			+ X				
− high − Y	e	ɛ		ə	ɔ		o
− high + Y	ɐ	a					
		− back (− round			+ back − round		+ back + round

The best candidates for features X and Y are [±tense] (or its successor [±Advanced tongue Root] (ATR) and [±Constricted Pharynx] (CP) respectively. Harmony can then be formulated:

29) $\begin{bmatrix} V \\ - CP \\ - \text{high} \end{bmatrix} C_0{}^+ \begin{bmatrix} \begin{bmatrix} V \\ \alpha \text{ tense} \\ \beta \text{ high} \end{bmatrix} & \text{STEM} & + & V \end{bmatrix} vb$.

$\downarrow$ $\begin{bmatrix} \alpha \text{ tense} \\ \beta \text{ high} \end{bmatrix}$ $\qquad$ $\downarrow$ $\emptyset$ $\qquad$ (Redenbarger 1977:268)

The formulation of Lowering had been complicated by the need to include a subcase lowering /i u/ to /ɛ ɔ/ in stressed syllables only in marked 3rd conjugation verbs (see sect. 1). This entailed formulating Lowering as a rule of stressed vowel lowering,

which therefore had to operate after the rules of
Stress assignment; but Harmony has to operate before
stress is assigned (see sect. 9). The natural com-
plementarity of the two rules was thus made more
complex, as the two rules could not operate simultaneously or adjacent to one another. Redenbarger's
solution is to formulate Lowering as a rule of Laxing, which converts /i u/ to an unused feature combination [+ high - tense], that is /I U/, at the
same time as converting /e o/ to /ɛ ɔ/. Neutralisation, formulated as a tensing rule

30) $\begin{bmatrix} V \\ - stress \end{bmatrix} \longrightarrow \begin{bmatrix} + tense \end{bmatrix}$

will convert atonic /I U/ back to /i u/, after which
a rule of Feature Adjustment (my label) converts the
remaining cases of /I U/ to /ɛ ɔ/:

31)   Feature Adjustment $\begin{bmatrix} V \\ - tense \end{bmatrix} \longrightarrow \begin{bmatrix} - high \end{bmatrix}$

        However, Redenbarger's neat analysis of mor-
phological rules does not give a good account of
Portuguese phonetics. He analyses [a] and [ɑ] as
front vowels on the strength of a single formant
analysis of EP tonic vowels, the figures in fact
showing that [a] is a true central vowel and [ɑ] a
front-central one:

32)   Formant values for EP tonic vowels (Martins
      1973)

	F1	F2
[ɔ]	530	994
[a]	626	1326
[ɑ]	511	1602
[ɛ]	501	1893

He does not distinguish between [ɑ] and [ɐ] (see
note 13) and he is forced to represent [ə] as a mid
vowel since his own rule of Feature Adjustment excludes high lax vowels. In this way he loses sight
of the fact that [a] [ɐ] and [ə] constitute a series
of central vowels differing only in height (and
partly overlapping as a result, cf. Strevens 1954:
14). The characterisation of /e-ɛ/ and /o-ɔ/ as
tense-lax pairs is not well supported from phonetic

data, since /ɛ ɔ/ are as peripheral as /e o/ (cardinal according to Strevens 1954) and are as long as /e o/ (Martins 1973).

Not surprisingly, then, the phonological rules do not fit in with Redenbarger's feature framework. The rules of Reduction are clearly a generalised raising process, in both EP and BP, yet they are represented as a mixture of tensing (/a/→[ɐ]) centralisation/laxing (/e/→[ə]) and raising (/e o/ ⟶ /i/u/). Similarly, the rule of NasVQ in BP is a raising rule, as BP [ɐ] is not to be equated with EP [ɑ].

For the latter part of our analysis, the feature system of (26) is preferable,[19] requiring only slight modification to preserve the distinction between [ɐ] and [ɑ]; for this purpose Redenbarger's feature [Tense] should be retained, to characterise [ɐ] as [+ low + tense]

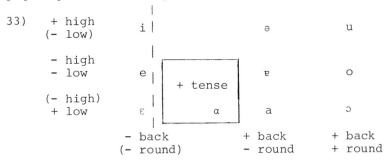

33)

+ high (- low)	i		ə		u
- high - low	e		ɐ		o
(- high) + low	ɛ		ɑ	a	ɔ

| | - back (- round) | + back - round | + back + round |

We now have an analysis where different feature systems hold for different sets of rules. The division of rules according to this criterion agrees with the division made on the basis of rule type and rule interaction in sect. 9, except that Neutralisation works with the 'morphological' feature system instead of falling in with the phonological rules.

The transition between the two systems does not require any additional machinery. The rule of Feature Adjustment is effectively a redundancy rule, as it makes the feature [±tense] redundant among high vowels. With only minor adjustments it can become a rule that restructures the feature system by making [±tense] and [+ CP] redundant everywhere in BP and in all but the low central vowels of EP:

34) Feature Adjustment (revised)

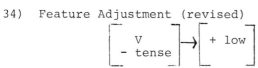

This formulation of Feature Adjustment not only
changes /I U/ to /ɛ ɔ/ but also revises the representation of /ɛ ɔ/ from [-high, -CP, -tense] to
[-high, +low, (-CP), (-tense)]. In EP the[+tense]
vowel [α] will be unaffected.

In terms of rule application, Feature Adjustment must follow Neutralisation, and feeds all the
phonological rules which use the new feature system.
Neutralisation, for its part, is in the odd situation of being a phonological rule using the 'morphological' feature system. In fact, these two rules
have a special function, as they are "transition
rules", rules which effect the transition from one
level or rule block to another. Their natural place
is thus between the two major blocks of rules, as in
the final rule scheme of (35).

35)   Root Vowel Quality
               Special Stem Formation
               Lowering
               Harmony
               NVQ
               Stress
               _____

               Neutralisation
               Feature Adjustment
               _____

               Nasalisation
               NasVQ
               Reduction

11. CONCLUSIONS

The complexities of Portuguese vowel alternations
have been shown to be not just a question of phonology or of verb morphology, but of the interaction
between the two. In particular, the marginal phonemic contrast of /a/ and /ɐ/ in European Portuguese
arises from the morphologisation of a phonological
rule, and a modification of the surface phonological
feature system in the direction of the deep morphological system.

Phonology versus Morphology

Romance verb morphology, as Romance inflectional morphology in general, presents a challenge to
the phonologist by its variety and complexity. The
balance and interaction of morphological and phonological rules is a major factor in this picture, and
is a significant part of the characterisation of
the various Romance languages. Portuguese shows a
complex morphological component matched by an equally
complex phonological component, in which it is similar to French (see for instance Dell 1980: ch. 4-6
on the phonology and morphology of schwa): in Spanish
(Harris 1969) and Italian (Bartholomew 1979) the
greatest complexity is in the morphological component.
The concept of transition rules allows us to
identify the point at which abstract and concrete
phonology meet. For Portuguese it is the rules specifying the quality of mid vowels; for Spanish the
rule of Diphthongisation (Harris 1969:116-8) which
operates after the morphological rules to convert
underlying lax /e/ and /o/ into the surface diphthongs /je/ and /we/, has all the marks of a transition rule. There is now no need for abstract and
concrete phonology to be seen as antagonistic and
mutually exclusive, since they can co-exist in separate, linked components. In this reconciliation,
as in many other developments, Romance linguistics
is ideally suited to show the way.

NOTES

1. The terms morphophonemics and phonology
have too many usages to stand undefined. Here,
phonology is used in a Praguean sense to cover not
only allophonic rules but also phonologically motivated neutralisation rules and phonotactic rules.
Morphology and morphological rule will be used to
refer to rules realising or operating upon morphological units or phonological units in grammatical
contexts. The term morphophonemics is taken in the
American structuralist sense (e.g. Hockett 1954) as
the set of mutation rules whose output is a phonemic
representation; it will be little used in this discussion as it cuts across my morphology-phonology
distinction. For other paths through this jungle,
see Matthews 1972 especially pp. 54-5; Sommerstein
1977:204-11.
2. For the purposes of illustration, EP is
represented by the Lisbon dialect and BP by Rio de
Janeiro. EP and BP forms are only distinguished

where it is relevant to the discussion; elsewhere,
EP forms are used for exemplification. Most of the
phonological differences between the two varieties
are in fact accounted for by the rules proposed.
In addition there are differences in the distribution and realisation of the /R/ and /r/ phonemes
(cf. Brakel 1974) and EP has a rule of e-centralisa-
tion by which /e/ is realised as [ɐ] in the diphthongs /ei/ and /ẽĩ/, and when followed by /ʎ ɲ ʃ ʒ /
in the next syllable.

3. The basic morphological structure of Portuguese synthetic verb forms is:

Root + Theme ⌐ + Tense/Aspect/Mood + Person/
        ⌐ STEM   Number

as illustrated by the form <u>falavas</u> 'you were saying':

/fal +   a   +   va   +   ʃ /
Root   Theme   Past   2nd pers. sg.
     1st conj.   Imperfect

The Theme or conjugation marker is: 1st conj. /a/;
2nd conj. /e/; 3rd conj. /i/. See Pontes 1972,
Parkinson 1979 ch. 3 for complete accounts of the
segmental morphology of Portuguese.

4. Metaphony is the traditional term used in
Portuguese for vowel alternations conditioned by the
quality of vowels in the following syllables. A
similar rule is found in Portuguese noun morphology.
The name is retained here as a label without explanatory value. There is a plethora of exceptions,
which do not affect the analysis given here: see
Mateus 1975:126-141 for the irregular verbs that fall
into this category, and Harris 1974:64 for some of
the regular ones.

5. Harmony incorporates the rule of Theme
vowel deletion by which the Theme vowel is deleted
when followed immediately by a vowel. (See Harris
1974, Redenbarger 1978 for justification of the rule).
It is in fact part of a wider rule of internal
sandhi of the form:

$$\begin{array}{cc} \left.\begin{array}{c}V\end{array}\right] & \left[\begin{array}{c}V\end{array}\right. \\ \downarrow_{\text{STEM}} + & \text{AFFIX} \\ \phi \end{array}$$

(cf. Pardal 1977:59)

The ad-hoc abbreviation [α F]....[α F] is used to represent an assimilation of tongue-body features.

6. Redenbarger's original formulation

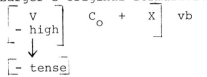

is too lax, since the configuration V C_0 + does not uniquely specify verb roots, and would allow the rule to operate on most non-final suffixes, including the Theme vowel. As the rule is intended to apply only to root vowels, there is no point in avoiding specific reference to morphological structure.

7. Nasal vowels, diphthongs and syllables closed by /l/ are not affected by atonic vowel reduction. The vowels /ɛ ɔ a/ are not completely excluded from atonic syllables, but their occurrence is exceptional and departs from a very regular pattern of tonic-atonic vowel correspondences.

8. A separate rule is required to neutralise the contrast of /e/ and /i/ in atonic final syllables in EP: this rule accounts for the realisation of the Theme vowel /i/ as atonic final [ə] as in fere /fer+i/ ['fɛrə].

9. This analysis has a long history starting with Trager 1943, Reed and Leite 1947, Câmara 1953, Barbosa 1965. For full generative analyses of this type see Brasington 1971, Mateus 1975, Parkinson 1979.

10. In EP the nasality of nasalised vowels is weak to the point of imperceptibility. In both varieties there is progressive nasalisation of vowels following nasal 'consonants, which has no effect on vowel quality.

11. The main members of this class are: dar (Special Stem /dɛ/), vir (/viɛ/), caber (/koubɛ/), trazer (/trousɛ/), saber (/soubɛ/), querer (/kizɛ/), fazer (/fizɛ/), poder (/pudɛ/), por (/puzɛ/), ter (/tivɛ/), estar (/stivɛ/).

12. The same stem is incorporated in the Pluperfect, Past Subjunctive and Future Subjunctive forms of these verbs. All attempts to identify a Past tense morph (e.g. Mateus 1975:164-9) founder on the impossibility of finding a morpheme or morphosyntactic feature common to the Preterite and Future Subjunctive: what we require is a lexical listing of the Special stems and a morphological rule indicating that marked irregular verbs have the structure [Special Stem + T/A/M + P/N] in these tenses.

13.   The phonetics of this aspect of Portuguese have been sadly neglected.   No account of Portuguese phonetics distinguishes more than two central 'a'-vowels.   Yet there are at least two varieties of the 'close a': in EP the vowel found in atonic syllables, mid, central [ɐ] is clearly distinct from the low-mid front-central [ɐ] found in N-vowels and diphthongs.   (See Martins 1973, Redenbarger 1978, Parkinson 1979:37-4).   In BP only [ɐ] seems to be found.

14.   Northern dialects of EP do not have this rule (Viana 1883:46).

15.   I found considerable variation between informants in this respect.   Two non-Lisbon informants both had some verbs (especially <u>remar</u> 'to row', <u>telefonar</u> 'to telephone') as exceptions to NVQ (with the cognate nouns <u>remo</u> 'oar', <u>telefone</u> 'telephone' also exceptions).   One of them had certain verbs, including Viana's example <u>tomar</u>, showing an alternation of /o/ and /ɔ/ identical to that found in 2nd conjugation verbs, e.g. <u>tomo</u> 'I take' ['tomu] <u>toma</u> 'he takes' ['tɔmɐ].

16.   This version of the stress rule is deliberately formulated to make a surface-true generalisation.   It is still a morphological rule, as it refers to morphological structure in two of its subcases.

17.   In most generative analyses the process of Nasalisation is bound up with the derivation of nasal vowels from VNV sequences, e.g. <u>irmã</u> 'sister' derived from /irmana/—→/irmãna/—→/irmãa/—→/irmã/. In this case, the rule of Nasalisation will be morphological, as it will be sensitive to a nonphonological distinction between 'nasalising N' in <u>irmã</u> and 'non-nasalising N' (e.g. /n/)in <u>mana</u> 'sister' ['mẽnɐ](BP ['mẽnɐ]) derived from /mana/.   For alternative accounts see Brakel 1979, Parkinson 1979 ch.4.

18.   See Sommerstein 1977:189.   Stifling is one of several principles stipulating that when two incompatible rules can operate on the same segment, the less general of them has precedence.

19.   It could be argued that a scalar feature of vowel height would give an even better account of Reduction.   See Lipski 1973 for such an argument, based on more complex AVQ rules in a different variety of BP.

Chapter 3

THE 'PAST SIMPLE' AND THE 'PRESENT PERFECT' IN ROMANCE*

Martin Harris

The evolution of the verbal system has always been
one of the principal concerns of historical Romance
linguists, and within this general field perhaps
no single topic has aroused greater interest than
the constantly changing inter-relationship between
two indicative paradigms which have been variously
labelled in the literature and which I shall refer
to by the time-honoured names of 'past simple' and
'present perfect'. The emergence in V(ulgar)
L(atin) of the paradigm HABEO FACTUM, and its opposition to the earlier C(lassical) L(atin) paradigm FECI has been widely discussed by Latinists;
the formal and semantic development of the derivatives of these two paradigms has been of great interest to both synchronic and diachronic linguists
concerned with particular Romance languages; and
the complex and fascinating interplay of tense and
aspect revealed by a study of these two paradigms
has often been noted by linguistic theoreticians.
The purpose of the present article is three-fold: to
attempt an integrated description of the (semantic)
evolution of these two paradigms from VL to the
present day not only in the standard languages but
also, where possible, in other regional varieties
and dialects; to seek to identify the parameters
which appear to have been operative at various
times; and to offer, where possible, explanations
for the changes which have been observed.

* I should like to thank Suzanne Fleischman, Ian
Mason, Ralph Penny, Glanville Price and Nigel
Vincent for their helpful comments on an earlier
draft of this paper.

'Past Simple' and 'Present Perfect'

Before turning to an examination of the data,
certain conceptual and terminological clarifications
are in order. First of all, it is imperative at
all times to distinguish clearly between form and
function, a distinction unfortunately not always
fully maintained in discussions of this topic. We
shall be dealing with two forms, FECI and HABEO
FACTUM and their derivatives, and we shall refer to
these indiscriminately either by their paradigmatic
labels or as the 'past simple' and '(present)
perfect' respectively. These formal labels are
used regardless of the semantic value of the paradigm in any given état de langue. At the same time,
the discussion will centre on various temporal
and/or aspectual categories, including those we
shall label 'preterite' and 'present perfect' (in
senses to be defined hereafter), along with their
various exponents. The distinction is crucial in
interpreting statements such as 'the (present)
perfect form in contemporary spoken French, j'ai
fait, serves, inter alia, as a preterite, thus
je l'ai fait hier', where 'present perfect' is of
course a formal label in this instance while
'preterite' refers to the meaning of the form in
context.
We shall be concerned centrally here with two
time-based semantic categories, although a number
of other elements of meaning, both temporal and
aspectual, will enter the picture from time to time.
The key distinction will be between on the one hand
a 'present perfect' category used to refer to an
action or state situated within a period of time
which includes the present moment or seen as being
still relevant at the present moment (these points
will be elaborated upon in what follows) and on the
other hand a 'preterite' category in which the
event or series of events designated by the verb
took place within a period of time which is wholly
past, is seen as complete rather than in progress
at the past moment in question, and is not represented by the speaker as having present relevance. These categories are at this stage deliberately rather imprecisely defined, since each is
made up of several semantic components which can,
as we shall see, be treated differently in various
languages at various times. It seems important to
stress also that no claim whatsoever is being made
for the universality of the categories in question;
while the distinct semantic components can, I would
confidently assert, be expressed somehow in any

language, for example lexically, the question as to
whether any or all of these features can be combined into 'bundles' which then function as a category given overt marking within the verbal system
of any particular language is of course very much
language-specific. (This is tantamount to agreeing
with the views expressed by Langacker (1976, esp.
pp. 319-24) that 'cognition - or conceptual structure - is essentially the same for the speaker of
all languages'; for this to be translated into
language, however, 'coding' must take place using
forms and structures specific to the language in
question.) Non-universality granted, however, the
verbal categories 'preterite' and 'present perfect',
appropriately and varyingly defined, are indispens-
able in any analysis of the Romance verbal system -
as indeed they are more widely, at least within the
Indo-European group of languages - and they will
accordingly be used here.

Let us now try to establish more precisely the
semantic value of our two principal categories.
The basic opposition is in terms of <u>present</u> <u>rele-
vance</u>. The present perfect category serves
primarily to mark the present relevance of an event
etc. which took place, began to take place or
failed to take place in the past. An appropriate
context for the verbal paradigm having present
perfect value in a particular language may be one
in which the period of time in which the event
occurred is still in progress, whether explicitly
('I have done it today') or implicitly ('I have
done it once', <u>i.e.</u> in my life, which is still in
progress.) (Note that the time of the event itself
is in principle irrelevant.) Certain adverbs
referring to periods of time still in progress may
strongly favour the use of present perfect, as may
certain 'recent past' adverbs (e.g. still, already,
yet, just, lately and the like in contemporary
British English, thus: 'have you seen him lately?').
Conversely, use of the present perfect category may
depend on speaker-judgement as to present relevance,
either in conjunction with, or independently of,
criteria such as the presence or absence of certain
adverbs as indicated above. The precise domain of
this category varies from language to language and
from time to time, as will be apparent from what
follows.

The preterite category, on the other hand,
subsumes events, or series of events, which took
place in a period of time which is, explicitly or
implicitly, wholly past (possibly the very recent

past), which are not marked as being presently
relevant, and which are not to be additionally
aspectually marked (e.g. as durative, habitual etc.)
thus 'I did it yesterday'/'I did it four times last
week'. (For a fascinating survey of possible links
between the evolution of the preterite in relation
to the imperfect in Romance, outside the scope of
this paper, cf. Posner 1961.)

The essential indeterminacy in the scope of
the present perfect category, thus defined, will be
immediately apparent. We shall see that where the
preterite: present perfect opposition is still
operative in Romance, the selection of the latter
category may be triggered off by semi-formal
criteria - e.g. the presence or absence of certain
adverbs - and/or by the subjective judgement of the
speaker as to the present relevance of his utterance. The particular conditioning factors will
need to be clearly specified in each case. To
illustrate the fluidity in this area, we may contrast two distinct varieties of English. In many
dialects, the adverbs listed above (already, just
etc.) are in themselves insufficient markers of
present relevance to require the use of the present
perfect paradigm: contrast the use made in many
forms of American English of 'I just did it'/'he
did it already' where British English would prefer
'I have just done it'/'he has already done it'.
Equally, whereas some dialects distinguish two
values of '(n)ever' and the like (as wholly past
time adverbs, and as adverbs having present relevance), others do not, with the consequential loss
of such distinctions as that between 'he has never
done it (but may yet do it)' and 'he never did it
(but now he never will)', to the profit of the
latter. In some forms of English, in other words,
the domain of the present perfect category, what is
and what is not seen as presently relevant, is
greater than in others, and this in turn clearly
affects the domain of the preterite category. In
the Romance languages likewise, as we shall see, it
is the inherent instability of the present perfect
category which everywhere underlies the evolution
of this small part of the past tense system.

The purpose of this brief introduction making
use in part of familiar English data is firstly to
serve as a reminder that the 'present perfect'
category, inasmuch as it relies upon the concept
of present relevance, is not in any sense an
absolute or objective category, and that the
relationship between any paradigm having such a

value and a paradigm with 'preterite' value is both
variable and potentially unstable. Of course, in a
language with two distinct paradigms the opposition
between which is based in part on the temporal
distinction defined above, there may well be other
elements of meaning of an aspectual nature, such as
'duration' or 'habitualness', which serve to keep
the two paradigms apart in addition to, or conceivably in lieu of, the temporal distinction to
which we have referred. Our survey of the situation
in Romance will need to take full account where
appropriate of such non-temporal distinctions also.
The second purpose of this introduction is to recall that we are dealing with semantic categories
which recur in various ever-changing guises not only
in all the Romance languages but certainly widely
elsewhere in other Indo-European languages and most
probably in many other language families also. Any
attempt, therefore, to explain the observed phenomena in Romance, synchronic or diachronic, exclusively in local terms referring to specific features
of the language or cultural history of one particular area is likely to be less convincing than one
which seeks to integrate the data under discussion
with comparable data from elsewhere. This way we
shall at least see which patterns, and which
changes, appear with any frequency. The extent
to which the observed changes can be <u>explained</u>,
however, is a very moot point, which will be
addressed briefly in the final part of this
paper.
  Let us now commence our presentation of the
Romance data by looking at Classical Latin. The
CL 'perfect' tense FECI represents an interesting
starting point, in that we have a single paradigm
which subsumes the functions of both the 'present
perfect' and the 'preterite' as just defined, and
as these are manifested in, say, British English or
Castilian Spanish. The FECI paradigm is one of
three - the others being FECERO, the 'future perfect' and FECERAM, the 'pluperfect' - formed on a
stem, the perfectum, which reflects the merger of
two earlier sets of Indo-European stems, the perfect
and the aorist. From the earliest texts, the FECI
paradigm had two values[1]: as a preterite and as
present perfect. The first of these uses calls
for little comment : it was the narrative tense
<u>par excellence</u>, it co-occurred with past time adverbs
and required historic concordance within the elaborate sequence of tense rules of the classical
language. The second is rather more complex, in

that the original primary value of the paradigms of the perfectum appears to have been aspectual, specifically - as the name implies - to refer to events that were, are or will be complete at the moment of time in question. Any event which is complete at a particular time reference point, however, must also be temporally anterior to that moment of time - if I had done it before he arrived, the 'doing' is clearly earlier than the 'arriving'. Any paradigms aspectually marked as perfective, therefore, are clearly marked also, implicitly at least, in respect of time, and there is a widespread tendency for this temporal element within the meaning to come to predominate over the aspectual element, a process well attested in more than one instance within Romance. In the case of the 'present perfect' value of the FECI paradigm in CL, it is difficult if not impossible to separate an aspectual value (completed at the present) from a temporal one (begun or effected at an earlier moment but still in progress at/relevant to the present moment). Latin grammarians[2] tended, perhaps on formal grounds, to see the former as predominant; subsequent developments in VL suggest however that the latter had become the more dominant value at least by the early centuries of the Christian era.

The reason for this last assertion is to be found in an examination of one of the best known of all the innovations within the Romance verbal system, namely the creation in VL of a range of compound paradigms formed with the verb HABERE and a past participle, one of which, HABEO FACTUM, incorporating the present tense of HABERE, is the antecedent of the 'perfect tense' in most contemporary forms of Romance. (For parallels in other Indo-European languages, cf. McCray 1979:147). The origins of this structure are found in earliest Latin, where the verb appears still to have its full value as a marker of possession (as in the Plautine example 'multa bona bene parta habemus' lit. 'many good things well obtained we have') and where the past participle is in effect adjectival, with appropriate concord with the relevant nominal. From this starting point, two important changes take place : the full semantic value of HABERE gradually diminishes (already in Ciceronian Latin, the structure is found with verbs like 'learn' 'discover' 'persuade' 'compel' etc.; cf. Ernout & Thomas, 1951: 223), and the degree of union between the two parts of the syntagm slowly becomes greater, to the point where we may rightly speak of a unitary (albeit

compound) paradigm within the indicative mood. Two
important corollaries of this are that the verb
HABERE when part of such paradigms changes in status
from full verb to auxiliary verb and the past participle becomes an integral part of the verb phrase,
permitting the abandonment of concord in many instances (cf.'haec omnia probatum habemus' in the
sixth-century <u>Oribasius Latinus</u>, with unmarked
'probatum' rather than 'probata'; for a recent discussion of this process cf.Ramat 1981), although
the latter change spread slowly and sporadically,
and is still not wholly complete today. As a final
stage in the development, discussed further below,
the structure came eventually to be used also in
the case of intransitive verbs. (The question of
why some verbs make use of <u>be</u> rather than <u>have</u> as
their 'perfect' auxiliary and all consequential
issues are set aside in this paper; see Vincent
(this volume).)

It seems clear that the original function of
these paradigms as they became part of the verbal
system proper was to mark aspect, that is, to stress
that some particular event or state was completed
or achieved. The fact that it was primarily to
express this aspectual value that the new form was
adopted seems to confirm our earlier claim that in
the case of the 'present perfect' use of FECI, it
was the temporal meaning ('present relevance')
which had come to predominate by the classical
period, leaving the way open for a new paradigm to
mark perfective aspect if such were felt to be
necessary. It hardly needs to be added that the new
paradigm, HABEO FACTUM, expressing analytically as
it did the two principal components of the meaning
of any present tense within a perfective aspect,
was perhaps singularly liable to be reinterpreted
as having primarily a temporal value, to wit
'present relevance'. The extent to which this
reanalysis did in fact occur in the development of
the Romance languages is the main theme of the next
part of this paper.

Let us then sum up the position as it must have
been in common VL, shortly before the break-up of
the Empire. One form, FECI, had two clearly specif-
iable temporal values, 'preterite' and 'past with
present relevance' ('present perfect'). A new form
HAVEO FACTUM had come into being and was in the
process of being grammaticalised with a primarily
aspectual value (cf. the <u>tener</u> + past participle
structure in modern Castilian), but with inescapable
temporal (i.e.present) connotations. It would seem

rash to attribute anything further than this to commom VL: although the position just described forms the starting point for subsequent developments throughout Romania, these developments reveal significant and in some cases substantial divergences from each other in the light of the differing analyses made of this essentially subjective and unstable area of meaning, and must therefore be dated after the time at which we can legitimately speak of Vulgar Latin.

Before looking at the differing patterns which are apparent in contemporary Romance, attention should be drawn to one factor which appears to be common throughout the entire language family, namely the entry into the basic indicative verbal system of each language of a 'present perfect' paradigm based on HABEO FACTUM (but cf. discussion below about the subsequent replacement of haver by ter in Portuguese), with a meaning which, although clearly retraceable to the value attributed to that paradigm in VL, is in most cases no longer primarily an exponent of the 'perfective aspect' in the sense discussed earlier. It is precisely to the value of these paradigms vis a vis the value of derivatives of FECI that we shall now turn.

An examination of the position in contemporary Romance reveals essentially four synchronically distinct patterns (with minor variations to be discussed below), where (i) is the common starting point, where (ii) represents the next stage of development and is attested almost everywhere, where (iii) may well emerge from (ii) - as has happened relatively recently in Castilian, see below - and where (iv) is a widespread, but by no means inevitable, development from (iii).

The four patterns may be summarised as follow:

(i) FECI retains all the functions it had in common VL, as just described. HABEO FACTUM remains restricted to present states resulting from past actions, and is not used to describe past actions themselves, however recent (Calabrian, Sicilian);

(ii) FECI retains most of the functions it had in VL, including reference to recent past events and to events occurring at a period of time still in progress. HABEO FACTUM does however begin to develop the semantic values which we have labelled 'present perfect', but at first only in highly specific circumstances; in addition to meeting the

'Past Simple' and 'Present Perfect'

primary criterion of taking place or at least starting in the past but having present relevance, an
appropriate use of the compound form will also be
aspectually marked as durative or repetitive ('I
have lived here/been living here all my life'; 'I
have often seen him at the theatre'). (Galician
and Portuguese; many varieties of South American
Spanish);

   (iii) FECI is restricted to preterite functions,
with HABEO FACTUM assuming, in addition to the
functions outlined above, the archetypal 'present
perfect' value of 'past action with present relevance'. (Recall that this subjective classification
has to be more specifically defined in respect of
each language.) (Castilian Spanish; some varieties
of langue d'oc and langue d'oil);

   (iv) FECI is restricted to formal registers and
may ultimately be lost entirely, HABEO FACTUM assuming, in addition to the 'present perfect' functions just mentioned, those which we have labelled
'preterite' ('aorist'). (In other words, the
(semantic) distinction between the 'present perfect'
and the 'preterite' is neutralised, the compound
paradigm coming to carry both meanings, exactly as
FECI had done in CL.) (Standard French, Northern
Italian, standard Rumanian).

   Let us now look at each of these patterns in
turn, starting with those areas of southern Italy,
where, although both the 'past simple' and the
'present perfect' paradigms are found, the range
of functions conveyed by the latter is extremely
limited. In the far south, for example, in
Calabrian and Sicilian, the 'simple past' is used
for single events, however recent and regardless of
whether the period of time concerned is still in
progress or not (e.g. with oji (oggi) 'today'), to
the exclusion of the compound form. When, however,
the present state resulting from a past action (or
inaction) is the focus of attention, the 'present
perfect' paradigm is appropriate. Rohlfs (1966-9:
para. 673), for instance, contrasts (Calabrian)
mi scrissi ('he has written/wrote to me (on some
unspecified occasion)') with non m'a scrivutu ('he
hasn't written to me (so I have no news of him)'),
or l'aju fatto ('I've done it (sometime in my life,
it is part of my experience)') with u fici ora
('I've just done it', lit. '...I did it now'). It
is clear that, more than anywhere else in the

50

Romance-speaking area, the present state rather than the past event leading to that state is central to the meaning of the paradigm[3]. In other words, the situation we described in (common) VL and that reported for medieval Sicilian by Ambrosini(1969: 154/5) ('il passato prossimo con valore temporale (i.e. past time value) è sostanzialmente estraneo al siciliano antico, anche in produzioni relativamente culte ... invece, il passato prossimo serve ad indicare non precendenza cronologica, ma condizione attuale...') has changed little if at all, and is therefore markedly different even from those other forms of Romance (e.g. Galician) where the domain of the compound paradigm is also relatively limited.

Turning now to areas where the value of the compound paradigm <u>has</u> changed, let us look first at those forms of Romance where a meaning 'past but with present relevance' has developed to some limited extent, but where the use of the paradigm remains heavily circumscribed. In standard Portuguese, for example, use of the <u>tenho feito</u> paradigm (for a discussion of the replacement of <u>haver</u> by <u>ter</u>, see below) is in general restricted to instances where a continuous state, or alternatively a continuous or repeated series of events, which began at some earlier moment, is still in progress either now or at some period of time which includes now, i.e. has not fully elapsed. In other words, not only must the action or state persist until the present - that is, present relevance is a necessary but not a sufficient condition to justify the use of this paradigm - but additionally an aspectual value of durativity or repetition is needed before <u>tenho feito</u> may be used, thus 'O que tens feito últimamente?' ('What have you been doing lately?'). The initial perfective aspect of HABEO FACTUM in Latin has been lost, here as throughout most of Romania, with the originally secondary temporal value coming to prevail. In the case of metropolitan Portuguese, however, not only must the temporal setting of the action be within a period which includes the present, but even then the paradigm is used appropriately only when additional aspectual criteria are met. (See Irmen 1966, esp. p.231, for a historical review of this development in Portuguese; Castilho (1966: 142) sees this development in terms of the aspectual value of the auxiliary extending to the entire syntagm). Expressed in the terms used earlier, the mere occurrence, or implicit postulation of, a present time adverb ('today' etc.), let alone a recent time adverb or presuppositions of the continued present existence

of the speaker and the like, is not sufficient to
trigger the replacement of fiz by tenho feito, the
latter accordingly being a heavily marked form.
(For a statement of this position, cf. Mattoso
Cammara 1972: 144-6; see also Thomas 1969: 131-3 and
for a more detailed survey Castilho 1966). There is
some evidence, however, that the tenho feito paradigm may be gaining ground somewhat, at least in
Brazil: Kahane and Hutter cite (1953: 20) examples
such as 'Tem visto Maria nestes últimos dias?'
('Have you seen Maria in the last couple of days?')
where there apparently is no necessary implication
of durativity or repetition to supplement the present time reference.

Those who describe the position in Galician
are divided in their analyses of the situation in
that dialect. Whereas it is widely accepted that
instances of haber + past participle are Castilian-
isms (e.g. Rojo 1974: 135) and while all agree also
that the ter + past participle structure is found
with the value of Castilian tener + past participle,
(a usage discussed below and not directly relevant
at this stage), opinions differ as to whether ter
+ past participle also has any of the values associated with the parallel paradigm just discussed
in Portuguese. Some claim categorically not: thus
Cotarelo Valledor (1927: 94): 'Por regla general ...
tiéndese en Galicia a no usar más que los tiempos y
formas simples de la conjugación.' A more balanced
view, however, seems to be that of Santamarina
(1974: 159-61), who demonstrates that grammaticalisation of teño feito is underway, particularly with
intransitive verbs, as a 'present perfect' with the
'repetitive' aspect mentioned above. (Santamarina
details clearly (loc cit) the consequences of the
co-existence in gallego of two heavily overlapping
syntagms having the form ter + past participle). A
similar conclusion emerges from the examples in
Rojo (1974: 128-32), who points up also (123) the
frequency of 'castellanismos y lusismos' particularly in written Galician. In sum, however, one cannot fully accept Rojo's claim (122) that 'el gallego
rechaza normalmente las formas compuestas'; in his
understandable anxiety to avoid equating Galician
teño feito with Castilian he hecho, Rojo fails to
acknowledge sufficiently in his general remarks -
though the evidence is certainly there in both his
own data and that of Santamarina - that teño feito
is now grammaticalised as an indicative paradigm in
gallego, but only in contexts in which the verb
refers to an event or state which has recurred more

'Past Simple' and 'Present Perfect'

than once during a period of time which began in the
past and is still in progress now.[4] A similar position appears to hold in Leonese: see for example
Millán Urdiales 1966: 174/5.[5]

In Portuguese, Galician and Leonese, then,
there does exist a 'present perfect' paradigm within the indicative mood, but with very precise limits
on what is accepted as (linguistically) present for
this purpose, and generally with added limitations
by way of aspectual restrictions on when the paradigm may be used.

Leaving aside now northwestern Spain, what is
the situation in other Spanish-speaking areas?
Broadly, we may say that all varieties make use of
the two paradigms in question and that all impose on
the 'present perfect' paradigm the requirement of
present relevance. The exact nature of this requirement, however, varies from region to region, with
Castilian, as we shall see, being at the most
'tolerant' end of the spectrum. In 'most of Spanish
America', according to Kany 1951: 161, 'the simple
preterite is frequently used... in cases where a
purist insists on the present perfect'. From the
examples he gives (no vino hoy for no ha venido hoy,
¿qué pasó? for ¿qué ha pasado?), it is clear that
in such forms of Spanish the criterion of 'present
relevance' is not met simply by the occurrence of
a present-time adverb (hoy) or by the fact that the
time setting is indefinite and thus by implication
comes up to the present. (In other words, the
British English opposition between 'what has happened?' and 'what happened?' is neutralised).[6] Kany's
well documented conclusions indicate that a relatively restricted interpretation of 'present
relevance' is general in Spanish American (cf. also
the full survey of Berschin 1974: 35/7), although
less markedly so in 'Peru, Bolivia and other limited
areas' (op. cit.: 162).[7] A similar picture is attested in the Spanish of the Canary Islands (Alvar,
1965: 315/6). An impressive and detailed analysis
of the use of the paradigms in Mexican Spanish is to
be found in Moreno de Alba (1978). Essentially, this
shows that in the case of the compound form, aspectual characteristics of durativity and repetition
are, as we saw earlier in Portuguese, very frequent
concomitants of the primary requirement 'starting in
the past but within a time period lasting until the
present', accounting for 90% of the attestations in a
large corpus, whereas past events not having these
aspectual characteristics but seen by the speaker
as relevant to the present account for only 4.4% of

the attestations.[8] These examples are stated by
Moreno de Alba (1978: 63) to be 'en cierta medida
excepcionales en el dialecto mexicano, pues la
mayoría de los hablantes prefiere usar, con este
valor, el pretérito [i.e. the past simple]'. There
is no reason to believe this analysis to be untypic-
al of what we have already seen from Kany's general
survey to be a very widespread[9] situation in Spanish
America.

There are, however, dialects of Spanish - of
which Castilian is of course the prime example - in
which the use of the compound form is not so heavily
constrained. The classic discussion is that of
Alarcos Llorach (1947), who rightly rejects the view
of Meyer Lübke (1890: III: para. 108) that the distinction between hize and he hecho is purely stylistic, the former paradigm being, in Meyer Lübke's
view, destined to the fate it has undergone in
(standard) French. Alarcos believes that it is possible to distinguish between the uses of the two
paradigms, thus: (1947: 127): 'Si el pretérito simple
es el pasado absoluto visto desde la conciencia
presente, el perfecto está visto a través del presente gramatical', i.e is used when present relevance is a pertinent factor. (For a discussion of
this widely accepted view, and appropriate further
bibliographical references, cf. Berschin 1976: 21/2).
Alarcos further believes that the distinction is
'puramente temporal, considerando el 'tiempo' no sólo
como una circunstancia objetiva, sino también como
un contenido de conciencia, y por ende subjetivo'
(1947: 114). He goes on to explain clearly when the
choice of paradigm is 'objective' and when 'subjective'; in the first case, it is adverbial complements
and the like which indicate clearly the presence or
absence of the present relevance which triggers off
use of one paradigm or the other, while in the second
case the choice of paradigm depends only on the
'tiempo subjetivo del que habla'.[10] In certain contexts, then, the use of either paradigm[11] is determined - as in English - by the occurrence of adverbs
which do, or do not, have present time relevance; in
other contexts - again as in English - only the
speaker's subjective judgement determines the presence or otherwise of 'present relevance' and hence
the choice of paradigm. (Certain adverbs do not
predetermine the choice of paradigm; in these cases,
the 'subjective' choice operates, as one would expect,
cf. Alarcos, op. cit.: 117).

'Past Simple' and 'Present Perfect'

Notice that, if Alarcos' analysis is correct -
as we believe it to be - then the value of the present perfect in Castilian (as also in Navarese and
Aragonese, according to Kany (1951: 161)) is dependent purely on temporal factors, albeit factors which
are at times subjectively determined. Indeed,
Alarcos explicitly rules out (1947: 113/4) the relevance of aspectual factors in this area of Castilian
Spanish: 'El aspecto de la acción ... no influye, al
parecer, en la preferencia por el perfecto simple o
por el compuesto'. In this respect, there is a clear
difference between Castilian and Mexican Spanish, a
point explicitly acknowledged by Moreno de Alba
(1978: 68). (For detailed surveys of the position
in contemporary Castilian, cf. Barrera-Vidal 1972
and Berschin 1974, the latter being informatively
and favourably reviewed by Rivarola 1980. A short
but suggestive presentation can be found in Skubic
1964).
It is perhaps worth stressing, in view of the
parallelism indicated above between Castilian and
English (and cf. also Stockwell et al. 1967: 139f)
that the mere fact that both languages use their
compound form to indicate past events with present
relevance should not be taken necessarily to suggest
translation equivalence in every case. It should be
abundantly clear by now how subjective the concept
of present relevance is; and detailed examination of
examples of Castilian Spanish show that the perception of present relevance does differ, at least
slightly, from that of at least this speaker of
British English. Thus, for example, the question
'¿cuándo ha llegao [sic] usted?' (Alarcos, 1947: 119)
would translate (for me) as 'when did you arrive?'
rather than *'when have you arrived?' , despite the
obvious truth of the assertion (loc. cit.) that
'para el que pregunta, la acción se ha producido
necesariamente en un momento indeterminado del
período comprendido entre un punto del pasado y el
momento presente en que se habla, en que está
incluído el presente'.[12] Interestingly, the other
example cited (¿Se ha ido tu padre?') will translate
with a present perfect ('Has your father left?'),
even when the answer is 'Yes, he left last night',
just as in Castilian. The essential fuzziness of
'present relevance' in the absence of over-riding
adverbials should be clear.
This distinction between the uses of the two
paradigms is relatively recent in the history of
Castilian (dating in popular speech from the latter
part of the sixteenth century), a fact which is

hardly surprising in view of the different situation
we have reported in much of the rest of the Spanish-
speaking world, and its development is very clearly
documented in the concluding section of Alarcos
(1947: 130-6); no point would be served in para-
phrasing that account here. Suffice it to say that
the patterns we outlined at the start of our survey
of Romance are all attested (op. cit.: 136), in
chronological order, except the very last, that is,
the loss, or severe stylistic restriction, of the
past simple paradigm.

Before leaving Castilian, we might ask whether
this ultimate stage - which we shall shortly note in
French, Northern Italian and Rumanian, - is about to
manifest itself in Castilian. Certainly, a number
of authors, from Meyer - Lübke onwards, have claimed
to detect an incipient reduction in the use of the
past simple, particularly in popular registers and
particularly in Madrid. Alarcos rejects this claim,
after careful consideration of the available data,
and indeed it seems difficult to sustain such a view.
While such a development would not be surprising in
the longer term, in view of what has happened so
widely elsewhere in Romania, it should nevertheless
be stressed that changes in other Romance languages
are merely suggestive; in themselves, they render a
change in Castilian neither imminent nor even
inevitable.

Before turning to those areas of Romance where
the evolution in usage of the compound paradigm has
gone even further, we should look at the situation
in dialects of the langue d'oil and langue d'oc
other than standard French, seeking to establish
first of all - in view of its demise from the standard spoken language - where the past simple paradigm
is still in use and, thereafter, how the two paradigms are distinguished. For evidence of the position
in non-standard spoken French, I am heavily indebted
to Ian Mason's impressive doctoral thesis (Mason
1977). As a prelude to a detailed analysis of the
relationship between the two paradigms at two points
within the bas normand dialect area, Mason surveys
the general position within the Gallo-Romance area
as reported in the Atlas Linguistique de la France
(1902-1910; henceforth ALF) and in various studies
since that date. The ALF reveals (map 976) a clear
division between simple and compound forms in the
case of il partit; this form is offered as the normal exponent for the preterite meaning in almost the
whole of southern France and in Normandy (to which
we may add also certain varieties of Walloon;

cf. for instance Remacle, 1956: II:55ff.), whereas
elsewhere a compound form is preferred. At the same
time, map 32 reveals that the compound form, the
'present perfect', is in use virtually everywhere in
a context where the reference is to an event which
began in the past but is still in progress at the
present moment - interestingly, in view of the
Galician/Portuguese position, an example with no
overtones of repetition. Not surprisingly in view
of what we know of standard French, map 1154 reveals
greater hesitation in the northern strongholds of
the fit paradigm in the case of a first person plural form; but in the occitan area, the simple form is
found here also. Overall, the evidence is so clear
that even the weaknesses inherent in the methodology
of the ALF (Mason, 1977: 165-8) cannot vitiate it.

The general picture reported by the ALF has of
course been updated subsequently by numerous monographs, although inevitably many regional forms of
French have been decaying rapidly during this period.
Essentially, one finds that, within the langue d'oil
area, the past simple paradigm is limited in occurrence to certain areas of Normandy (including the
Channel Islands) and Wallonia and adjacent areas,
with residual status in parts of central-western
France such as Vendée and Poitou (Mason, 1977: 187).
In the Franco-Provençal area, the past simple paradigm has apparently receded markedly during this
century (op. cit. 193), a situation repeated in many
forms of eastern Occitan (Blinkenberg, 1939, 1948;
cf. also the observations in Dauzat 1946: 78). The
past simple survives, however, in at least certain
varieties of Gascon (where however the position is
complicated by the existence of the anà + infinitive
structure (cf. the discussion of this structure
below)), and perhaps best of all in western Occitan,
where it is clearly in contrast with the present
perfect. (See Camproux 1958: 34/5 for a detailed
analysis of the relationship between the two paradigms in gévaudanais).

Where one turns to a consideration of the use
of the two paradigms in those areas where both have
retained their vitality, one finds the - essentially
subjective - criterion of present relevance once
again dominant. Where - as in Val de Saire, one of
the points investigated by Mason (1977) - the past
simple is, as a result of prolonged interaction with
the standard language, clearly marginal to contemporary usage, it is nevertheless available for use in
classic preterite contexts, e.g. a series of past
events reported in a narrative. Elsewhere, however,

- for example, in Jersey French (Mason 1977), in La Gleize (Walloon) (Remacle 1956: II:55/6)[13] or in gévaudanais (Camproux 1958: 35) - the two paradigms are clearly distinguished, and the use of the compound paradigm depends on 'present relevance' as conceived by the speaker.

We may now conclude our survey of the present position in Romance by considering, more or less together, standard French, Rhaeto-Romance, northern Italian (including the standard language) and standard Rumanian. In each of these languages, the scope of 'present relevance' gradually came to be so broad as to subsume ultimately all those past events and states which had hitherto been within the domain of the past simple. That this change took place in the spoken language is in no way surprising: it is not at all difficult to imagine that the concept 'perceived as having present relevance by the speaker' came, in certain areas, to encompass all past events reported in colloquial speech. As Klum (1961: 168) puts it: 'En employant le passé composé, on incorpore les événements, fussent-ils d'une époque tout à fait écoulée, avec l'actualité présente: il y a association psychologique...' Be that as it may, in French until the sixteenth century, the specification of a period of time no longer in progress - even one as recent as last night - generally[14] required the use of the past simple; rather suddenly thereafter the past simple was lost from (Parisian) speech, to the point where it was already the butt of ridicule by the time of Molière. As Dauzat puts it (1937: 103): 'au xviie siècle, le passé simple était en pleine crise dans la langue populaire ... il était sorti, à Paris, de l'usage parlé courant (peuple et petite bourgeoisie) dès le xviiie siècle'. (For a detailed survey of the history of the two paradigms in French, cf. Foulet 1920). Wilmet (1976: 61-82), in discussing these two paradigms, distinguishes discours from narratif, and points out that the latter permits a moving away from the 'speaker-here-now' perspective more easily than the former and hence can more readily retain a paradigm marked as not having present relevance. Be that as it may, in standard French, the past simple is now wholly restricted to the written language and even there is found with any frequency only in the third person.

In the case of Italian, the French situation is long established also in the dialects of the north, (Bourciez 1967: para. 446(c) speaks of the development as 'déjà très avancée vers la fin du xvie siècle'; cf. also Rohlfs 1966-9, para. 673), while in central Italy including the standard language the encroachment by the compound paradigm on the erst-while domain of the past simple is more limited; as a result, while the neutralisation of the opposition of present relevance is an increasingly normal feature of popular everyday language (cf. Tekavčić, 1970: 16; for a more cautious view, cf. Lepschy and Lepschy, 1977: 220); the past simple is still widely used particularly in writing (cf. the views of Wilmet, cited above) with its value 'past not relevant to the present' unimpaired.[15] (For a full discussion of the position in contemporary Italian, cf. Blücher 1974 and Tumler 1980). The use of the past simple may thus be seen as stylistically conditioned in contemporary written Italian, though by no means as markedly so as in French.

In standard Rumanian (though not in certain southern dialects), the forms of the past simple are now restricted to historical narrative within the literary language, having been lost progressively from various spoken dialects. (See, for example, Gr. Limb. Rom., 1966, paras. 227/8 for a statement of the present position; for a historical survey, cf. Şiadbei 1930). In Rhaeto-Romance, the past simple was found in early texts, (Bourciez, 1967, para. 523(a)) but has now been lost. It is thus of course true that in the spoken registers of all these languages, the wheel has come full circle: just as Latin FECI had two values in CL, so too do the 'perfect' paradigms in French, Rhaeto-Romance, northern Italian and Rumanian. Both the history of the Romance languages and our own intuitions lead one to suppose that the wheel will continue to turn.

We have now surveyed the current usage of the derivatives of FECI and HABEO FACTUM in contemporary Romance and will shortly attempt to present a very brief integrated overview. Before so doing, however, we might just glance for a moment at three topics essentially tangential to our main theme.

Firstly, we need to observe the inter-play between derivatives of TENERE and those of HABERE in Romance. In southern Italy, Sardinia and Iberia in particular, the former clearly rivalled the latter as far back as Latin (Bourciez, 1967, para. 246(b)), originally no doubt with the same full possessive value that HABERE had at first had. In general, the structures based on TENERE retain this value (see below), with consequential full agreement of the past participle functioning as a predicative adject-ive; thus Cast. tengo escrita la carta ('I have the letter written'). In Galician and Portuguese,

however, <u>ter</u> (<TENERE) underwent the same evolution
as had HABERE in VL, becoming the normal auxiliary,
at the expense of <u>haver</u>, by the seventeenth century.
The earlier structure, with quasi-possessive meaning
and participial accord, has however survived also.
In contemporary Portuguese - though not at earlier
periods, cf. Irmen 1966: 224-9 - the distinction
between the two values is clearly made; contrast,
for example, <u>tem escrito a carta</u> ('he has been writing the letter') with <u>tem escrita a carta/tem a
carta escrita</u> ('he has (got) the letter written').
In Galician, on the other hand, there appears to be
considerable overlap, clearly described, for example,
in Santamarina 1974: 159-61. It may well be this
polyvalency, coupled with the fact that the <u>teño
feito</u> paradigm in Galician, even when it is fully
grammaticalised, clearly has markedly different values from <u>he hecho</u> in Castilian, which has led to the
view of some analysts, discussed and rejected above,
that there is no compound perfect paradigm in
Galician.

The second point to note is that the loss of
the past simple paradigm from the spoken language
of much of France, parts of northern Italy (Rohlfs,
1966-9: para. 673) and much of Rumania (Iordan-Orr,
1970: 336n.1) has led directly to the creation of
a set of double compound forms, of the type <u>j'ai eu
fait</u>. The formal mechanism whereby they come into
being is clear: if the 'past simple' is everywhere
replaced by the compound paradigm, the same will
happen even where the original past simple was itself an auxiliary; thus <u>j'eus fait</u> becomes <u>j'ai eu
fait</u>. The use made of these forms is, however,
inconsistent, varying from dialect to dialect and
even, apparently, from idiolect to idiolect: they
tend in any event to be ignored by normative grammarians. They are nevertheless available as part of
the input to any new cycle of changes which may affect the past tense system in the future, for instance
as a new marker of present relevance! (For a detailed analysis of the use of these forms in one
language, cf. Foulet, 1925 and Cornu 1953; for further discussion, see Harris 1970 and the references
cited there).

The final point concerns the unexpected use of
the auxiliary verb 'go' (<u>anar</u>, <u>aller</u> etc.) + infinitive with preterite value, above all in Catalan[16]
but also in <u>gascon</u> (Marcuèze-Pouey 1955) and
<u>béarnais</u> (Bourciez 1967: para. 319(c)). The original
value of this paradigm - found at first more widely,
e.g. in northern France; Gougenheim, 1951: 136 -

60

'Past Simple' and 'Present Perfect'

seems to have been inchoative; the most widely accepted explanation for its evolution into a 'preterite' paradigm, unexpected both in pan-Romance and
more general terms, is that suggested by Colón 1961:
173, in brief, a combination of a verb of motion to
add immediacy coupled with use of the historic present of the auxiliary for a similar purpose (cf.
pop. Eng. 'then he goes and messes it all up!').
Such a paradigm would have first been used in contexts having present relevance, then extended its
range in a now familiar way.
   Returning now finally to the principal theme of
this analysis, the interrelationship between two
verbal paradigms in Romance, what general conclusions
can one draw? The evidence is, I believe, overwhelming that we are dealing here with a single
phenomenon, albeit one which manifests itself at
different times and in different ways in various
languages. (What is more, this phenomenon is in no
way limited to Romance, as we have seen; cf.
Meillet's famous analysis (1926: 149-58), Schogt
(1964), and for a more recent comparative survey of
the position in Indo-European, McCray 1979). Put
at its simplest, verbal periphrases marking the
present results of past actions -- such as exist in
all languages at all times - are prone to grammaticalise as 'present perfects', i.e. paradigms which
denote past events seen as having present relevance.
(Comrie (1972: 52) makes it clear that, across languages, verb forms marking the perfective aspect are
particularly prone to become primarily temporal in
value, precisely because they inevitably express a
relation between two time-points; for a more general
tendency for tense to develop from aspect, both
diachronically and during the acquisition process,
cf. Fleischman 1982 and the references cited there).
We have seen, however, that 'present relevance' is
not necessarily an objective category; while there
may well be certain preferences governed, for instance, by the presence or absence of certain adverbs,
or additional conditions imposed to limit the domain
of the paradigm in question - as with the aspectual
requirements in Portuguese, for example - there remains, often at least, an area in which the choice
depends on what Alarcos, speaking of Castilian,
describes simply (1947: 125) as 'sentimiento personal'. An exactly similar point is made by Camproux
1958 (cited by Mason, 1977: 200): the distinction
between es mort i o tres ons and mouriquet i o tres
ons will depend very much on the context in which
it is uttered and the impression the speaker wishes

to convey (cf. the distinction in English between
'he has been dead for three years (now)' and 'he
died three years ago'); Terrell (1970: 29), cited by
Berschin (1974: 26), speaks felicitously of 'different conceptualisations of the same reality.' Once
this 'subjective' element, inherently instable, has
entered the system[17], then it is at any time possible - though clearly not inevitable -- for the domain
of 'present relevance' to expand above all in speech,
for psycholinguistic reasons along the lines suggested earlier by Klum, the end result being the event--
tual severe restriction or even exclusion of the
earlier past simple paradigm. At any point after
the whole process has started, it is open to a language to create a new 'perfective' structure, as has
occurred with <u>tengo hecho</u> in Castilian (McCray 1979:
152 calls this 'a kind of ebb and flow, of tense to
aspect and back again'); at any point after the last
stage has been reached, the 'present perfect become
preterite' may no longer suffice in cases where it
is found necessary unambiguously to mark present relevance, and a new paradigm tends towards grammaticalisation: thus <u>je viens de faire</u> or perhaps <u>j'ai eu
fait</u> in French.[18] (For a detailed survey of a directly parallel cycle involving go-futures, where very
similar factors are clearly at work, cf. Fleischman
1982). Finally, a given formal change may lead
almost accidentally to other consequential changes
- as with the creation of the <u>temps surcomposés</u> in
very largely those areas of Romania (and in German
too; cf. Hauser-Suida and Hoppe-Beugel 1972: 254ff)
where the 'past simple' has yielded to the 'perfect'.
These new paradigms may well 'hover', as it were, on
the edge of the system until some later change creates a slot for them - or they may never enter fully
into the mainstream of the language.

To what extent, finally, can these changes be
explained? It seems to me that the factors just
outlined provide a <u>general</u> explanation of what can
be observed. There exists a set of closely related
elements of meaning, which are not always objectively
distinguished from one another, and where semantic
drift of a familiar kind within a relatively fluid
semantic area is frequently attested. Meaning shift
in the case of one paradigm may well open the door
for the creation of a new paradigm, which will in
turn be drawn from an adjacent semantic area. More
specifically, in talking about the past - as also
about the future - speakers tend to orientate themselves in terms of the present, and to use verb forms
marked semantically - and very often morphologically

also - for present relevance. Such paradigms may in
due course expand their role so much that the forms
they complemented are threatened or even lost, in
which case the 'new' paradigms cease to be specifically
marked for present relevance. So once again new
forms are needed and the wheel turns once more. At
times, one formal change will in itself be the explanation of another, a development which may in
turn have the potential - realised or not - to alter
the system as a whole: thus with the temps surcomp-
osés. (For a similar development in the history of
French, cf. the emergence of ce livre, as opposed
both to le livre and ce livre-ci/la, discussed in
Harris 1977: 255/6).
    None of this can, however, be taken to be an
explanation of why particular changes take place in
particular languages at particular times. Here we
are, it seems to me, in a field where fully satisfy-
ing explanations are often not to be found. The
causes may at times be linguistic - e.g. phonetic
erosion may irretrievably compromise a particular
form - but do not appear to be so in the case at
hand. Arguments based, as they have been particularly in the case of French, on such language specific
features as anomalousness of forms are inherently
implausible: why should sixteenth century French
speakers find a set of forms easy but seventeenth
century French speakers find them insuperably difficult? And why do Galician peasant farmers cope
with forms too difficult for a Frenchman?[19] Similarly, the postulation of a sudden deterioration in the
intellectual capacities of the average Frenchman, as
is clearly implicit in the analysis proposed by Imbs
1960: 89,[20] hardly seems convincing. Even arguments
based on typological change such as those advanced
in Harris 1978 have only limited explanatory value:
the general preference for preposed auxiliaries
which we would expect in contemporary Romance appears
to affect certain idioms sooner and more generally
than others and therefore cannot of itself answer
the specific questions we are currently addressing.[21]
    Defeatist though it may seem at first sight, it
seems more realistic to argue that, within the
general framework outlined above for which reasonably plausible explanations are available, the implementation of particular changes - or their non-
implementation - is due to combinations of socio-
historical factors which often cause them to be in
practice - and possibly in principle, if one accepts
the arguments in Lass 1980 - inexplicable. The
precise historical, social and socio-linguistic

factors which caused a well-established paradigm to
be dropped rather quickly in French in the sixteenth
and seventeenth centuries may well never be known,
since the data is simply not available to us. Even
in the case of current or future progress - and despite the very significant progress in sociolinguistic
research in this area in the last decade or so - it
would be rather difficult to predict when, or to
explain precisely why, for example, he hecho might
suddenly oust hice in Castilian (if this were to
happen) or why the past simple should suddenly res-
trict the domain of the perfect in British English
(if this were to happen). My own feelings on the
issue of explanation are summarised in Harris
(forthcoming b): there may in principle be a socio-
cultural explanation available for such changes,
but there are so many variables at work that our
chances of capturing them in any particular case are
at present remote and, when we are dealing with a
wholly past event, non-existent. We must rather
satisfy ourselves with presenting wherever possible
an integrated view of a whole series of changes as
we have done here, providing a clear and explicable
framework within which the observed changes have
occurred, and accepting that the exact timing and
nature of a particular change in a particular language may possibly be beyond our capacity to explain
convincingly at present; this is the area in which
we can most look forward to progress in the years
to come.

ACKNOWLEDGEMENT

It was as a student in Joe Cremona's Romance Philology
tutorials that my interest was first aroused in the
historical morphosyntax of the Romance languages,
and in particular in the relationship between the
various verbal paradigms. It is therefore singularly appropriate that one of the principal topics
within this area should be the subject of my tribute
to Joe on this occasion.

NOTES

1. To say this does not imply that the values were consciously distinguished by a Latin speaker, any more than an average French speaker is aware of two values for ai fait. Our claim is simply that a distinction made frequently elsewhere in Romance - and indeed in later Latin - was neutralised in CL, one form being thus bivalent. The evidence of the sequence of tense rules (cf. Harris 1978: 134) shows clearly that the paradigm could be used on either the past or the non-past time plane. The analysis advanced here differs radically from that proposed by Serbat (1975, 1976), who insists that FECI can never have a 'present' value and is therefore exclusively a past tense. Leaving aside the irrefutable syntactic evidence provided by the sequence of tense rules (cf. in this connection Poirier 1978: 371), Serbat's discussion is in any event vitiated by a failure to distinguish between some absolute concept of the present and a 'psycholinguistic' concept of 'present relevance', a recurrent theme of the present paper. Serbat's views deserve more detailed comment than is possible here as do those of Vairel (1978); suffice it to say here that one can surely accept a bivalent FECI paradigm à la Meillet without claiming that the 'present perfect' value is in any sense (synchronically) prior or indeed the sens propre in any sense, and without necessarily accepting the 'explanations' advanced by Meillet (see below). As for one of the questions which Serbat directs at Meillet (1976: 332 'comment une forme exprimant l'achèvement au moment où l'on parle peut-elle s'employer pour une action passée sans relation avec le présent?'), I hope at least a partial answer will emerge in what follows. (A similar remark applies to the comment of Vairel 1978: 391). That it does in fact happen should be more immediately obvious to a French speaker than to most!

2. For a recent discussion of the views of Latin grammarians on the topics in question here, cf. Serbat (1976).

3. Bourciez speaks of the almost total absence of HABEO FACTUM from the far south (1967: para. 446), a fact which he attributes to the prolonged persistence of Greek. The paradigm is however attested, as we have seen, and the analysis presented here appears to account for these attestations.

4. There seem to be no examples in the work cited of the teño feito paradigm being used - with an appropriate verb - to mark the durative aspect

(i.e. the duration of a state) of the 'present
perfect' tense rather than the repetitive aspect.
If this is more than an accidental gap in the corpus,
it represents an interesting distinction between
Galician and Portuguese.

    5. Penny suggests (1969: 157) in his analysis
of the habla pasiega that 'como en dialectos leon-
eses hay tendencia a evitar el perfecto compuesto.'
He continues: ' hay vacilación continua, en el nivel
individual, entre el perfecto simple y el compuesto.'
If there is really 'vacillation', this seems to
suggest dialect interference, under the influence
presumably of Castilian. It may be, however, that
use of the paradigms is in fact conditioned, but
conditioned by factors such as we have discussed for
Galician/Portuguese rather than by those appropriate
in Castilian.

    6. Interestingly, Kany draws attention (1951:
162) to what he calls 'familiar American English'
did you do it? in place of have you done it? Once
again we are dealing with different interpretations
of the concept of present relevance in different
varieties, or even idiolects, of the same language.

    7. Lapesa (1980: 588) reports a marked
increase in the use of the compound paradigm in NE
Argentina and part of Bolivia, possibly foreshadow-
ing developments similar to those in French, N. Italian
and Rumanian, discussed hereafter.

    8. The remaining instances of the use of the
present perfect paradigm are accounted for by what
Moreno de Alba calls 'valores secundarios'(1978: 63).

    9. The data adduced by Berschin (1974) for
Columbian Spanish, citing Florez (1963), suggest
that the domain of the present perfect there is
broader than in Mexican Spanish. To be more specific, the perfect is found with indefinite time
periods including the present (e.g. 'aún no ha
llegado') but not with definite time periods even
when they are still in progress (thus 'llegó hoy'
rather than 'ha llegado hoy'). Florez specifically
distinguishes this greater use of the perfect from
that of 'mucho hispano-hablantes.' For further
discussion, cf. Berschin 1974: 36-40.

    10. One is reminded of the conclusion of Paiva
Boléo (1936: 51) that 'se torna assaz difícil ...
precisar os motivos da distinção, por serem mais de
natureza linguístico-psicológica que de ordem
gramatical'.

    11. We therefore agree with Alarcos in reject-
ing the opinion of Lenz (1925) that it is only the
use of the compound paradigm which is subjectively

determined. On the contrary, it is the choice which
is subjective, in the absence of any adverbs etc.
which pre-empt that choice.
  12. Of course, if the event is known to be
past, '¿cuándo compraste este libro?' is perfectly
acceptable, as one would predict.
  13. Thus: 'Il (le parler wallon de La Gleize)
distingue nettement les deux temps, avec les réserves
bien connues ... Le passé défini ... marque les
faits successifs, sans impliquer aucune idée de
durée, ni aucun rapport avec le présent ...; il
s'applique non seulement à des faits éloignés, mais
aussi à des faits rapprochés, même à ceux de la
veille ... Le passé indéfini exprime que l'action
est accomplie par rapport au présent, ou tout au
moins il implique un rapport de l'action accomplie
avec le présent ... ' (Remacle, 1956, II 56-8).
  14. It is interesting to recall that in Old
French, the 'present perfect' paradigm was already
used at times, at least in poetry, apparently inter-
changeably with the 'past simple' to denominate
wholly past events; in prose, this development
apparently first appears towards the end of the
thirteenth century (Bourciez, 1967, para. 318(c)).
(For comments on the relationship of the two paradigms in Old Provençal, cf. Sutherland 1959: 45).
Recall also the very restricted usage of the imperfect in Old French, for whose values the past simple
was widely attested (cf. Garey 1955). It may well
be that this ambivalence in the value of Old French
fit opened the door to a relatively easy advance on
the part of a fait.
  15. It follows that ho fatto has two values
in contemporary Italian, at least in certain registers. This point is discussed in Tekavčić (1970:
16 n.35), although for theoretical reasons he is
unhappy about incorporating this dual value within
his analysis. Cf. also note 1.
  16. The vaig cantar paradigm rivals rather
than replaces the simple paradigm in Catalan. Badía
Margarit (1962: para. 151) describes the position
thus: 'con la excepción del valenciano y también,
aunque menos, del balear (que mantienen el perfecto
simple, coexistiendo con el perifrástico), todo el
resto del domínio lingüístico catalan sustituye el
tiempo simple por el perifrástico en el habla
corriente'. The use of the simple paradigm in
speech is 'afectado', and the periphrastic paradigm
has been gaining ground in writing throughout this
century: 'hoy el catalan literario emplea indistint-
amente uno u otro de ambos tiempos de modo que la

opción se ha convertido en un recurso estilístico'.
The two paradigms then are contrasted stylistically and/or dialectally rather than semantically.
Taken together, they are opposed to the 'perfect'
paradigm in a way not dissimilar to that in Castilian,
except that the requirement to use the perfect in
respect of a period of time still in progress, explicitly or otherwise, is more nearly absolute. We may
therefore contrast ha traballat molt where the
subject is still alive with va traballar molt (or
the simple equivalent) where the subject is (probably) dead (or at the very least no longer working in
the field in question). For a discussion of the
relationship between the paradigms, cf. Badía Margarit
(1962: paras. 205/6).

17. McCray, talking of Indo-European in general, highlights both the semantic instability and
the cyclical nature of the changes under discussion
(1979: 146): 'The perfect expressed a semantic
reality which lay between those of aorist and present, indicating the present result of past action.
Suspended between the poles of a stable linguistic
dichotomy, not fully belonging to either, a form
with such hybrid semantic would surely be subject
to much diachronic change. ... Nevertheless semantically it was quite well preserved. In several
linguistic systems the category of the perfect was
constantly being given new formal identity while
still retaining the ancient semantic value and
syntactic function'.

18. As Vairel (1978: 384) points out, this is
what happened in VL, leading to the grammaticalisation of the very HABEO FACTUM paradigm we have
been discussing. This does not, however, prove,
pace Vairel, that FECI functioned exclusively as a
past tense in CL, (a point apparently conceded on
p.405) merely that it could not serve unambiguously
as a marker of present relevance, for which value
therefore a new paradigm was progressively introduced. The parallel between CL and modern French is
very clear.

19. Recall that we are opposing only the
suggestion that conjugational difficulties actually
caused the evolution which we have noted in contemporary French and elsewhere. The more perceptive
analysts who have appeared to suggest morphological
complexity as a causal factor turn out on closer
examination to have claimed something rather different: once the two paradigms (fis/ai fait) are in
effect synonymous, then the compound paradigm has
clear morphological and systemic advantages over

the simple. Thus Foulet (1920: 296): 'Le passé
défini, <u>du jour où il cessera d'être indispensable</u>
(italics added), n'a aucune chance de se maintenir
definitivement dans l'usage'. Similarly, Meillet
(1926: 155) makes it clear that the issue of morphological complexity arises only after the initial
distinction of meaning has been obscured. Thus
morphological factors explain the retention of one
form rather than another only when the opposition of
present relevance has already been lost, and are not
to be seen as the primary cause; indeed, 'on est
amené à éliminer toutes les causes qui seraient
particulières à une langue (op. cit.: 156). (It has
to be said this distinction is not always made as
clearly as it might be, particularly by those who
summarise Meillet's views). The fact that, as has
been widely noted by many scholars, a development
similar to that in French has also taken place in
many German-speaking areas should cast further doubt
on the attribution of any primary causal role to
morphological factors. (For a fascinating analysis
of the position in contemporary German from a perspective easily reconcilable with that adopted here,
cf. McLintock 1978 esp. pp.32-3). Meillet's only
suggestion as to the cause of the central change,
the loss of the meaning distinction itself, is that
it is somehow the inevitable concomitant of the development of our civilization to move from 'mot-forme
variable' to 'mot fixe' (1926: 156-8; see discussion
in Iordan-Orr 1970: 306-7). As an explanation, this
suffers from the same general weakness as a typological approach (cf. note 21). Furthermore, and more
specifically, it not only fails to explain the vig-
orous retention of the past simple in much of the
Spanish-speaking world, but even less can it explain
the apparently growing use of the past simple at the
expense of the perfect in many forms of English.
This last development is however less surprising
once one accepts the inherent subjectivity of the
concept 'present relevance' in many cases.
    20. Imbs 1960: 89: 'Il est manifeste que le
bon usage du passé simple suppose non seulement un
bon dressage grammatical mais aussi tout un mode de
pensée, voire une esthétique ... Il est difficile de
préciser dans quelle mesure la complexité de cette
élaboration intellectuelle a contribué à éliminer le
passé simple du français parlé commun ...' The use
of a paradigm becomes 'intellectually complex' only
after instinctive use has ceased and the rules are
learnt at school or elsewhere; this factor cannot
therefore play a causal role. One might however

accept the suitability of the label 'mode de pensée' with respect to whether or not one distinguishes in a particular état de langue between events seen as having present relevance and those not so seen. (Paiva Boléo, 1936: 113 speaks of 'diferente representação mental'). The question that we have been addressing is: what causes this mode de pensée to change?

21. The point is made in Harris (forthcoming a) that typology provides a framework for predicting the form a change is likely to take in a given language at a given time, insofar as change takes place at all. It cannot predict when, or even whether, a particular change will in fact occur.

Chapter 4

THE DEVELOPMENT OF THE AUXILIARIES *HABERE* AND *ESSE*
IN ROMANCE*

Nigel Vincent

1. The replacement of inflected forms by periphrases
is a notable characteristic of the evolution of Latin
into Romance, two commonly cited examples of which
are the development of *habere* + past participle into
Romance forms variously labelled as compound or
perfect, and the expansion of *esse* + past participle
from its limited role in the classical language to
the status of a general exponent of passive. Sand-
wiched somewhere between these two, but not so
frequently discussed, is the use of *esse* + past
participle to mark the perfect of a class of intransitive verbs as exemplified in French *je suis tombé*
'I have fallen' and Italian *è uscita* 'she has gone
out'. Three principal weaknesses, however, mar the
completeness of an otherwise rich philological
tradition.

    (i) An atomistic tendency to deal with the
three constructions in isolation one from another.
Thus, for example, Bourciez (1967:266ff) treats the
two uses of the periphrases with *esse* in two sections
of a single paragraph, followed by a separate paragraph devoted to the one with *habere*. Such a pro-
cedure permits an adequate documentation of the facts,
but inhibits any unified explanation of the evolution.

* A version of this paper was first presented at
Romance Linguistics Seminar IX in January 1981. I
am grateful to the following people who commented on
it either at that time or subsequently: Jim Addams,
Martin Harris, Giulio Lepschy, Chris Pountain, Max
Wheeler.

Lausberg (1966:319ff) falls into the same trap,
although with a different division of labour in that
he takes the two perfects together and the passive
separately, thereby rupturing the formal (and, as
will be argued below, semantic) unity of *amatus est*
and **ven(u)tus est*.

This same defect manifests itself in a more
extreme form in a concentration on *habere* + past
participle to the (almost) total exclusion of the
esse perfects. The reasons here are various. Some
scholars more or less dismiss the problem out of
hand, as when Price (1971:226) observes simply "a
somewhat similar development gave rise to forms
such as je suis venu". Harris (1970, 1978) in
different vein uses *habeo factum* as a portmanteau
for all compound perfects, since his concern is to
explain the emergent structural role of such a
syntagm rather than the detailed mechanism of its
evolution. In many other cases, ranging from the
succinctly expressed exchange between Kuryłowicz
(1931, 1937) and Nicolau (1936) to the profusely
documented studies of Thielmann (1885) and Happ
(1967) - the last-mentioned with a valuable review
of the intervening literature - the focus of attention is solely the periphrasis with *habere*. Even a
scholar of the stature of Benveniste (1968:86) can
write: "The typical periphrasis for the Latin perfectum is based on *habere* + past participle". There
are noteworthy exceptions - including Meyer-Lübke
(1899:310ff), Diez (1876:264ff), Herzog (1910),
Sneyders de Vogel (1927:252ff) and Nyrop (1930:
Ch.7) - to which we shall return, and there is even
the occasional monographic treatment such as Benzing
(1931) devoted to *esse* and its reflexes, but it
remains true to say that the ancestor of Modern
French *ils sont partis*, Italian *sono partiti*, etc.
has been treated as the poor relation. This omission, which is especially serious in work of a more
theoretical cast over the last half century, in turn
forbids a properly integrated account of all three
constructions.

(ii) Where *esse* and *habere* perfects do both
figure, the discussions are all too often bedevilled
by an uncritical retention of the overly simple
traditional distinction between transitive and
intransitive verbs. Lausberg (1966:319) is typical
in this regard: "Obsérvese que, de acuerdo con su
significación, *habere* se limita al principio a los
verbos transitivos, mientras que *esse* forma el

perfecto de los verbos intransitivos".
Scattered here and there are to be found intimations
that such a neat bifurcation will not suffice, as
for instance Tekavčić (1972:296): "È da notare
tuttavia che non tutti gli intransitivi prendono
l'ausiliare *essere*." Further distinctions are necessary within both classes, as revealed by Lucot's
(1940) brief but incisive remarks and by the occasional use of the term 'verbes neutres' - e.g.
Sneyders de Vogel (1927:116ff) - to identify a sub-
group of intransitives.
    A prime requirement, therefore, is an adequate
theory of verbal classification which will allow for
more subtle distinctions than those that are traditionally made. Such a theory will have to account
for the relations between *esse* and *habere* and thus
provide the basis for an understanding of which
verbs evolve with which of the alternative periphrastic constructions. In fact, general treatments
of the grammatical relation between 'be' and 'have'
are available - notably Benveniste (1960), Allen
(1964) and Bach (1967), but they have not been
applied in detail to the Romance situation. On the
other hand, there is also a long series of studies
dealing, albeit generally on synchronic grounds,
with the problem of predicting verb-auxiliary pair-
ings: thus, among others, Porena (1938) and Leone
(1954, 1970) for Italian, and Clédat (1903), Pichon
(1934), and Cohen (1960) for French. We shall seek
to capitalise on this tradition in what follows.

    (iii) Finally, a more general criticism concerns
the theoretical underpinnings of the mechanism of
change by which verbs like *habere* and *esse* (and,
indeed, others - cf. Green, Pountain (this volume))
get drawn into periphrastic uses. The traditional
label for this process is 'grammaticalisation' (see
Meillet 1912, especially p.142ff for an early discussion), or, more idiosyncratically, 'mechanisa-
tion' (Lausberg 1966: paras. 583 and 855). Once
again the manuals are annoyingly vague when the
question is pressed beyond the terminological stage.
Tekavcić (1972: para. 837.1) does essay a brief
definition, and Lausberg (1966:319), in a passage
already cited, talks of the development of *habere*
accompanying transitive verbs as 'de acuerdo con su
significación', but he does not elaborate his
argument further.
    We are not alone in recognising this problem.
Manoliu (1961) contains numerous apposite though not
always clearly phrased observations, and Benveniste

(1968:86-9) presents a lucid analysis of the dilemma,
even if his solution seems less satisfactory, for
reasons which will emerge below. That the time is
ripe for detailed studies of grammaticalisation taking into account both general linguistic and particular philological problems is evident too from the
recent work of Givón (1979: especially Ch.5) and
particularly that of Traugott (forthcoming) and her
associates - see, for example, Shepherd (forthcoming),
Wiegand (forthcoming).

To sum up, then, our aim in the present paper
is to outline a brief theoretical background (Section
2) against which to see the internal relationships
between *habere*, *esse* and the past participle in
Classical (Section 3) and Vulgar Latin (Section 4)
followed finally by a broad survey of developments
in the individual Romance languages (Section 5).

2. We have already remarked that the terms most
widely used in previous attempts to classify verbs
and then predict their co-occurrences with either
habere or *esse* are transitive, if the verb in question takes both a subject and a direct object, or
intransitive if it only requires a subject. Alternatively, we may say that intransitives are verbs
that construct grammatically with only one noun-
phrase (NP), whereas transitives require two or more.
Consider now the following examples from English:

> (1) Tom was burning garden rubbish

> (2) The garden rubbish was burning

We note that in (1) *was burning* accords with our
definition of a transitive verb, while in (2) it
behaves as an intransitive. Furthermore, the object
NP of (1) is identical to the subject of (2): more
generally, if 'X is burning Y' then 'Y is burning'.
Observations such as these suggest that we need to
distinguish not simply the grammatical relations of
subject and object, in terms of which our definition
of transitive and intransitive was given, but also
semantic relations between the participants the NPs
identify and the processes or states denoted by the
verbs. To this end, we will say, in a straightforwardly traditional sense, that *Tom* is the Agent in
(1), and for the semantic role of *garden rubbish* we
reserve the term Neutral, for reasons that will become clear as we proceed. Note then that in (1) and
(2) *garden rubbish* retains the same semantic relation
but differs in grammatical function. For a converse

case compare:

    (3)   Tom was smoking a Havana cigar

    (4)   The cigar was smoking in the ashtray

    (5)   Tom was smoking

Now (3) seems clearly parallel to (1) and (4) to (2), but (5) would more normally be taken as akin to (3) and not (4) (though of course it could have the latter interpretation!). In other words, *Tom* in (3) and (5) and *the cigar* in (4) - but not in (3) - all exemplify the grammatical relation of subject although their semantic roles are not necessarily the same. The verb *smoke*, unlike *burn*, may take either an Agent or a Neutral as its grammatical subject, and if the Agent is expressed, the Neutral is optional in object position. Hence, a full lexical specification for a particular verb in a particular language will have to state not only what grammatical and semantic relations are required, but also how the two are connected. For a recent underlining of the theoretical importance of this see Bresnan (1980).

    As far as syntactic relations are concerned, we shall not have cause to refer to more than subject and object, for which traditional usage and definitions will suffice. With regard to semantic relations, the situation is rather more complex, and we shall avail ourselves of recent work in what has come to be known as Case Grammar (Fillmore 1968, 1971, 1977; Anderson 1971, Gruber 1976), according to which verbs and adjectives - or more generally predicates - may be classified on the basis of the semantic relations they contract with their associated NPs or 'arguments'. An archetypically transitive verb like *hit* takes an Agent and a Neutral, with an optional Instrumental, thus:

    (6)   The carpenter hit the nail (with a hammer)
            AG   NEUT   INST

Put requires Agent, Neutral and Locative:

    (7)   Fred put his slippers under the chair
           AG   NEUT   LOC

A verb like *own* may then be analysed as expressing a kind of abstract location:

> (8)   My brother owns these horses
>   LOC   NEUT

A verb taking the same arguments but in the opposite grammatical positions is *belong*:

> (9)   These horses belong to my brother
>   NEUT   LOC

Hold is parallel to *own* but with both a physical and an abstract sense:

> (10)   This bottle holds the elixir of life
>   LOC   NEUT

> (11)   Arnold used to hold the record for eating
>   LOC   NEUT
>
>   cold hot dogs

And so on. Notice in passing that whereas *possedere* 'own' in Italian always takes *avere* as its auxiliary, *appartenere* 'belong' often takes *essere*. It is at this point that a connection between case frame and auxiliary choice begins to emerge. However, more of this below.

The reader will have noted that all the examples (6) to (11) contain an occurrence of NEUT(ral), a case which we named but did not define at the outset of our discussion. The reason for this is that the definition is essentially negative: Neutral is the case of the argument which is, so to speak, semantically inert, and thus takes its interpretation from the meaning of the verb rather than from any independently definable case function such as Agentivity, Location, etc. That there is such a case is generally agreed, but a bewildering multitude of names have been suggested. Fillmore (1968:25) defines a case called Objective in the following terms: "the semantically most neutral case, the case of anything representable by a noun whose role in the action or state identified by the verb is identified by the semantic interpretation of the verb itself..." Stockwell, Schachter and Partee (1973:38) change the label to Neutral but retain the same definition, while Anderson, having identified his Nominative

(1971:37) as "the notionally most neutral case",
replaces it with the term Absolutive in Anderson
(1977:38) and says that it is "roughly Fillmore's
Objective". Central to the theory of semantic relations presented in Gruber (1976) is that of Theme.
Although no full definition is offered, various
tests are suggested whereby the theme may be recog-
nised. Thus, with verbs of motion the Theme is the
NP which undergoes the motion, while in verbs expressing a location the Theme is the NP of which a
given location is predicated. These tests tie in
very well with Fillmore's definition quoted above,
and indeed Fillmore himself does sometimes (e.g.
1972:12) use the term Theme. There seems little
doubt, then, that an 'inert' NP functioning within
the case structure of a verb is a genuine linguistic
category. One reason behind our decision to adopt
the label Neutral in this study is that it calls to
mind the already mentioned 'verbes neutres' (Sneyders
de Vogel 1927:116ff), a sub-class of intransitive
verbs characterised, amongst other things, precisely
by the fact that they take *être* in the compound
perfect. In our terms, 'verbes neutres' are those
which take a NEUT in subject position, thus clearly
distinguishing them from other intransitives such as
bark, *swim*, etc. with Agent subjects, and also sep-
arating the use of *smoke* in (4) above with NEUT as
subject from its use in (5) with AG filling the
subject slot.
    The final case which we shall need to recognise
is dubbed by Fillmore (1971:42) Experiencer, and the
nearest he gives to a definition emerges in the following remark: "Where there is a genuine psychological event or mental state verb, we have the Experiencer". The intention is to identify a relation
appropriate to the subjects of verbs like *believe*,
think, *know*, etc., where reference to an Agent seems
out of place. Thus:

(12)   John believed that the new law was unjust
       EXP   NEUT

(13)   Tom persuaded John that the new law was
       AG   EXP   NEUT
       unjust

Note in passing that Neutral also serves as the case
for sentential complements of verbs of thinking, saying, etc., a point to which we shall return below.

The interest of the class of verbs with Experiencer subjects in the present discussion is that they correspond almost exactly to one of the sub-classes of transitives identified by Lucot (1940) in a contribution as penetrating as it is brief. He writes (247-8):

> Les verbes transitifs ne sont pas sur le même plan. S'ils signifient tous une action qui passe sur un objet grammatical, ils se divisent cependant en deux groupes. Le sens des uns est tel que les conséquences de l'action intéressent le sujet (= our Experiencer - NV); l'objet n'ajoute qu'une détermination qui ne se trouve pas touchée par les conséquences ... Les autres expriment une action qui porte directement sur l'objet, soit qu'elle produise cet objet, soit qu'elle lui fasse subir un changement (= our Agent as subject - NV)."

The importance of this distinction lies in turn in the fact, noted by several scholars including Meyer-Lübke (1899: Vol. III, para. 289), Kuryłowicz (1931), Bourciez (1967: para. 126), Benveniste (1968: 87) as well as Lucot (1940:249) himself, that the earliest uses of the *habere* + past participle construction where a possessive nuance is no longer observable are with verbs such as *cognitum* 'know', *compertum* 'discover', etc.

Bearing in mind, then, the double system of verbal classification based on grammatical relations (Subject and Object) and on case relations (AG, LOC, EXP, NEUT), we are now in a better position to proceed to an analysis of the evolving Latin situation. It should be stated at once, however, that what follows does not seek to explicate the structural relationship of the evolving compound forms to the inflected forms inherited from Latin. We assume in this regard an account along the lines suggested by Harris in the previous chapter. Our concern here is rather to elucidate the steps by which the constructions with *habere* and *esse* developed from their original meanings and uses into the perfective meaning required by them in their new structural role. In other words, it is an investigation into the working out of that process of syntactico-semantic change traditionally labelled grammaticalisation.

3. Turning our attention first to *habere*, we may
recall that this verb is lexically specified to
require two NP's or arguments, a Locative and a
Neutral, as exemplified in the following sentences:

    (14)   tantas divitias habet   (Plautus)

             great   riches   he-has

                   NEUT   LOC

    (15)   locus ille nihil habet religionis (Cicero)

             place that nothing has of religion

             LOC   NEUT

    (16)   hostis   habet   muros (Vergil)

             the-enemy are-in-possession-of the-walls

             LOC   NEUT

    (17)   terror habet   vates   (Statius)

             fear   possesses the-prophets

             LOC   NEUT

    (18)   rogavi quid haberat in animo (Cicero)

             I-asked what he-had in mind

                   NEUT LOC

Of these, (14) is an instance of simple possession,
with the subject of the verb expressing, so to speak,
the location of the wealth. (15) has an overtly
locative subject and the predicate states a property of the place thus identified. In (16) it might
appear that *muros* refers to a place, and therefore
should be in the Locative, but the meaning of the
sentence is more forceful than the mere assertion
that the enemy are on the walls - it rather expresses the location of the walls as being within the
territory held by the enemy. (17) can then be interpreted in similar, albeit somewhat more abstract,
vein, while in (18) the locative subject is more
closely specified in the prepositional phrase *in
animo*. There are, then, various nuances here, but
a common structure is underlyingly detectable.
    In another set of examples, including as we
shall see the ancestor of the perfect periphrasis,
the second (NEUT) argument of *habere* is further
modified, e.g.:

(19)   cum   talem virum in potestatem habuisset
(Sallust) since such-a man in his-power   he-had
                              NEUT   LOC

(20)   miserrimum ego hunc habebo   amasium
(Plautus) very-sad   I   this shall-have lover
                          LOC   NEUT

(21)   me segregatum habuisse, uxorem ut dixit,
          I aloof   have-kept wife   as he-said
          LOC
          a me Pamphilum   (Terence)
          from me Pamphilus
                  NEUT
          'I, his wife - as he said, have kept
          Pamphilus aloof from me'

(22)   inclusum in curia   senatum habuerunt
(Cicero) confined in senate-house senate they-had
                              NEUT   LOC

The possible modifiers of the object of *habere* as
evidenced here are: adjectives (20), past participles
(21 and 22), and prepositional phrases (18 and 19);
in other words, exactly the class of forms which can
occur after a subject and the verb *esse* in a simple
predicational sentence. Thus:

(23)   horum   omnium fortissimi sunt Belgae
(Caesar) of-these all most-brave are the Belgians

(24)   castra sunt in Italia contra rempublicam
          a-camp is   in Italy against the-republic
          conlocata (Cicero)
          sited

(25)   in potestatem esse alicuius   (Cicero)
          in the-power to-be of-someone

Such a state of affairs is, of course, not coinci-
dental since the case generally assigned to subjects
of sentences with *be* and its equivalents in various

languages is precisely the Neutral case (cf. Anderson 1971:38, 85ff). The logic of this position is that the subjects in examples (23) - (25) are indeed semantically 'inert'. A property is predicated of the Belgians in (23), while the abstract location of a person is expressed in (25), and we may recall in this connection Gruber's test for his Theme as the NP of which the location is predicated. Moreover, once it is granted that *esse* is a verb taking Neutral case in subject position, a number of other elements in the pattern fall into place. First, we now see why *esse* can be used as a passive auxiliary (24), since the traditional grammatical definition of passive is a construction in which the object (to all intents and purposes the equivalent of our Neutral) is promoted to subject position.

We can explain too the role of the participle. This is generally agreed to have begun life as a purely adjectival form, as the following quotations attest: "The perfect participle passive of Latin is in origin an adjective in -*to*- which was neutral as to voice." (Palmer 1954:280), and again, "The verbal adjectives in -*to*- refer to abiding qualities or states, e.g. *tacitus, doctus, scitus*." (ibid. p.327). "Le rôle du participe passé passif est joué en latin par un ancien adjectif verbal en *-to-. Cet adjectif indiquait que le sujet avait la qualité exprimée par le verbe; il pouvait avoir le sens actif aussi bien que le sens passif..." (Ernout 1945: 344)

Adjectives, being generally items which express properties or attributes of objects, naturally co-occur with the Neutral case, whether or not the relationship is mediated by *esse*. The latter was, of course, optional in sentences of the form:

(26)   felix qui potuit rerum   cognoscere causas
(Vergil)   happy who could of-things know the-causes

        'Happy is he who ....'

However, as Ernout and Thomas (1951:para. 171) note, the use of forms of *esse* to relate subject and adjectival predicate was on the increase throughout the history of Latin.

The findings of this section, then, may be summarised under three heads:

(a)   *habere* is identified as a two-place verb taking LOC as subject and NEUT as object;

(b) *esse* is correspondingly a one-place verb taking NEUT as its subject;

(c) the participle is an adjectival form co-occurring with NEUT.

We now proceed to a consideration of the evolution of these structures into Vulgar Latin and Romance.

4. Consider the following example cited among others by Tekavčić (1972:para. 835) and typical of those adduced in the literature as exemplifying the kind of constructions with *habere* which eventually give rise to the Romance periphrastic perfects:

(27)   in ea   provincia pecunias magnas
       in that province capital great
                                  NEUT
       collocatas habent   (Cicero)
       invested   they-have
                  LOC

As Tekavčić notes, (27) means 'they have great capital invested in that province' and not (or not yet, at any rate) 'they have invested great capital ...'. In other words, we have here another instance of the by now familiar LOC and NEUT combination with *habere*. What then of the case structure of *collocare*? Consultation of the relevant entry in Lewis and Short (1879) reveals that in the overwhelming majority of citations *collocare* requires three arguments. Thus:

(28) a) occupato   oppido   ibi   praesidium
        having-occupied the-town there a-garrison
                                     LOC   NEUT
        collocavit   (Caesar)
        he-placed
        AG

     b) in prioribus libris satis collocavi
(Tacitus) in earlier books enough I-have-set-down
         LOC   NEUT   AG

82

      c) istam conloca cruminam in collo plane

(Plautus)   that place   purse   around neck plainly

           AG   NEUT   LOC

In our terms we can say that *collocare* takes AG (subject), NEUT (object) and LOC (prepositional phrase). Recall now that the participial form must modify a NEUT, and hence in the present instance imposes a passive interpretation on the *collocatas*, and we are in a position to diagram the structure of (27):

    (29)

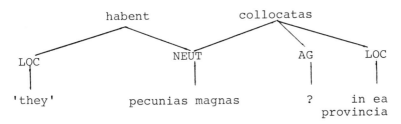

The LOC-subject of *habere* is of course expressed in the inflection, but the AG-subject of *collocare* is nowhere expressed. This omissibility of the AG is another consequence of the use of the NEUT-subject participial form, and it allows two possible interpretations to the sentence in (27) according to whether the investors of the money were the same people as the current possessors or not. Whichever of these readings we assign is a matter of pragmatics relating to our knowledge of the context of use rather than strict semantics.

    Consider another Ciceronian example:

    (30)   auctoritate   legum   domitas

           by-the-authority of-the-laws tamed

           habere   libidines

           to-have the-passions

which we diagram thus:

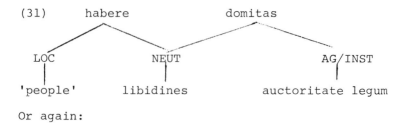

(31)   habere   domitas

  LOC   NEUT   AG/INST

'people'   libidines   auctoritate legum

Or again:

(32)   ibi   castellum Caesar habuit constitutum
        there a-camp   Caesar he-had built

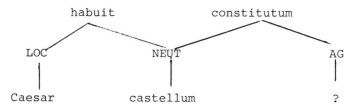

      habuit   constitutum

  LOC   NEUT   AG

Caesar   castellum   ?

In all three examples it is clear that the NEUT is the 'hinge' between *habere* and the accompanying verb in the participial form, and equally clearly, the LOC of *habere* and AG of the participle are not necessarily one and the same (unless of course one thinks that Caesar built his own camps!).

We are now in a position to be more precise about the mechanism by which the grammaticalisation of *habere* + past participle takes place. We have only to assume that in most instances the circumstances will dictate the identification of the LOC of *habere* with the AG of the participial verb, and it is then but a short step for this habitual identification to become a grammatically required one. In other words, *habere* no longer selects its own LOC but fills that position in its structure by promotion of the unexpressed AG of the verb to which it is attached by the NEUT 'hinge'.

Two important consequences follow from an account of the kind we have just outlined:

(i)   It predicts that verbs where the two roles in question cannot be other than identical will be in the vanguard of the change. Such is indeed the case for verbs with EXPERIENCER-subjects (cf. pp. 7-8 above), e.g.: *cognosco* 'I know', *comperio* 'I

learn, discover', *perspicio* 'I inspect', *persuadeo*
'I persuade', etc. As Lucot (1940:249) observes,
"Il est frappant dès lors que ce soit dans ce groupe
de verbes qu'apparaisse d'abord la périphrase par
habeo et le participe en *-to-*."

(ii) It explains why only transitive, or more
exactly two-place, verbs are involved in the *habeo*-
periphrasis. *Habere* is a two-place verb, as we
have seen. It can in the classical language construct with one-place predicates, notably adjectives
- e.g. (20) above and many similar examples - since
the LOC is filled independently. Once, however, we
require both identity between the LOC of *habere* and
the AG or EXP of its dependent verb and a NEUT as
'hinge', then only two-place verbs can fill the bill.
Put another way, the grammaticalisation of *habere*
involves the retention of its grammatical roles -
subject and object - but the loss of its independent
semantic role of LOC. This is a variant of a process which has occasionally been referred to as
semantic 'bleaching' (cf. Vincent 1980:56).
     Only at a later stage do the one-place verbs
parabolare or *dormire*, etc. become incorporated into
this construction.
     It is now time to bring the periphrasis with
esse into the story. We take for granted the independently motivated decline of the Latin inflectional
perfect (cf. Harris, this volume), which applies to
all verbs. However, as we have just indicated, the
habeo-periphrasis can only come to the rescue where
two-place verbs are concerned, so a complementary
pattern is required for one-place verbs.
     Formally, of course, the construction of *esse*
plus past participle was already common in Classical
Latin in at least two functions.

(a) The syntagm *amatus est* expressed the perfect passive, thereby representing a minor breach in
the otherwise inflectional passive inherited from
the Indo-European middle. It is a commonplace that,
whatever else needs to be said about it, the passive
construction involves the object of the active verb
becoming subject, with the agent either remaining
unexpressed or being relegated to a prepositional
phrase accompanying the main predication. It is
also true that the grammatical object of active,
transitive verbs is generally the most semantically
'inert' of the verbal arguments and corresponds to
what we have been calling NEUT. Given these two

observations, it follows that passives will normally and typically involve Neutrals as subjects, and this in turn will provide a rationale for the use of *esse* in the passive periphrasis.

(b) Parallel to passives in form but not in meaning according to the traditional classification are the so-called deponent verbs such as *locutus est*, *profectus est* etc. A full semantic breakdown of these is beyond the scope of the present study, but we may note some pieces of evidence in favour of analysing some deponents at least as having the NEUT-subject pattern.

1. Many deponents have the typical movement or change-of-state element of meaning which, as we have already seen (Section 2) leads writers like Fillmore, Gruber, etc. to identify a NEUT. e.g. *gradior* 'I step', with compounds such as *progredior*, *ingredior*, etc.; *labor* 'glide', *proficiscor* 'set out', *sequor* 'follow', *morior* 'die', *nascor* 'be born', *ordior* 'begin', etc.

2. Etymologically deponents go back to the medio-passives, and indicate in Ernout and Thomas' (1951:173) words 'une activité qui émane du sujet ou qui le concerne', rather than pure agentive action. Note too that many of the surviving middles in Latin are in the same semantic class as those identified above - e.g. *minui* 'diminish', *mutari* 'change', *verti* 'turn'.

The combined effect of these patterns and models is that there is both a formal parallel and a semantic pressure available to favour the development of periphrastic expressions like **ven(u)tum est*.

Synoptically, then, the contents of this section may be represented in tabular form:

Morphosyntactic category	Case of subject	Auxiliary

PERFECT

PASSIVE

AG _____ *habere*

NEUT _____ *esse*

The detailed working out of this scheme of things in the various parts of Romania will concern us in the next section.

5. Our account so far has highlighted the mutual interrelationships between the two periphrases in Latin, and the way they come to impose a bipartition on the verbs in that language. We begin our chron-icle of the changing balance between the two with Rumanian, where the salient fact is contained in the abruptly simple statement that the *esse* + past participle construction does not survive in the modern language. Apparent evidence to the contrary is provided by examples such as:

(33) o casă a fost zidită langă pârău

a house has been built beside the-stream

However, as Guillermon (1953: para. 98) - from whom this example is taken - notes, sentences of this form are a modern innovation based on imitation of nineteenth-century French and Italian literary mod-els, and the historically continuous and more typi-cally Rumanian rendering is:

(34) s'a zidit o casă langă pârău

with passive being expressed by the etymologically reflexive form *s'a zidit*. The widespread use of the 'voix pronominale' - see Lyons, this volume, for a modern account - in lieu of a periphrastic passive is the first consequence of the loss of the *esse* construction in Rumanian. The second is that all verbs take *a avea*, the reflex of *habere*, as their perfect auxiliary, regardless of their case struct-ure and semantic classification. More precise det-ails of the changes are difficult to establish in view of the length of the pre-literary period, but for an attempt to disentangle the situation see

Vincent (in preparation). Moreover, the Rumanian evidence offers valuable confirmation of the essential unity of *esse* + past participle which we argued for in Section 4. The construction either does not survive at all or it survives in both its roles, as in the Western Romance languages (including Italian), to which we now turn our attention.

Modern Italian, showing itself to be the most conservative of the daughters of Latin in this as in many other respects, retains a fully-fledged and grammatically productive contrast between *avere* and *essere* as auxiliaries. We display in (35) typical sets of verbs which take *essere* in Italian.

(35) a) *andare*   'to go'
        salire   'to go up'
        uscire   'to go out'
        venire   'to come'
        scendere   'to go down'
        entrare   'to come in'

     b) *restare*   'to stay'
        rimanere   'to remain'
        stare   'to be, stand'

     c) *nascere*   'to be born'
        morire   'to die'
        cominciare 'to begin'
        finire   'to end'

     d) *ingiallire* 'to turn yellow'
        ingrandire 'to get fat'
        invecchiare 'to age'
        dimagrire   'to slim'

     e) *accadere*   'to happen'
        succedere   'to happen'
        convenire   'to suit'
        bisognare   'to be necessary'

Some obvious semantic generalisations emerge from this list. The examples in (35a) and (35b) are respectively verbs of motion and verbs of position or location. As such they naturally fall into the general category of verbs with NEUT as subject (cf. the discussion in Section 2). The items in (35c) are traditionally labelled as 'change-of-state' verbs. In other words there is a kind of abstract movement from one state to another involved in their semantics, and therefore they too may appropriately

be regarded as having subjects in the NEUT case.
With reference to a particular example in this section, it is instructive to compare *nascere* and its
translation into English with an, in origin at least,
passive construction *to be born*. (35d) includes
verbs built on adjectival bases, and they all denote
a transition into the state defined by the adjective.
The relevance of NEUT is once more clear. Finally,
in (35e) we find the so-called 'impersonal' verbs,
whose subject is a proposition rather than an individual. Case grammarians generally concur that embedded sentences are introduced via the NEUT case
(cf. Anderson 1977:63, Fillmore 1968:28, Stockwell
et.al. 1973:505ff), and so we can establish the
generalisation that verbs in Italian with NEUT
subject take *essere* as an auxiliary. This leads to
some interesting minimal pairs. Consider:

(36) a) Il vaso ha   traboccato (di vino)
             LOC   NEUT
         the vase has overflowed with wine

     b) Il vino è   traboccato (dal vaso)
             NEUT   LOC
         the wine has overflowed from-the vase
                   (is)

These examples are from De Felice and Duro (1975),
who comment 'aus(iliare) *avere* quando il sogg(etto)
è il recipiente; aus. *essere* quando il sogg. è il
liquido'. Such a clause in the dictionary entry
should not really be necessary. The peculiarity
of *traboccare* is rather that either of its associated cases may become subject, but the generalisation still holds that when, and only when, the
NEUT takes the subject position the auxiliary is
essere.
     An old favourite of the Italian pedagogical
tradition is the contrast between *sono corso a Roma*
and *ho corso a Roma*. We can now see that the difference resides in taking the subject as NEUT - the
thing which moves, and as AG - the athlete indulg-
ing in his chosen sport. There are further ramifi-
cations to the situation in Italian which we cannot
follow up here (see Porena 1938, Leone 1954, 1970
for more extended discussion and exemplification).
In particular, while *volare* 'to fly' displays the
same auxiliary patterns as *correre*, other verbs of
motion - e.g. *nuotare* 'to swim', *viaggiare* 'to

travel' - seem not to. However, the general position is clear and interesting, since it give evidence of the original Latin semantic opposition still
being alive on Romance soil. Conversely, by inspec-
ting the facts of Italian we can get some understanding of how this construction must have emerged in
the post-classical period.

By comparison with Italian, Modern French
shows a rather impoverished state of affairs, with
être still active with only a handful of verbs - 22
according to Grévisse (1980: para. 1534). In addition he records another fifty or so where the choice
between *être* and *avoir* depends on a construal of
the verb as denoting 'state' or 'action'. Examples
are: *aborder, augmenter, baisser, changer, décamper,
diminuer, grandir, pourrir, vieillir*, etc. Even
then, Grévisse (1980:757, note 89) observes: 'Beau-
coup de ces verbes ne se conjugent, en fait, qu'avec
avoir...Quand ils prennent *être*, c'est que le participe passé est employé comme un simple adjectif.'
However, his distinction between state and action
is reminiscent of the example of Italian *correre*
above. Interestingly, *courir*, the French cognate
of *correre*, does not appear on Grévisse's list for
the modern language. In Old French usage varied,
as the following examples attest (all from Togeby
1974: para. 217):

   (37) a) ele est fuie

        'she has fled'

        (Modern French: elle a fui)

     b) c'estoit la cause pour laquelle

        it was the reason for which

        ils estoyent courus (Amyot)

        they had   run

     c) un ange qui pour nous prendre estoit

        an angel who to us   take   had

        vollé des cieulx (Ronsard)

        flown from heaven

     d) J'y   suis courue en vain (Racine)

        I-there have run   in vain

By contrast, Togeby notes that 'en ancien français
avoir pouvait s'employer avec *aller* pour indiquer

la durée de l'action', citing:

(38) a) Sire, vous avez assez   alé

sir   you   have enough gone

b) J'ay   tant alé

I-have so far gone

In general, however, the situation in Old French seems to have been more like that found in Modern Italian, and the direction of evolution since that time has been for more and more verbs to fall under the scope of *avoir*, so that the choice of auxiliary today can only be seen as the fossilised residue of a grammatically active opposition. This tendency towards the elimination of *être* in favour of *avoir* has been taken even further in Canadian French, as the investigations reported in Canale et.al. (1978) have shown. The figures set out below indicate the percentage of use of *avoir* as the auxiliary for the verbs listed in a series of tests administered to schoolchildren.

(39) Verb	Grade 2 (Age=8)	Grade 5 (Age=11)	Grade 9-12 (Age=15-18)
tomber	100	83	80
rentrer	92	100	82
rester	100	75	86
sortir	100	85	53
venir	79	73	32
arriver	69	56	24
partir	25	43	50
revenir	40	45	0
REFLEXIVES	46	25	27
aller	53	10	3

From occasional reports in the literature one imagines that these results could have been replicated from many varieties of regional and popular French, and they provide a modern parallel for a stage which has already been reached and indeed passed in the Iberian peninsula.

In Modern Spanish we note first that there are no surviving uses of *ser* as a temporal auxiliary, and second that *tener* is offering competition as an alternative to *haber* in circumstances which seem to be a re-run of the evolution of *habere* itself in the later stages of Latin. The relevant data has been extensively and illuminatingly compiled by Benzing

(1931), who documents first the widespread use of *ser* with the familiar classes of state and motion verbs in Old Spanish - e.g. *ir, andar* 'to go'; *venir* 'to come'; *llegar, arribar* 'to arrive'; *correr* 'to run'; *finar* 'to end'; *morir* 'to die'; *na(s)cer* 'to be born'; etc. - and second the gradual rise of *haber* from the thirteenth-century on, until by the end of the sixteenth-century there are only relic uses of *ser* in its auxiliary function. In similar vein, Keniston (1937) records 59 examples of auxiliary *ser* in his survey of sixteenth-century Spanish, distributed through the period as follows:

(40)   1500 - 1525   27

      1525 - 1550   20

      1550 - 1600   12

What is true for Spanish also holds for Catalan. Badía Margarit (1962: para. 156) cites examples more or less exactly parallel to those we have given above for Spanish.

We have already had cause to mention that in Spanish *tener* is now frequently found in sentences like the following (from Harmer and Norton 1957:356):

(41) a) tenía formado otro   concepto de la

        he-had formed another concept of the

        guerra

        war

    b) el capitan B - y el teniente C -

        Captain   and Lieutenant

        tienen absolutamente terminados los

        have   completely   finished   the

        preparativos

        preparations

In fact the Spanish construction is only available for transitive verbs, but already in Portuguese the cognate *ter* has completely replaced *haver* in all but the most literary register, regardless of whether the verb in question is 1-place, 2-place or even reflexive. Thus compare (from Willis 1971):

(42) a) tenho estado em Lisboa
       I've been   in Lisbon

     b) Têm   viajado   muito
        they've travelled much

     c) ainda não tinha chegado
        still not he-had arrived

There are, it should be added, semantic differences
between the use of the *ter* periphrasis in Portuguese
and the corresponding construction in Spanish, but
as they do not affect the general point we are making, we will not go further into them in the present
study.

We conclude at this point our necessarily rapid
survey of Romance auxiliaries. The narrative has
proceeded from East to West - beginning with Rumanian and ending with Portuguese - not simply for
traditional reasons nor for the sake of expository
elegance, but because we thereby see laid out in
their full geographical spread the stages of a historical continuum. Rumanian, of course, puts itself
outside the general pattern by the early - and as
yet unexplained - loss of the *esse* periphrasis, but
the other languages arrange themselves neatly in a
progression from the conservatism of Italian to the
extreme of innovation in Portuguese. Diagramati-
cally, we can portray the situation thus:

(43)

	Ital	OldFr	OldSp	ModFr	CanFr	OldPort	ModSp	ModPort
ESSE	———————————————— – – – – – – – – →							
HABERE	——————————————————————————————————— – – →							
TENERE						– – – – – – ——————————→		

Obviously, the above can represent only an initial
approximation. More detailed research would be
necessary to show, for example, whether Modern
Spanish is more or less advanced along the line of
change than Old Portuguese - the assignment to the
relative positions in (43) is in part impressionistic. But it is our belief that a cline similar, if
not identical, to the one set out here does indeed
reflect a diachronic reality, and hence represents
a positive - and so far as I am aware - original
finding of the research synthesised in this study.
A fuller survey would entail more careful investigation of a number of problems, notably those relating to the patterns detectable in non-standard dialects, where, as often, change has proceeded more
rapidly. Thus, there are regional French patois
where *avoir* has almost if not completely supplanted
être, and Southern Italian dialects where the use
of *tenere* closely parallels modern Spanish. Full
coverage of these facts would require a separate
volume - one which I hope eventually to write - but
the gross profile of auxiliary development is none-
theles plain to see.
   One grammatical environment for auxiliaries
which has not so far figured in our discussion is
the compound tenses of reflexive verbs, the reason
being that reflexives exhibit sufficient syntactico-
semantic properties of their own to merit separate
treatment. The crucial point is that relexives in
Romance, and indeed other languages, have at least
two uses:

   a) As a kind of medio-passive, permitting the
agentive role of the subject to be reduced or even
allowing non-specification of the agent. This is its
function in familiar French examples such as *le
beurre se vend ici*, and the one which lies behind
the Italian and Spanish 'impersonal' *si/se* constructions. Essentially, these are structures in which
NEUT is promoted to subject position, and so, by
our earlier hypothesis, the auxiliary *esse* would be
appropriate. (For further discussion and references
regarding this use of the reflexive, see Lyons, this
volume.)

   b) As a genuine transitive verb in which the
direct object happens to be identical to the subject.
This gives rise to both reflexive and reciprocal
interpretations, so that, for example, French *les
soldats se sont tués* may mean either 'the soldiers

killed themselves' or 'the soldiers killed each
other'. Whichever is relevant in a given context,
however, the fact is that the construction involves
a two-place verb being used transitively. Therefore, *habere* should in strict logic be required, and
indeed it is found, as the following examples indicate:

(44) a) quant ele s'a   bien lavée
         when she herself-has well washed

     b) Conan s'a   bien défendu
                himself-has well defended

These French instances - cited after Herzog (1910:
175) - are matched by similar cases in Italian:

(45) a) questi due cavalieri s'aveano
         these two knights   each other-had
         lungamente   amato
         for a long time loved

     b) Bito s'avea   messa la piu ricca
             (on) himself-had put   the richest
         roba di vaio
         cloak of fur

Two further examples from the same source - the
thirteenth-century *Novellino* - well illustrate the
ambivalence of the reflexive construction in regard
to auxiliary choice:

(46) a) che si   era posto in cuore
         that himself was put   in heart
         di provarsi
         to test himself

     b) io m'hoe   posto in cuore di cosí
         I myself-have put   in heart to thus
         fare tutti i giorni
         do   every day

Here the reflexive expression *porsi in cuore* 'to decide' takes *essere* in (46a) and *avere* in (46b). What ultimately seems to decide the case in favour of *essere/être* as the only auxiliaries for all uses of the reflexive in Standard Italian and French (but not in the dialects) is the statistical preponderance of the medio-passive over the genuine transitive use.

Our explanation of the auxiliary patterns with reflexives is not far removed in essence from that offered by Herzog (1910). It is important to follow him too in emphasising that the use of *haber* with reflexives in Spanish - and even more so the corresponding use of *ter* in Portuguese - does not represent a survival of the transitive reflexive usage discussed and exemplified in (b) above. The modern Iberian auxiliaries are innovations after the post-sixteenth-century loss of *ser* in the peninsula which we have already documented. Before that time reflexives took *ser* there as well. The Rumanian use of *a avea* is not parallel to the Spanish and Portuguese, since the *esse* periphrasis was never an option there, but it is equally unlikely to be a relic of the earlier transitive pattern (see Vincent, in preparation).

In conclusion, there are three points to be made by way of comment on the data presented here. In the first place, the continuum shown in (43) offers a nice example of a syntactic parameter along which the various Romance languages can be ranged from most conservative to most innovative. It can thus be set beside the more familiar phonetic and morphological scales by which the Romance languages have traditionally been classified. Secondly, it is of interest that with regard to this dimension of change French is *not* the one which has moved farthest from the Latin starting-point. Indeed, French in the matter of auxiliary usage shows itself to be one of the more conservative dialects. Finally from a general linguistic point of view, we find here evidence of a gradual syntactic change of a kind that some recent theoreticians - notably Lightfoot (1979) - have sought to deny. The ensuing theoretical issues are taken up again at greater length in Vincent (1982). Such a blend of Romance and general linguistic considerations could not be more typical of the teaching of Joe Cremona, and it therefore makes it all the more fitting that this article should be contained in a volume dedicated to him.

Chapter 5

THE STATUS OF THE ROMANCE AUXILIARIES OF VOICE

John N   Green

A welcome side-effect of the recent surge of
interest in universals and language typology has
been the new impetus given to previously neglected
areas of historical linguistics, notably the aeti-
ology and mechanisms of morphosyntactic change.
Linguists investigating how languages renew their
grammatical resources have enriched an already extensive battery of explanatory constructs (such as
restructuring/reinterpretation, the transparency
principle, learnability theory) with at least three
far more traditional notions: the role of metaphor,
grammaticalisation and gradience. The purpose of
this article is to examine the usefulness of these
notions in accounting for the evolution of part of
the Romance auxiliary system. Accordingly, we shall
begin with a fairly detailed synchronic analysis of
what might be called the 'peripheral' passive constructions in Castilian Spanish (that is, excluding
those conjugated with ser and estar, for some remarks on these, see Pountain (this volume)); after
a brief examination of parallel structures in other
Romance languages, we shall turn to what can be re-
constructed of their historical development, ending
with some more general observations on the status
of auxiliaries as transitional categories.
     The area of Spanish grammar on which we shall
concentrate is not conspicuously well described in
the literature, and modern usage in particular is
poorly recorded. There are only two monograph
treatments available (Matthies 1933 and Roca Pons
1958) and a number of fragmentary studies which,
although some are excellent in themselves (like
Bull's 1950 analysis of the contrastive ranges of
quedar and quedarse), were not designed to show
interrelationships or systemic coherence. A

significant difficulty (and one which the present
article may be felt not entirely to escape) is the
proper delimitation of the field, and in this respect it is instructive to compare the - often brief -
treatments offered by standard reference grammars.
    The 1931 edition of the Academy Grammar makes
no mention of the less common auxiliaries in its
section on the passive (para. 275), and elsewhere
has only two very brief and unrelated comments.
The first of these, having remarked that only
haber and ser are properly speaking auxiliaries, [1]
but that some other verbs can occasionally fulfil
that function, goes on to say (para. 92): 'El
citado verbo tener, e igualmente dejar, estar,
quedar y llevar, son auxiliares también para la
formación de los tiempos compuestos ...' then
giving one example for each verb.[2] The second,
implying that finite past participle constructions
are equivalent to predicative adjectives introduced
by a copula, continues (para. 200): 'Lo mismo que
estar, se construyen con un adjectivo predicativo
muchos verbos intransitivos, como andar, dormir,
llegar, seguir, venir, ir, etc. ...', but gives
only one illustration, from Cervantes, of a past
participle conjugated with one of these verbs
(venía fatigado). Given the overlap of estar and
the presence of the intransitive quedar in the
first group, the two comments taken in conjunction
appear to commit the Academy to the view that a
minimum of ten verbs can be pressed into service
as auxiliaries and that the resulting constructions
are all fundamentally of the same type. The draft
of a new grammar published by the Academy in 1973,
though in general much superior to its predecessor,
marks only a meagre advance in the areas which
concern us here. In a much fuller section on verbal periphrases, where the aspectual functions of
different auxiliaries are now noted in connection
with verb + gerund structures,[3] there is still no
mention of the same auxiliaries (ir, venir, andar)
used to form passives. An adjacent paragraph does
however observe, 'Los verbos llevar, tener, estar
y ser, y a veces traer, quedar y dejar, forman
perífrasis verbales como verbos auxiliares, desposeídos por lo tanto de su significado propio' (1973:
449; para. 3.12.6b). We shall attempt to demonstrate below that the parallelism of structure
implied by this grouping cannot be upheld on syntactic grounds.

The treatment in Ramsey (1894/1956) is much better exemplified but scarcely less fragmented than that of the Academy: the section on the 'Passive Voice', after illustrating the differences between ser and estar, suggests that 'the expression may be varied by substituting for estar one of the following verbs': ir, andar, verse, hallarse, encontrarse, quedar, quedarse, sentirse, presentarse, mostrarse (para. 21, 33). In a quite different context, Ramsey remarks that the use of tener with a past participle, 'often denotes the subsistence of the state produced by the action' (para. 18, 5); in a further section he notes that 'llevar is sometimes idiomatically used like tener in the manner of an auxiliary ...' (para. 27, 25), and elsewhere exemplifies the parallel use of dejar but without explicit comment (paras. 18, 4; 27, 16). Harmer and Norton (1957₂) achieve better cohesion, grouping the verbs in terms of their substitution relations: hence they observe in the chapter devoted to the passive: 'Ser and estar followed by the past participle may be replaced by verbs such as hallarse, ir, quedar(se), verse' (para. 206), and, in a different section, that 'Tener is sometimes used to replace haber in the compound tenses of transitive verbs' (para. 343) and 'Dejar and llevar may also be similarly used as substitutes for haber' (para. 344).

The other principal Spanish-language reference works have in general a better overall view of verbal periphrases without necessarily being more explicit on the sub-class which concerns us here. Thus, Bello-Cuervo (1970₈) discuss the use of andar and venir as auxiliaries with the gerund, but only mention in passing their use with the past participle. This tendency to concentrate on gerundival periphrases, often to the complete exclusion of participial ones, is further evidenced in the early editions of Seco (1953), in Gili y Gaya (1961a) and even in the up-to-date compendium of Alcina Franch-Blecua (1975).[4] Gili y Gaya does, however, draw attention to participial combinations with llevar, tener, traer, quedar and dejar stressing their perfective value (paras. 99b and 100), while later editions of Seco, supplemented by M. Seco, give the same list as Gili y Gaya, together with the same statement about perfective value, but adding that the substitutability of an adjective for the past participle in these structures means they should be treated under the much more general rubric of predicative complements ('oraciones cualitativas'

in his terminology - paras. 140 note and para. 143
note).[5] The picture which emerges from two rather
more specialised works, though better fleshed-out,
is not fundamentally different: Criado de Val
(1958$_2$) and Lamíquiz (1972) both emphasise grammaticalisation as the factor responsible for creating
new auxiliaries and both sketch taxonomies in terms
of aspectual relations. Lamíquiz seems particularly unwilling to commit himself on the size of
the class of 'semiauxiliaries' (only ir, ponerse,
volver, acabar and seguir are cited, none in conjunction with a past participle) whereas Criado,
having stated that the class is relatively large
and that Spanish has a rich variety of periphrases
involving verbs of action or movement, gives on at
least five occasions an illustrative list which,
after the fourth or fifth verb, tails off into a
cryptic 'etc.'. Indeed, aside from the four verbs
whose grammaticalisation he considers entirely
consolidated (haber, ser, estar and tener, para.
127), only three others seem to be exemplified in
participial constructions: andar, vivir and salir -
not the most obvious selection.

Given an undoubted element of cross-derivation
in the comments we have so far discussed, it is
perhaps surprising that so little notice has been
taken of Hanssen's observation, which though made
as long ago as 1910, still accords closely with
modern usage (see below): 'Zum Ausdruck der abges-
chlossenen Handlung dient estar mit Part. des
Passivs. Neben estar steht quedar. Andere Bedeu-
tungsnüancen bringen die Hilfsverben ir, andar,
venir, continuar, seguir, welche dauernde Handlung
bezeichnen' (1910: para. 36, 3).

The difficulty of delimiting the field of
investigation, and the importance of doing so, are
brought into sharp focus by the two monographs to
which we earlier alluded. The apparently crisp
limits set by Matthies' title (1933) - verbs of
motion with past participles - are belied by the
space he devotes to estar, quedar and vivir, while
neglecting continuar, seguir and - most important -
venir. Despite copious exemplification and an
overtly historical dimension, there is no attempt
to explain why a particular group of verbs should
be singled out for grammaticalisation. Rather,
Matthies propounds a narrow theory of aspect and
attempts to account for all his examples in terms
of the imperfective/perfective dichotomy, andar/ir
representing the archetypal imperfective (substi-

tuting for 'sein') and <u>salir</u>, faintly assisted by
<u>llegar</u> and <u>caer</u>, representing the perfective ('wer-
den'). This procrusteanism is vigorously attacked
by Amado Alonso (1939) in what amounts to an unfav-
ourable review article on Matthies, taxing him with
errors of fact and omission,[6] but concentrating
chiefly on methodology: Matthies' wrong-headed conclusions are directly attributable to the way he has
circumscribed his field of investigation, preferring
spurious formal ressemblance to the semasiological
criterion he ought to have used. (We are bound,
however, to note that in the brilliant and far-
ranging studies of <u>salir</u> and <u>andar</u> he offers by way
of counterpoint, Alonso does not follow his own
advice so far as to suggest a better delimitation
of the extent of 'grammaticalisation' in Spanish).
The other major monograph by Roca Pons (1958), avoids
similar strictures by making no claims to compre-
hensiveness. It is in fact more a series of loosely
connected essays, in which a general conceptual
framework is established for the investigation and
classification of auxiliaries, followed by detailed
case studies of <u>tener</u> and <u>estar</u>, with vignettes of
<u>hallarse</u>, <u>verse</u> and the now archaic <u>se(d)er</u> and
<u>yacer</u>, and brief mention of some less common items.
Roca Pons excludes from his purview verbs of motion
and those which - like <u>quedar</u>, the now archaic
<u>fincar</u> and <u>restar</u>, and the transitive <u>dejar</u> -
'sirven, sobre todo, para la expresión de un aspecto
puntual terminativo' (1958: 386), though he has
elsewhere published separate articles on <u>andar</u> (1954)
and <u>dejar</u> (1955).
    Summarising so far, we may say that all the
major reference works agree to recognise an indeterminate class of verbs with certain auxiliary-like
characteristics, but that their recording of present
day usage is at best patchy. Probably as a direct
result, none is prepared to offer a reasonably
complete list of the verbs involved, and such illustrations as are given betray disagreement on the
extent of the phenomenon and on the verbs most prom-
inently used. In practice, investigators seem to
have found difficulty in setting well-motivated
confines to their research,[7] although only Alonso
and Roca Pons (the latter mindful of the censure
meted out by his illustrious predecessor to Matthies)
elevate this to the status of a major methodological
issue. Undeniably, delimitation represents a genuine problem. This is because the semi-auxiliaries
lie precisely at the intersection of at least four

systems: on a morpho-syntactic level, those of
aspect and voice; on a semo-syntactic level, that of
qualitative ·(or appositive) predicates; and in terms
of lexical relationships, the 'full' lexical value
of the items pressed into service as auxiliaries.
The position is further complicated in the case of
semiauxiliary + past participle constructions - in
contrast to the colligations with infinitives or
gerunds - by the indeterminate status of the past
participle. While it is clearly incumbent on individual researchers to make plain the relative importance they attach to these interacting systems, and
hence the delimitation appropriate to their stand-
point, the decision itself must be justified on
model-theoretic, not merely methodological, grounds.
It is not a self-evident truth, pace Alonso, that
semasiological criteria are to be preferred to
grammatical criteria.

Against this rather murky background it seemed
appropriate to assemble some information on modern
usage.[8]   Such an inquiry would hopefully yield
answers to at least the following questions:

1)   Which are the most common verbs able to
perform auxiliary functions?

2)   What is the overall frequency of this type
of construction?

3)   Do examples occur freely in different
varieties, or is their occurrence tied to particular
registers?

4)   Does the overall distribution support the
grouping of these constructions with passives?

5)   What grammatical constraints are discernible (types of subject, concord, tense/aspect configurations)?

6)   What semantic constraints, if any, operate
between semi-auxiliary and lexical item?

To be fair, few of the works we have so far mentioned
share the conceptual orientation implied by these
questions (Criado de Val 1958 representing a prom-
inent exception); it seems nevertheless worthwhile
to point out that in none of them are the questions
systematically answered - indeed, for the most part
they go unasked.

In attempting some answers, I have drawn on two sets of examples. The main corpus, which I assembled some years ago as part of a wider investigation into passive usage in modern Spanish, is described and analysed in two earlier articles (Green 1975, 1979). It consists of eight texts, all composed since 1960 and representing three register types, with a total length of almost 200,000 words.[9] Although the text selection is in no statistical sense random, the method of data collection (exhaustive recording of examples identified by purely formal criteria) allows the analytical findings and derived projections to be treated with a measure of confidence. Using this corpus, answers can be attempted to questions (1) through (5) above, but the number of examples recorded permits only a very tentative reply to (6). In order to check the conclusions reached, I collected a subsidiary set of examples, all drawn from newspapers published in August/September 1981; since these do not represent exhaustive coverage and are not relatable to word-length, they are kept separate from the main corpus in the statistics which follow. In both cases, the criterion for including an example was designed to be as formal as possible - a past participle conjugated with some verb other than ser, estar or haber. Even so, practice revealed some doubtful cases, especially where there was a fair degree of separation between verb and participle; in such cases I erred on the side of generosity so as to maximise the chances for rarer verbs to be represented.[10]

The main corpus yielded 203 examples from 199,550 words of running text, a mean density of 1 : 983. The number of 'auxiliaries' was 24, and the number of participles 152 (their combinations are set out in the Appendix). In the subsidiary corpus, an additional 41 examples were collected; these featured 9 'auxiliaries' - all of which had been recorded in the main corpus - together with 32 participles, 11 of which overlapped with those in the main corpus. Aggregating the two sets of scores, the list of 'auxiliaries' in descending frequency order is:

quedar	54	(43 + 11)
tener	33	(32 + 1)
ir	27	(22 + 5)
verse	27	(20 + 7)
hallarse	14	
resultar	12	(2 + 10)
sentirse	11	

andar	10			
seguir	9			
venir	8	(5 +	3)	
ver	6	(5 +	1)	
encontrarse	6	(4 +	2)	
notarse	5			
permanecer	4			
llevar	4	(3 +	1)	
aparecer	2			
caminar	2			
continuar	2			
pasar	2			
quedarse	2			
encontrar	1			
mantener	1			
parecer	1			
presentarse	1			

$$\overline{}$$

244   (203 + 41)

As will be apparent, aggregating the two sets of examples makes a negligible difference to rank order - only the position of <u>resultar</u> is altered and it seems justifiable to conclude that this verb occurs chiefly, though not exclusively, in a newspaper 'reporting' mode.

Several discrepancies come to light when this list is compared with what can be extrapolated from the reference grammars and studies discussed above. Firstly, the importance of <u>quedar</u> is much underestimated; secondly, some verbs of quite high frequency are omitted from nearly all the treatments - witness <u>verse</u>, <u>hallarse</u>, <u>resultar</u>, <u>sentirse</u>; and thirdly, the converse, quite a large group of the verbs quoted do not appear in this sample. While failure to be represented in a sample of this fairly modest size does not, of course, impugn the grammaticality of other combinations, it does cast doubt on the wisdom of making a verb like <u>salir</u> (unattested here) into the lynchpin of one's linguistic analysis, as does Matthies.

To the best of my knowledge, there is only one other corpus-based study of auxiliary frequency with which my results can be compared, that of J. de Kock (1975). His criteria for inclusion are broadly similar, but the corpus is not: though larger than mine, it draws exclusively on the published essays of Unamuno, thus gaining in analytical accuracy at the expense of stylistic breadth. In this literary sample, de Kock found 61 separate items which could

be considered in some sense auxiliary to an accompanying participle, over half of them appearing only
once; the most frequent, after <u>ser</u> (145) and <u>estar</u>
(87), were: <u>ir(se)</u> 23, <u>quedar(se)</u> 20, <u>sentirse</u> 20,
<u>creerse</u> 11, <u>verse</u> 11, <u>vivir</u> 11, <u>parecer</u> 10, <u>andar</u> 9,
<u>venir</u> 8. Although the high incidence of <u>creerse</u>
and <u>vivir</u> is surprising (and can probably be ascri-
bed to Unamuno's individual style) the other frequencies and the rank order accord reasonably well
with those of my own sample, and certainly the discrepancies would not bolster up any of the published
accounts.[11]
It would be misleading to attempt to answer
questions (2) - (5) without reference to register,
since there is a good deal of internal variation in
the corpus which can be attributed to this factor
(for the justification of the three-way register
division see footnote 9). Table 1 records the raw
incidence of each of three example classes, and re-
lates this to word-length by means of a density
score. Figure 1 represents the proportional incidence per register, expressed as a bar chart.[12]
Over the whole corpus, the 'semiauxiliary' class is
the least frequent, but this is due to the skewing
effect of the reporting register: in both the others,
the incidence of semiauxiliaries falls midway between
those of <u>ser</u> and <u>estar</u> constructions. In spite of
this register-determined variation, it remains true
that the semiauxiliary class is distinctly more
stable than either of the others - a fact immediately
apparent from Figure 1. We can therefore answer
question (3) in the affirmative: examples of semiauxiliaries do occur freely in all the varieties
sampled and any constraints imposed by register are
confined to a rather narrow band.
Tables 2 and 3 show the occurrences of semiauxiliaries analysed by: register, animacy of grammatical subject, concord pattern, and tense-paradigm.
The easiest parameter to interpret is concord, which
serves neatly to divide the semiauxiliaries into two
sub-classes. On this evidence, one can make an
absolutely exceptionless statement for each verb, as
to whether it requires the past participle to concord
with the grammatical subject (GS) or with the object/
complement (GO). It may be objected that this is
not a very exciting finding: all that has been
achieved is a formal validation of the traditional
category of transitivity. But there is a little
more at stake. Firstly, in cases where the semiauxiliary is reflexive, the concord pattern clearly

Table 1. Frequency by register

register	occurrences			word-length	densities		
	ser	estar	semi-aux		ser	estar	semi-aux
reporting	231	59	38	47,000	1:203	1:797	1:1237
creative	64	192	110	104,500	1:1633	1:544	1:950
expository	91	47	55	48,050	1:528	1:1022	1:874
total	386	298	203	199,550	1:517	1:670	1:983

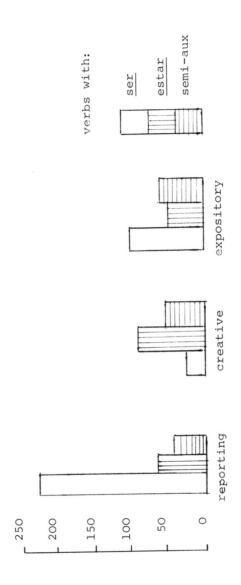

Figure 1. Example types by register

	Register			Grammatical subject		Concord		Total
	report.	creat.	expos.	anim.	inan.	GS	GO	
andar		9	1	7	3	10		10
aparecer	2			.	2	2		2
caminar		1	1	2		2		2
continuar		2		1 ,	1	2		2
encontrar	1				1		1	1
encontrarse	1	1	2	2	2	4		4
hallarse	1	3	10	5	9	14		14
ir	2	11	9	12	10	22		22
llevar	3				3		3	3
mantener			1	1			1	1
notarse		5		5		5		5
parecer			1		1	1		1
pasar		2		1	1	2		2
permanecer		4		4		4		4
presentarse	1				1	1		1
quedar	15	13	15	10	33	43		43
quedarse		2		2		2		2
resultar			2	1	1	2		2
seguir		9		8	1	9		9
sentirse	1	9	1	10	1	11		11
tener	6	22	4	28	4		32	32
venir	2	2	1	2	3	5		5
ver	2	2	1	4	1		5	5
verse	1	13	6	16	4	20		20

Table 2. Semiauxiliaries by register, animacy and concord

	Pres		Fut		Imp		Perf		Pret		Plup		Cond		Infin		PsPrt	
	An	In	An	In	An	In	An	In	An	In	An	In	An	In	An	In	An	In
andar	3	1			4	1				1								
aparecer		2																
caminar	1				1													
continuar		1			1													
encontrar		1																
encontrarse	1	1				1			1									
hallarse	2	7	1		2	2												
ir	6	5		1	6	2										2		
llevar		3																
mantener															1			
notarse					2				3									
parecer		1																
pasar										1					1			
permanecer	2				1				1									
presentarse		1																
quedar		17		5	1	3	1		6	3	1	1			2	2	1	
quedarse					1				1									
resultar					1	1												
seguir	1		1		4	1			2									
sentirse	2	1			5				2						1			
tener	14	2			14	1										1		
venir	1	2			1	1												
ver			1						2				1		1			
verse	2	1			3	1	1		4	1	1				6			
Totals	35	46	3	6	47	14	2		22	6	2	1	1		12	5	1	
%	39.9		4.4		30.0		1.0		13.8		1.5		0.5		8.4		0.5	

Table 3. Semiauxiliaries by tense paradigm, subdivided by animacy

distinguishes grammatical reflexivisation (or
'medialisation') from a lexical property of the
verb: the pairs <u>encontrar</u>/<u>encontrarse</u> and <u>ver</u>/<u>verse</u>
represent quite different syntactic structures,
<u>quedar</u>/<u>quedarse</u> do not.[13]   Secondly, all transitive
verbs in Spanish can be conjugated with <u>haber</u> to
form compound tenses without thereby requiring or
even permitting concord, and given that this represents a major departure from the position in Old
Spanish (where concord was frequent, though not
obligatory, with <u>haber</u>), the present-day pattern
is best interpreted as a rather efficient two-way
marking system.   Essentially, and with very few
exceptions, concord shows that the past participle
is passive.   Thus, presence of concord systematically marks the participle for passivity while its
absence marks the complete grammaticalisation of
<u>haber</u> + participle, in which the participle is
interpreted as [+ perfective, - passive]; at the
same time, obligatory concord on the objects of
some transitive verbs (<u>tener</u>, <u>encontrar</u>, etc.)
serves as an overt reminder that in these constructions the verbs are not fully grammaticalised and
retain a part of their normal lexical meaning.
    The animacy/non-animacy of the grammatical
subject is, I would argue, a particularly clear
index of the degree of grammaticalisation in the
case of verbs whose 'normal' lexical meaning denotes
an intentional act or process for which 'being alive'
is a logical prerequisite (such as <u>andar</u>, <u>caminar</u>,
<u>ir</u>, <u>venir</u>, <u>ver</u>).   One could be forgiven for expect-
ing that colligations of these verbs with inanimate
subjects would result in semantic deviance, if not
outright ungrammaticality.   Just conceivably, this
was true in the very remote past (though it would
have to be more remote than the classical Latin
period, as we shall see below).   More likely, it
has always been possible to exploit these apparently
impermissible combinations to indicate personification or to achieve some other stylistic effect.
What interests us here, is the point at which this
metaphorical extension of the original sense becomes
so frequent - so stereotyped, almost - that successive generations of speakers fail to notice the
metaphorical overtones and reanalyse the verb as a
mere carrier of grammatical information.   Once the
grammaticalisation process is under way, and a
degree of polysemy is established in the verb, it
seems probable that the persistence of animate-
subject combinations - indeterminate as between an

'auxiliary' function and the 'original' lexical
meaning - is the factor which prevents a complete
lexical split. Verbs able to maintain this deli-
cate balance will remain 'semiauxiliaries'. Those
whose period of lexical split is followed by the
atrophy of the original lexical value - a process
Pulgram (1978) convincingly documents in the case
of haber - will develop into true auxiliaries.
     In the present corpus, as Table 2 shows, most
of the verbs occur with both types of subject,
regardless of the 'illogicality' of an inanimate
subject for many of them. For hallarse and quedar
there is a marked preponderance of inanimates,
arguing for advanced grammaticalisation. Among
verbs of motion, ir and venir seem equally happy
with animate or inanimate subjects, while llevar
(which admittedly only occurs three times) seems to
favour inanimates. At the opposite end of the
scale, the restriction of notarse, quedarse, sentirse[14] and probably caminar to animate subjects is
almost certainly not fortuitous; these are verbs
capable of taking a participial complement in much
the same way as an adjectival predicate, but for
the moment no more.[15]
     We should presumably not wish to say a con-
struction was fully grammaticalised if, despite
reasonably frequent occurrence, it was strictly
confined to one particular linguistic mode. The
register system could thus provide a mechanism
of propagation for the construction and, at the
same time, an index of its diffusion. The inclusion of the register distribution in Table 2 is
intended only as a rough guide to range, but the
figures do allow us to draw some tentative conclusions on the degree of grammaticalisation attained
by various verbs. Most obviously, the verbs with
the highest overall frequency also have quite a
full range: although only one verb, verse, appeared
in all eight texts, ir occurred in seven, quedar
and tener in six, sentirse in five. Some less
frequent ones also have a good range: the four
examples of encontrarse were each in a different
text, and the five of transitive ver came from four
texts. While not proving that grammaticalisation
is well advanced for these verbs (it would be
foolhardy to make any such claim on a sample of
this size), their distribution is nevertheless
consistent with such a view. It contrasts markedly
with the distribution of: notarse (five occurrences
all in the same text, and probably attributable to

the author's individual style), <u>permanecer</u> (two occurrences in each of two literary texts) and <u>seguir</u> (nine occurrences spread over three literary texts) - verbs which, moreover, are attested almost exclusively with animate subjects.

Set out in Table 3 is the information available to answer the question: do tense/aspect constraints operate on semiauxiliaries? On this chart, occurrences are broken down according to the traditional tense paradigms, each subdivided for animacy of grammatical subject. Although after this subdivision the numbers in many cells are very small and must be treated with appropriate caution, the exercise does produce a good scatter and strongly suggests that animacy and tense-form are independent variables, with no appreciable mutual influence.[16] Overall, examples are heavily concentrated in the present (39.9%) and imperfect (30%), with the preterite (13.8%) and infinitive (8.4%) trailing well behind. While this skewed distribution cannot be random and is certainly significant, we should not lose sight of the fact that occasional examples are thrown up in every category. Now, if it were claimed by a linguistic theory that examples of the type found in this corpus are all statives and should be derived transformationally from underlying action-passives - as has certainly been claimed for constructions with <u>estar</u>[17] - we should not expect to find any occurrences at all in perfective tense-forms. So, although the idea has its attractions, the overwhelming preponderance of imperfective tense-forms (more than five to one) cannot be accounted for by a syntactic theory of derived stativity, because this would wrongly predict that the observed 16% of perfective-tense examples were all ungrammatical. Nor can it be argued by way of defence that the tense distribution in this sample is the result of conflating patterns which are quite clear-cut for individual verbs: as is apparent from Table 3, eleven verbs occur in perfective tenses, all of them producing similar or greater numbers of imperfective examples. The evidence, then, points to three conclusions: firstly, despite the high frequency of imperfective tenses, most semiauxiliaries retain the freedom to participate in perfective constructions; secondly, and as a direct result, the theory of derived stativity must be rejected; and thirdly, the observed concentrations must be explained in terms of semantic/pragmatic properties of individual verbs rather than grammatical constraints on the construction.

Before examining the behaviour of individual verbs, we should return to our earlier question (4): does the overall distribution support the grouping of semiauxiliary constructions with passives? In many ways, this is the most difficult question to answer, requiring value judgements at every stage. We noted from Table 1 and Figure 1 that examples of this type occur in all texts sampled, that they are more stable by register than passives conjugated with either ser or estar, and that they rarely represent the most frequent of the three categories[18] In terms of concord, the semiauxiliaries subdivide into two groups, the larger of which matches the concord pattern of ser- and estar- passives. For the minority group, the pattern arguably reflects a 'normal' passive at a deeper syntactic level (that is if mantiene cerrada la puerta is envisaged as deriving from an underlying structure of the approximate form mantiene (la puerta está cerrada)). As regards the animacy of the grammatical subject, the semiauxiliary class records the lowest incidence of inanimate subjects, roughly 40% : 60% (compared with estar 52% : 48%, ser 81% : 19%;[19] this is however still a very high reading when compared with the 'normal' selectional restrictions on these verbs in their non-auxiliary uses, and represents a major shift towards the subject pattern typical of passives.[20] In respect of tense/aspect preferences, we have seen that the semiauxiliaries concentrate heavily in the imperfective tenses; in this, they mirror very closely the distribution of estar- passives (though with a slightly higher incidence of preterites, further accentuated in the non-systematic data of the subsidiary corpus), but differ considerably from ser- passives, for which preterites constitute the largest category.[21] Two other criteria, not so far mentioned, deserve examination: the separability of the participle from its semiauxiliary and the incidence of agentive phrases. A strong argument in defence of the view that semiauxiliary constructions are passives, and a counter-argument to the charge that they are 'merely' adjectival complements with more elaborate copulas, would be a demonstration that they co-occur freely with agentive or instrumental phrases. Unfortunately, my earlier investigation showed that these phrases - regardless of their potential grammaticality - are not very common with any kind of passive (1975: 356), so that expectation on the

present corpus cannot be high. Nevertheless, of
the 203 examples, 22 (or 10.8%) appear with agents
expressed by por and a further 6 (2.9%) have instrumental phrases introduced by de. This compares
with figures of 24.7% for passives with ser (the
larger part confined to the reporting register) and
of 14.6% for those with estar. Nor can there be any
doubt that most of these instances are directly
comparable with fully-specified passives using the
conventional auxiliary; witness:

1)   Las piernas y la curva del vientre iban
señaladas por los pantalones negros (text 2C)

    'Her legs and the curve of her stomach
were accentuated by the black trousers'

2)   El monarca iba acompañado de dos
secretarios, que tomaban nota de sus observaciones
... (text 3C)

    'The monarch was accompanied by two
secretaries who noted down his observations ...'

3)   No había el menor peligro de que un
buceador resultase alcanzado por el disparo, pues
la bala perdía todo su poder de penetración antes
de recorrer un metro de agua (text 3C)

    'There was not the slightest danger that
a diver would be hit by the shot, for the bullet
would lose all its power of penetration within a
metre's underwater travel'

4)   La medida y forma del espacio quedan defin-
idas, en cada caso, por la situación de las masas
contenidas en él; ... (text 3B)

    'The extent and form of space can be
defined, in every case, by the relative position
of the masses within it; ...'

A similar picture emerges when the semiauxiliary
constructions are compared with conventional passives on the basis of the degree of separation
between verb and participle. A short subject-NP
or single-word adverbial element is intercalated in
25 examples, representing 12.3% of possible sites
(in the subsidiary corpus there were a further
three examples, representing 7.3% of that corpus);

these figures compare with an intercalation rate of
14% for estar-passives but only 3% for ser-passives.
Again, the semiauxiliaries fall within the observed
range of variation, nearer to the distribution of
estar than of ser. The evidence, then, points to a
similar conclusion on every one of the parameters
examined; the semiauxiliary constructions are sub-
stantially comparable with estar-passives and share
some important characteristics - chief among them
concord patterns - with ser-passives. In other
words, the semiauxiliaries can only be excluded from
the class of 'passives' if it is maintained that all
copula + past participle combinations are equatable
with predicative adjectives, and that Spanish accordingly possesses no 'analytic passive'. In my
view, that would be manifestly absurd.

The last remaining question concerns the
semantic constraints operating on semiauxiliaries.
There are at least two levels on which this can be
interpreted: the compatibility - in purely lexical
terms - of verb and participle, and the stronger,
quasi-syntactic constraints to which some verbs
seem susceptible. Taking the latter point first,
recall our earlier conclusion that the semiauxiliaries - as a class - have the freedom to participate
in both perfective and imperfective structures,
while exhibiting a very strong preference for imper-
fectives (Table 3 shows eleven verbs with examples
in both categories, including quedar which occurs
in almost every possible slot). Notwithstanding
this general conclusion, and the probability that
only their low frequency prevents some other verbs
from producing perfective examples (resultar, for
instance, appears several times in the preterite in
the subsidiary corpus; see Appendix part III),
there is a handful of verbs whose confinement to
imperfective structure does not seem fortuitous.
These are: tener (32 + 1 occurrences), ir (22 + 5),
venir (5 + 3) and possibly llevar (3 + 1).[22] I
have been unable to find modern examples of these
verbs used as passive auxiliaries in the perfective
tenses.[23] An explanation sometimes favoured, and
perhaps going back to Letelier (1893), sees the
durative nuance inherent in these and similar verbs
as fundamentally incompatible with the punctual overtones always conveyed by perfective tenses. This has
the weakness of supposing logico-semantic considerations to be paramount in language, and fails to
explain why inherently imperfective verbs can ever
be used in punctual tenses. A better explanation

would be that the 'durative nuance' of such verbs serves to indicate the relevance to the moment of speaking, of an event, process or series of events now remote in time; witness:

5) ... Enrique Segura, que tiene dedicada una sala con veinte retratos (text 1)

'... Enrique Segura, who has a gallery devoted to twenty of his portraits'

6) Bele tenía solucionado el problema de los ejercicios: ... (text 2C)

'Bele had the homework problem solved: ...'

7) Tenía fijadas las fechas de varios [examenes], entre ellos la Historia (text 2C)

'He had the dates of several fixed in his mind, among them History'

8) [todas las latas] ... llevan troquelada la fecha de envasado (ABC 25.9.81)

'all the tins ... have the canning date stamped on them'

All of these refer to single events ((7) perhaps refers to a series of events) in what is past time at the moment of speaking/writing, but with consequences which are still valid: because Bele once had an inspiration about coping with her homework, she now knows what to do, despite being tired, rather hung-over and late for class; because the cans had the date stamped on them, shoppers can now identify which ones are suspect. These interpretations are only possible if there is a temporal gap between the event and the time of its relevance. This, I believe, is the real reason perfective tenses do not occur, for a perfective tense would have to be interpreted as simultaneous with the event being reported by the participle and thus, if acceptable at all, would defeat the object of using tener or llevar in the first place.
    Turning now to the lexical compatibility of semiauxiliary and participle, it may seem rash to attempt any general statements on the basis of so restricted a corpus. There is, however, good reason to believe that lexical juxtapositions are

subject to far less rigid constraints than grammatical processes, so that even an enormous corpus might only enable one to talk in terms of 'favoured patterns'. Be that as it may, the present corpus does provide illustration of two significant processes - semantic adaptation and the gelling of idiomatic combinations. The two most frequent combinations in the corpus are <u>verse obligado</u> (eight examples in five different texts plus an extra one in the subsidiary corpus) and <u>ir acompañado</u> (five examples in four different texts) which clearly represent a stage of cohesiveness associated with idioms, and simultaneously illustrate some important semantic tendencies. Roca Pons (1958:376) comments on the frequent matching of <u>verse</u> with <u>obligado</u> and avers that the meaning is not a straightforward resultative, but carries connotations of 'sentirse obligado'. This seems to me to miss the point: 'feeling' obliged might also be the result of 'being' obliged, but is not necessarily synonymous with it. The overwhelming evidence of the present sample is that <u>verse</u> is used with animate subjects to indicate helplessness in face of some external event or pressure which is almost invariably undesirable. Aside from <u>obligado</u>, <u>verse</u> provides the auxiliary for: <u>abocado</u> 'confronted', <u>apurado</u> 'exhausted', <u>asaltado</u> 'assaulted', <u>atendido</u> 'awaited', <u>condenado</u> 'condemned', <u>envuelto</u> 'enmeshed', <u>postergado</u> 'left behind', <u>privado</u> 'deprived', <u>rebajado</u> 'humbled/cheapened', <u>reducido</u> 'reduced', <u>rodeado</u> 'surrounded', <u>sentado</u> 'seated [against one's will]', <u>sobrepasado</u> 'overtaken', <u>sometido</u> 'subjected'.[24] There is only one instance of something desirable being predicated by <u>verse</u>: a girl in one of the novels (text 2C) is said to feel elated to 'verse admirada', but even here it seems that passivity is being stressed - she is pleased to find herself admired, but had taken no special measures to bring this about. Even though these examples show a very clear preference pattern for <u>verse</u>, it must be emphasised that it is no more than a preference - not a selectional restriction even, and certainly not a grammatical constraint. There is absolutely nothing ungrammatical about <u>se vio felicitado de todos</u> 'he was congratulated on all sides', but it carries a slightly jarring nuance and, apparently for that reason, tends to be avoided.

Ir acompañado illustrates the first of two
discernible processes of semantic adaptation -
harmonisation and dissimilation. Ir is a verb of
motion, acompañar strongly implies motion, so they
form a natural pair and can be juxtaposed without
any violence to the 'normal' meaning of either
element. Acompañado occurs five times in the main
corpus, invariably with ir and always with an instrumental phrase introduced by de; it occurs twice in
the subsidiary corpus, both times with venir, thus
maintaining the harmony. The unusual aspect, and
the one which argues for a degree of grammaticalisation, is that five of these seven instances have
inanimate subjects, subjects - that is - not 'logically' capable of movement or accompaniment; witness:

9)   Y no se acierta a comprender cómo es
posible que pueda presentarse esa idea ante los
españoles sin venir acompañada de la más terminante
repulsa ... (Sur, 5.9.81)

'It is quite incomprehensible that this
idea should even be mooted before the Spanish
people without at the same time being categorically
rejected ...'

A similar harmony can be found in the tendency of
hallarse and encontrarse to combine with participles
indicating location and static position (sometimes
enforced), hence: hallarse adentrado 'absorbed in',
agrupado 'grouped together', empotrado 'squashed in',
encerrado 'shut in', enfrascado 'bottled up',
equilibrado 'balanced', estacionado 'parked',
instalado 'installed', parado 'stopped/stationary',
situado 'situated' and, twice with encontrarse,
encarcelado 'imprisoned'.[24] The opposite tendency
of dissimilation is less common and seems chiefly
confined to verbs of motion. Various commentators
(the Academy, Ramsey and Gili y Gaya among them)
have mentioned attenuation of meaning in the semiauxiliaries without being very precise about what
'attenuation' implies. What they do not say is that
it may be a two-way process, affecting both auxiliary
and lexical item. The most dramatic example is a
colloquialism in one of the novels (2A):

10)   - Voy muerta - suspira

'"I'm flaked out", she sighs'[literally:
'I'm going dead']

Only marginally less eye-catching are the following collocations:

11)   La ciudad andaba ajetreada como de costumbre ...   (text 2A)

'The city had a restless look about it, as usual ...' [literally: 'went about fidgeted']

12)   Por veredas y caminos andan desperdigados Institutos de Investigación y jardines agronómicos, raíles de tranvías, y un reactor nuclear, ... (text 2C)

'Scattered about the highways and byways are Research Institutes, experimental farms, railway tracks, and a nuclear reactor, ...' [literally: 'go/walk scattered']

13)   ... este cine, que anduvo desnortado durante casi cincuenta años ... (text 3D)

'... this film industry, that drifted aimlessly for nearly fifty years, ...' [literally: 'went about de-northed', i.e. without a reference point]

These and similar examples could perhaps be dismissed as transparent metaphors carefully constructed by style-conscious novelists or university lecturers. But one can hardly dismiss the following grammaticalised uses of venir, in reporting and expository contexts respectively:

14)   Esta diferencia ... viene motivada por la inferior infraestructura de España   (text 1)

'This difference can be accounted for by the inferior infrastructure of Spain'

15)   ... la situación de un punto viene dada por dos guarismos (text 3B)

'... the position of a point is given by two values'

In (14) and (15), the original metaphor is still discernible if one stops to look for it (so, (15) could perhaps be rendered - 'the position of a point can be arrived at ...'), but the rather mundane context makes an intentional metaphor most unlikely; rather, venir has been grammaticalised to the point where it can serve quite unobtrusively as a passive auxiliary.[25]

The constructions we have so far examined are neither recent developments in Spanish nor exclusive to it. On the contrary, most Romance varieties have at least some constructions in common with those we have documented for Spanish, though the general phenomenon of semiauxiliaries appears never to have been investigated on a pan-Romance scale. So, for instance, Diez in his section on the passive (1860: 198-199) mentions the reflexes of stare/restare/remanere in Italian, Occitan, Spanish and Portuguese (the two latter using the lexical equivalents fincar and quedar), identifies ire/andare as a 'southern' usage, exemplified in the same four languages, and has a longer passage on venire, said to be common in Italian but not unknown in Spanish and Portuguese. Meyer-Lübke (1899: 329-333) covers similar ground, but also mentions the FIT CANTATUS type of N. Italy and has a major section on venire, described as 'vereinzelt im Spanischen und Portugiesischen, häufiger im Italienischen, ganz besonders verbreitet im Graubündnerischen' (330). Bourciez, noting occasional examples of VENIT LAUDATUS and FIT LAUDATUS in Latin, avers, 'La première resta fréquente en Italie et en Rhétie; la seconde semble s'être confinée et développée de bonne heure surtout dans la Haute-Italie' (1967: para. 245c), later exemplifying the generalised pattern with venire in Engadinisch varieties (para. 530). Any future pan-Romance treatment, aside from remedying the obvious gaps in coverage of the principal manuals, could profitably employ a two-way classification roughly dividing Romania into north and south zones. All varieties have access, in some measure, to reflexive constructions to express passives, but thereafter the northern zone is largely confined to a single auxiliary for the analytic passive, while the southern admits a much greater range of semiauxiliaries - all of them, for that reason, only partially grammaticalised.[26]

Dating the emergence of semiauxiliary constructions must to a large extent depend on subjective interpretation of sparse attestations and has in the past proved controversial. On the one hand, the wide diffusion of similar patterns in the modern Romance languages argues, if not for a common origin, at least for a strong inherited

tendency; but on the other, the considerable
diversity of lexemes now favoured, and the difficulty of finding indisputable forerunners in Latin,
argue for a development post-dating the collapse
of the Empire. It is certainly true that semiauxiliary constructions seem well established by
the earliest Romance texts; this is documented for
Spanish by Matthies (1933) and Roca Pons (1958),
for Italian by Kontzi (1958) and Setterberg-
Jörgensen (1943) and for Ladin by Ettmayer (1921).
This last article was however written as a counter
blast to Meyer-Lübke's implication that the passive
periphrases with verbs of motion can be traced
directly back to Latin;[27] Ettmayer advances a
highly conjectural alternative explanation curiously
based on the 'supine of purpose' construction.
Against this, Löfstedt (1938-39) assembles a number
of classical examples from Virgil, Ovid, Juvenal
and Propertius with venire used as a copula with
nominal and adjectival complements, and just two
examples from Propertius which appear to be incon-
trovertible forerunners of the modern construction:
non impune illa rogata venit (1,5,32) and irritata
venit quando contemnitur illa (1,10,25).
     Turning now to the development of the semi-
auxiliaries in Spanish, some insight can be gained
from my earlier diachronic study of exponents of
the passive (1978). Here, a 10,000-word sample of
running text was taken from nine prose texts,
beginning with the Alfonsine Crónica and progressing
at roughly equal intervals to a Baroja novel of
1908.[28] As in the corpus of modern Spanish, the
criteria for including examples were made as formal
as possible, and all past participles conjugated
with some verb other than haber were counted. The
full list of verbs occurring is given in the
Appendix (Part IV). Figure 2 shows as a graph
the relative incidence of passives with ser, estar
and all other auxiliaries. Making allowance for
the rather eccentric distributions in Persiles and
Feijóo, it is clear that the use of ser as a passive auxiliary has been in steady decline since the
Old Spanish period, while the use of estar and the
semiauxiliaries has shown a modest rise.[29] It is
unfortunately impossible to control for register
effects in earlier stages of the language and, as
we have seen, if the graphs were produced beyond
Baroja to include the modern corpus, there would be
appreciable differences in their trends, depending
on where the 10,000-word sample was drawn. Judging

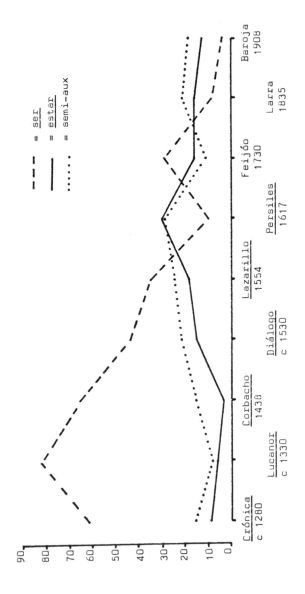

Figure 2. Diachronic profile of ser-passives, estar-passives and semiauxiliary constructions

on the distribution recorded in Figure 1, however, the major variation should be located not so much in the fairly stable semiauxiliary class, as in the _ser_-passives, where a sample excluding the reporting register would show a further fall but one drawn entirely from newspapers would probably show a rise.

For present purposes, the essential thing is merely to demonstrate that small numbers of the semiauxiliary class occur steadily from the Crónica onwards. Although there is some fluctuation in concord patterns with haber in the early texts, no fluctuation is discernible for any other auxiliary, so that the class can be subdivided - like the modern corpus - according to whether concord is required with the grammatical subject or object. The ratio of animate to inanimate subjects stays almost exclusively in favour of animates until the early 16th century text, the Diálogo being the first to exhibit thoroughly modern patterns in this respect. The two inanimate subjects recorded in the Crónica represent variants on the same phrase - quand sannuda anda la mar 'when the sea runs angrily' - a context in which the personification could well be imitated from ancient sources and in which the metaphor appears both transparent and intentional. Certainly, there is a marked difference between these instances and the two potentially modern combinations to be found in the Preface to the Valdés Diálogo:

16) ... paréceles que enteramente va perdida la fe

'... it seems to them that faith has been completely lost' [literally: 'goes lost']

17) Viendo, pues, yo por una parte quán perjudicial sería ... si esta cosa assí quedasse solapada, ...

'Seeing, on the one hand, how damaging it would be if the matter were to remain hushed up in this way, ...'

From this text onwards, there seems to be a gradual spread of inanimate subjects to verbs with which they were not previously attested, but inanimates as a class, except in the possibly atypical Feijóo text, do not approach either the absolute frequency

or the 40 : 60 ratio with animates which we earlier
showed to be typical of the modern corpus. It seems
likely, then, that at least in literary prose, the
regular colligation of semiauxiliaries with inanimate
grammatical subjects is of comparatively recent date.
The majority of the lexical items now most
frequently serving semiauxiliary functions (see
Table 2 above) are attested from the earliest texts.
Verbs of motion and location were early candidates
- witness the appearance of andar, fincar, ir,
llevar, venir in the Crónica, together with a
healthy sprinkle of tener examples and a single
occurrence of verse which in my view clearly shows
a degree of grammaticalisation at this early date:

18)   E ellos cuando se uieron coytados dexaron
se dentro caer, e quisieron ante seer quemados que
morir a manos de los romanos

'And when they found themselves sorely
pressed, they jumped down [into the flames] and
preferred immolation to death at the hands of the
Romans'

The semantic constraints on the availability of
verbs for service as semiauxiliaries are neatly
illustrated by the replacement of a now archaic
fincar by quedar from the 16th century Diálogo
onwards - the semantic shift of quedar presumably
not being complete much before this date.
The primacy of semantic relationships in
determining which verbs can be utilised as semiauxiliaries, must be our first and most general
conclusion. This is vividly emphasised by the pre-
dictability of new recruits to the modern list of
semiauxiliaries when compared with those attested
in the historical samples (see Table 2 and the
Appendix). Virtually all the verbs fall into two
broad groups - the majority into movement and
location, the minority into perception. Hence,
knowing the availability of andar, caer, ir, salir
and venir, one could predict with some confidence
the acceptability of combinations with caminar,
continuar, pasar and salir. Likewise, fincar and
quedar imply permanecer and resultar; hallar implies
encontrar; llevar and traer imply mantener, and so
on.[30] At a fairly obvious level, therefore, the
history of Castilian provides further confirmation
of the widely attested tendency for locative expressions to be grammaticalised into temporal/aspectual

ones (see Pottier 1961/1968: 197; Lyons 1977: 718).
Nevertheless, noting the availability of a
set of verbs for grammaticalisation is not equivalent
to explaining how this is effected, nor, more fundamentally, why it is necessary. I have tried to show
that for the Spanish semiauxiliaries grammaticalisation began with a stage of metaphorical extension.
This can operate in two ways: the first is through
extension of lexical collocations (thus <u>verse
rodeado</u> 'to see oneself surrounded' could be understood literally, but <u>verse asaltado</u> '... assaulted'
does not necessarily entail sight of the attacker,
and <u>verse obligado</u> '... obliged' can only be
understood metaphorically); the alternative is
through extension of grammatical colligations (thus
a verb whose lexical meaning 'logically' requires
an animate agent is permitted to take an inanimate
subject). In principle, this latter process has
access to any intransitive verb and can be viewed
as a powerful mechanism for maximising functionality
in language. The same process was responsible for
the generalisation of the original 'true' reflexive
from exclusively animate constructions, via metaphorical uses with inanimates, to the fully-fledged
Romance mediopassive. Here, as in the case of
intransitives of motion and location, grammaticalisation once set in motion could advance fairly
quickly and unimpeded by any serious risk of ambiguity.
The grammaticalisation of the whole periphrasis,
as opposed to that of the finite verb alone, is a
much broader issue, and one which cannot be properly
examined here. The evolution of the periphrastic
past tenses with <u>habere</u>, via a surface reanalysis
of an originally passive expression, is by now
quite well understood (see Vincent, this volume),
and it seems to me that the passives with semiauxiliaries share the identical opening stages.
Crucial in this respect is the ability of the past
participle to function as a surface adjective.[31]
Given the fairly free word order of Latin and Spanish, numerous opportunities can arise for originally
independent adjectival phrases (deriving from
deeper level passives) to be reinterpreted as
grammatically dependent on the main verb. Consider:

19) Comitatus amicis, magnam per viam venit

Acompañado de sus amigos, viene por la
calle mayor

'Accompanied by his friends, he comes along the main street'

19') Venit, comitatus amicis, per magnam viam

Viene, acompañado de sus amigos, por la calle mayor

19") Venit comitatus amicis (per magnam viam)

Viene acompañado de sus amigos (por la calle mayor)

A reanalysis on these lines requires only that listeners fail to hear or correctly interpret any intonational cues marking off the adjectival phrase in (19') from the rest of the sentence. Notice, in particular, that the necessary word order could occur quite naturally, without the need of new syntactic mechanisms to 'feed' the embryonic structure. A similar process, I believe, is responsible for the transitive (GO concord) periphrases, though in this case there has been an additional step to mark the grammaticalisation: the past participle has gravitated to the verb, just as it did in the _haber_ past tenses, but so far without loss of concord. In modern Spanish, there is now a strong preference for placing the participle immediately after the auxiliary, even though this means anticipating concord with an object not yet mentioned. In the modern corpus, for instance, all six examples of transitive _ver_ show this order: _verán enclavadas ... magníficas instalaciones_ 'they will see magnificent installations sited ...'; _ver convertida la Roca ..._ 'to see the Rock converted ...'; _vi realizados mis deseos_ ' I saw my wishes fulfilled'; _vio reflejadas sus figuras ..._ 'he saw their faces reflected ...'; _España vería acrecentado su territorio ..._ 'Spain would see its territory increased ...'; _ve desperdigados sus nobles esfuerzos_ '...sees its noble efforts frittered away'.

Granted a degree of grammaticalisation, the question remains: do auxiliaries constitute a category at all? Opinions vary considerably, running a complete gamut from de Kock's (1975) suggestion that auxiliaries of whatever kind constitute one large gradient category, to the claim that surface 'auxiliaries' all derive from underlying full verbs - advanced for English by Pullum and Wilson (1977) and for Spanish modals by Klein (1968). As often

happens, these would-be polar positions have more
in common than either shares with an 'intermediate'
analysis like that of Pottier (1961), which rests
on a three-way classification: full verbs like
comer, estudiar ... which could not conceivably
be auxiliaries; verbs able to function as auxiliaries, like ser, querer, ir ...; and auxiliaries
proper 'que no son verbos ... soler, y generalmente
haber ...' (1961/1968: 196). This notionally-
based taxonomy has a curious consequence: it
establishes a class of 'auxiliaries', separate from
'verbs', whose only indisputable member, soler, is
morphologically indistinguishable from numerous
regular verbs, while some members of the bi-func-
tional class (ser, ir and presumably haber) have
the most irregular and salient morphology. We have
not so far distinguished 'morphological differenti-
tion' from 'grammaticalisation', but the distinction
is valid and necessary for some languages. In
Rumanian, for instance, a voi has two morphologi-
cally-differentiated conjugation patterns discrim-
inating between its use as a full verb and an
auxiliary. Castilian has no parallel. It has
developed no morphological distinctiveness to set
apart grammatical and lexical uses of the same
verb, much less any invariant morphology for auxiliaries - such as the preverbal tense/aspect
markers found in French creoles. This morphological
criterion, taken in conjunction with our earlier
observations on the apparent open-endedness of the
class of verbs able to act as 'semiauxiliaries',
strongly favours a gradient analysis for Spanish.
(Indeed, the class of potential 'auxiliaries' is so
large that no language, we might argue, would ever
want to grammaticalise them all.) At one extreme
of the gradience would be verbs like haber which
have lost virtually all trace of lexical meaning,
and at the other, verbs like mostrarse and notarse
which have lost virtually none of theirs. A treatment along these lines would represent a synchronic
reflection of a diachronic process still possibly
incomplete. The drift from OV to VO order and from
postposed to preposed auxiliaries may eventually
culminate in a small class of invariant auxiliary
particles, but in view of the two millennia needed
to reach the present position, the furthest we can
speculate is that the culmination is still a little
way off.

NOTES

1. 'Se llaman <u>auxiliares</u> porque sirven de
auxilio para la formación de los tiempos compuestos,
y también porque con el verbo <u>ser</u>, uno de los
comprendidos en esta denominación, se suple la voz
pasiva de los transitivos, que propiamente no la
tienen en nuestro idioma. [...] Los verbos propiamente auxiliares son <u>haber</u> y <u>ser</u>...' (Gramática de
la RAE 1931: 48).

2. The examples are: <u>tengo pensado ir a</u>
<u>Badajoz</u>; <u>lleva entendido que jamás lo consentiré</u>;
<u>está mandado que se hagan rogativas</u>; <u>dejaron dicho</u>
<u>que vendrían mañana</u>; <u>quedó resuelto que se haría</u>
<u>tal o cual cosa</u>. Despite the superficially similar
structure, it should be apparent even from the scant
context given that there are two distinct constructions: the grammatical subjects of <u>está</u> and <u>quedó</u>
are in apposition to their complement clauses (put
differently, the subject could be taken to be the
postposed NP), whereas <u>tengo</u>, <u>lleva</u>, <u>dejaron</u> have
an animate subject actually or potentially different
from that of the dependent clause. We return to
this point below.

3. '<u>Ir</u>, <u>venir</u>, y a veces <u>andar</u>, añaden a la
duración del gerundio las ideas de movimiento,
iniciación o progreso...' (1973: 448)

4. Their major section on 'Bipredicaciones con
unidad de sentido (1975: 777-782; para. 5.4) is
principally concerned with aspectual relations,
classifying <u>estar</u> / <u>seguir</u> / <u>andar</u> as 'duratives'
and <u>ir</u> / <u>venir</u> as 'progressives' but only when col-
ligated with the gerund. In the summary chart
provided (781), only three verbs, <u>haber</u> / <u>tener</u> /
<u>ser</u> are shown as colligating with the past part-
iciple.

5. There is considerable cross-fertilisation
in these accounts, usually but not always acknowledged. For a particularly blatant example, compare
the statement quoted earlier from the new draft of
the Academy grammar (<u>Esbozo</u> 1975: 449, para. 3.12.6b)
with the antecedent statement in Gili y Gaya:
'Los verbos <u>llevar</u>, <u>tener</u>, <u>estar</u> y <u>ser</u>, y a veces
<u>traer</u>, <u>quedar</u> y <u>dejar</u>, forman frases verbales en las
cuales funcionan como verbos auxiliares, desposeídos
por lo tanto de su significado propio...' (para. 99b).

6. Matthies' monograph was not in general well
received. E. Keniston complained that it begged too
many questions and was preoccupied with stylistic
nuances to the exclusion of genuine linguistic
analysis: <u>HR</u> 3 (1935: 173-177). The review by

Romance Auxiliaries of Voice

A. Rosenblat though better natured is really no more
enthusiastic: RFE 20 (1933: 406-408).
7. The enviably neat presentation achieved, for
instance, in Rallides' analysis of the tense-aspect
system of standard South American Spanish owes less
to the Diver 'form-content' model he uses than to a
conscious decision to exclude the really messy data:
'Furthermore, we shall not consider those morphemes
which have not become completely grammaticalised,
i.e. viene cantando ... anda buscando ... and other
verbs of motion and state used in this kind of
construction' (1971: 9). Interestingly, these constructions are being sharply set off from the está
cantando type, which is treated as fully integrated
within the system.
8. The abundant examples in Matthies (1933) and
Roca Pons (1958) are predominantly literary and
heavily weighted to the period from 'classical' to
19th century Spanish. The illustrations in Alonso
(1939) are presumably all intended as current usage,
though it is evident that a wide range of styles and
registers are represented, but not documented as
such. A brief article by Fish (1964) seems also
intended to illustrate modern usage, but its jumble
of examples, all bereft of attribution, makes no
attempt to sort out different types of construction.
There are brief but perspicacious comments on llevar,
ir and venir in Lorenzo (1971₂: 113-116).
9. The texts are:
(1)   9 consecutive issues of the news bulletin
      España semanal, Madrid, October - November 1967.
(2A) J. Goytisolo La Chanca (novel, 1962)
(2B) J. J. Plans Alejandro Casona (dramatised
      biography, 1965)
(2C) J. A. Payno El curso (novel, 1962)
(3A) A. Fernández Suárez España, árbol vivo (1961,
      first 10,000 words)
(3B) Einstein   )(both 1961, in the
(3C) El sexto continente } Enciclopedia popular
) ilustrada series)
(3D) El cine español (unscripted university lecture,
      1968)
The sample is heavily biased in favour of written
Spanish (the more regrettable as no documentation
on spoken usage appears to exist). The texts are
grouped into three registers: 'reporting' (1),
'creative' (2A - C), 'expository' (3A - D), this
grouping being confirmed by applying the Chi-square
significance test on such parameters as: relative
density of examples, relative frequency of example-
types, tense-aspect configurations, grammatical

129

subjects, etc. (for details, see Green 1979). On this basis it was shown, contrary to expectation, that the university lecture (3D) was not significantly different from the written 'expository' texts (3A - C).

10. For the benefit of any reader sufficiently interested to make comparisons with the findings of my earlier article (1975), it should be pointed out that the new corpus is unfortunately not co-terminous with the earlier 'class C$_2$'. The latter was an 'all-the-rest' category, from which some examples have now been removed. One set of results has also been much altered by a change of policy: in assessing the animacy of the grammatical subject, examples like tengo pedidos diez libros are now treated as animate because of the main verb subject, whereas formerly they were counted as inanimate since libros was viewed as the subject of a deeper-level clause (tengo + (diez libros están pedidos)). Although I believe there are valid syntactic grounds for the earlier classification, using a deep-level analysis in this case may be felt to conflict with the formal-surface criteria used elsewhere; the change has therefore been made in the interests of harmony.

11. It is difficult to derive more information from de Kock's article, as the data are presented in support of a theoretical point (the definition of an auxiliary) rather than for their own sake. Probably some steps have been inadvertently omitted, since at present some of the figures appear not to add up.

12. Calculated by taking the raw scores of the reporting register and proportionally reducing the others to represent a word length of 47,000.

13. This is not of course to suggest that quedar / quedarse are freely interchangeable any more than other so-called 'optional' reflexives (see Bull 1950, 1952). No other examples occur in the present corpus (e.g. ir / irse, caer / caerse) so despite the few clear passives with agents adduced by Bull for quedarse (1952: 470-472), it seems that the auxiliary function of the reflexive member of the pair is at best rare and, just conceivably, being eliminated.

14. The sole example of sentirse with an inanimate grammatical subject is clearly a personification: España ... se siente hermanada en la esforzada lucha para lograr el aumento constante y progresivo del bienestar de nuestros pueblos (text 1) - literally: 'Spain feels herself sistered...', freely: 'Spain feels she has acquired a sisterly ally in the

constant struggle to achieve progress and advance-
ment in the well-being of our peoples'. Even a
transparent personification may however mark the
first stage of grammaticalisation.

15. There is however one example showing the
possibility of a more overtly passive construction
using notarse: Se notó embarazado por la intimidad
de su confesión 'He realized he was embarrassed by
the initimacy of her confession' (text 2C).

16. Only in the case of quedar are there unexpected concentrations - both present and future have
only inanimates.

17. For a refutation, see Green (1975: 352),
Luján (1981) and, for Portuguese, Querido (1976).

18. Only one of the eight texts (2A) has semiauxiliaries marginally in the lead, and this may be
accounted for by the abnormally low incidence of
ser-passives - unusual even in a 'creative' text
(ser 1, estar 19, semi-aux 21).

19. Figures taken from my earlier article (1975:
353-354). The animacy ratio now given for semiauxiliaries appears to represent a major discrepancy
from that reported earlier for class C_2; the difference is due to the change of policy discussed in
footnote 10 above.

20. Owing to pressure of space, I have excluded
from discussion a more detailed breakdown of the
person category. Overall - and remembering that
second person verbs are likely to be underrepresent-
ed throughout the present sample - the person
distribution of the semiauxiliaries is similar to
that of estar- passives (with a slightly higher
proportion of third person singular animates), and
markedly dissimilar from that of ser-passives.

21. Figures from Green (1975: 350, table 2).
The relevant scores for estar-passives were: present
39.6%, perfect 0.3%, imperfect 42.4%, preterite 5.2%;
and for ser-passives: present 15.6%, perfect 22.2%,
imperfect 6.8%, preterite 23%.

22. There is one conditional example of ir in
the subsidiary corpus which is difficult to classify.
Hallarse (14 occurrences) is also confined to the
imperfective tenses, though there is one preterite
for its near synonym encontrarse, and Roca Pons
(1958: 367-368) quotes several preterites for
hallarse, none of them absolutely modern.

23. For ir, there would of course be problems
of recognition in the preterite, which is identical
to that of ser; the other tense-forms are clearly
distinguishable. Roca Pons (1958) quotes a few
examples of tener used in the preterite, none more

recent than the 17th century and only one syntactically comparable with the constructions being studied
here.
    24. The translations are appropriate for the
particular examples of the corpus; it is not claimed
that these would always be the most natural equivalents.
    25. In sentence (14) I translate <u>viene motivada</u>
by 'can be accounted for'. Nigel Vincent reminds
me (personal communication) that Italian grammarians
have sometimes recognized a modal value in <u>venire</u>,
which of course is much more common as a passive
auxiliary in Italian than in Spanish. Certainly in
Spanish, this is not frequent. I suspect that it
may be an inferred connotation rather narrowly confined to generics and gnomic presents - circumstances under which other passives can also appear to be
modal, witness: <u>iter non celeriter faciendum est</u>
'the journey is not to be done quickly' implying
'you can't do it quickly', or <u>cela ne se fait pas</u>
'that isn't done' implying 'you mustn't do it'.
    26. The justification for grouping together the
northern varieties is functional, despite the differing choice of auxiliary. French, which has developed a wide range of periphrases for other purposes,
seems remarkably unadventurous about the passive -
in considering verbs of motion, Diez and Meyer-Lübke
are only able to point to a very sporadic use of
<u>s'en aller</u> with the past participle. The <u>venire</u>
construction has ousted reflexes of <u>esse</u> throughout
the southern Swiss dialects (Meyer-Lübke 1899:
para. 308; Rohlfs 1975: para. 90) and most Ladin
varieties (Ettmayer 1921). Modern Rumanian uses
<u>a fi</u>, representing a diachronic fusion of <u>esse</u> and
<u>fieri</u>. Among the southern group, Italian is by far
the best described in the literature though most
accounts concentrate on <u>andare</u> and <u>venire</u> (see,
among others, Lepschy - Lepschy 1977: 141-142,
Herczeg 1966, Leone 1966, Lo Cascio 1968, van Molle-
Marechal 1974; on the gerundival constructions with
similar auxiliaries Blücher 1973 - which comes to a
parallel conclusion to that of Rallides 1971, discussed
in footnote 7 above; and, on diachronic aspects,
Kontzi 1958 and Setterberg-Jörgensen 1943). On
Catalan, Badia (1962, I: para. 196) exemplifies
periphrases with <u>tenir</u>, <u>quedar</u>, <u>restar</u> and <u>deixar</u>,
stressing their terminative and resultative values,
but does not mention the verbs of motion. Portuguese
is briefly discussed by Azevedo (1975) and very well
documented by Dias da Costa (1976), from whose account Portuguese emerges as the nearest parallel to

Castilian, except of course for its generalisation
of <u>ter</u> as the normal past tense auxiliary, and for
an apparent reluctance to use <u>vir</u> + past participle
nowadays.

27. I cannot myself find the offending passage
in Meyer-Lübke, unless the implication is so
general that <u>any</u> phenomenon of wide diffusion is
held to be traceable to Latin. Ettmayer is sure
not: '.. so viel ich sehe, im Latein nirgends ein
Beleg zu finden ist.' and 'Auch die Verbindung von
<u>venire</u> mit einem Adjektiv ist unlateinisch' (1921:
<u>44).</u>

28. The texts were:
  <u>Primera crónica general de España</u>
    (abbreviated: '<u>Crónica</u>'), c 1280
  <u>Libro de ensiemplos del Conde Lucanor</u>
    (<u>Lucanor</u>), c 1330
  <u>El arcipreste de Talavera o el Corbacho</u>
    (<u>Corbacho</u>), dated 1438
  <u>Diálogo de las cosas ocurridas en Roma</u>
    (<u>Diálogo</u>), c 1530
  <u>La vida de Lazarillo de Tormes</u> (<u>Lazarillo</u>),
    1554
  <u>Los trabajos de Persiles y Sigismunda</u>
    (<u>Persiles</u>), 1617
  Two essays by Feijóo (<u>Feijóo</u>), c 1730
  Three articles by Larra (<u>Larra</u>), 1832-35
  <u>La dama errante</u> (<u>Baroja</u>), 1908

29. This impressionistic response can be more
formally demonstrated by means of the product-moment
coefficient, which registers a strong inverse relation of <u>estar-</u> to <u>ser</u>-passives (reading -0.734), a
weaker but still detectable inverse relation of the
semiauxiliaries to <u>ser</u>-passives (-0.394), and a
fairly strong positive correlation between the
<u>estar</u>-passives and the semiauxiliaries (+0.664).

30. The 'perception' contingent is not much
enlarged - <u>notarse</u>,confined to a single author,
seems an uncertain recruit. The non-occurrence of
other 'central' perception verbs is probably explained by the availability of an alternative strategy -
<u>se oyó alabado</u> 'he heard himself praised' is only
marginally acceptable and would be replaced by <u>se</u>
<u>oyó alabar</u>, using a non-inflected infinitive. The
infinitive construction appears to be mandatory with
an agentive phrase: <u>se dejó llevar por sus impulsos</u>
'he allowed himself to be swept along by his
impulses', but not *<u>se dejó llevado por</u>...

31. In many traditional grammars it is of course
designated 'verbal adjective' rather than 'past

participle'. As will by now be apparent, I believe it is better treated as a transitional category, not representing an adjective in syntactic deep structure.

APPENDIX

Part I: Participles of the main corpus having two or more occurrences

	Auxiliaries requiring concord with subject															with object				
---	andar	aparecer	caminar	continuar	hallarse	ir	notarse	parecer	pasar	permanecer	quedar	seguir	sentirse	venir	verse	encontrar	llevar	mantener	tener	ver
abandonado											1								1	
abarrotado	2		1																	
abrazado										2										
abierto											1								2	
acodado			1						1											
acompañado				5																
apurado	1														1					
cansado								2					1							
cerrado											1							1		
citado											2									
convertido											2									1
dicho											1								1	
defendido													1			1				
definido											2									
desconcertado											2									
distribuído											1					1				
doblado	1			1																
entendido																			4	
fijado											1								1	
inadvertido									2											
obligado															8					
parado			1								1									?
perdido									1		1									
preocupado	2																		1	
provisto				2																
reflejado											1									1
regado											2									
satisfecho				1							1									
sentado													1		1					
señalado				1							1									
sometido			1	1															1	
tendido														2						
vestido		1		2																

Part II: Participles of the main corpus having one occurrence.

aborrecido	+ tener	desesperado	+ andar	meditado	+ tener
abrigado	+ sentirse	desilusionado	+ sentirse	montado	+ ir
aclarado	+ quedar	desmayado	+ andar	muerto	+ ir
acrecentado	+ ver	desnortado	+ andar	motivado	+ venir
adentrado	+ hallarse	desorbitado	+ tener	ofendido	+ sentirse
admirado	+ verse	desperdigado	+ andar	paralizado	+ quedarse
aferrado	+ permanecer	despreciado	+ sentirse	pasmado	+ seguir
agarrado	+ ir	dirigido	+ ir	pensado	+ tener
agarrotado	+ tener	dividido	+ presentarse	plagado	+ ir
agotado	+ notarse	dormido	+ seguir	planteado	+ tener
agradecido	+ sentirse	duplicado	+ quedar	postergado	+ verse
agrupado	+ hallarse	echado	+ ir	prefigurado	+ quedar
aislado	+ permanecer	embarazado	+ notarse	preparado	+ tener
ajetreado	+ andar	embarcado	+ ir	previsto	+ tener
alcanzado	+ resultar	embobado	+ quedar	privado	+ verse
alejado	+ quedar	emparejado	+ andar	pulverizado	+ quedar
alelado	+ quedar	empotrado	+ hallarse	realizado	+ ver
amenazado	+ encontrarse	encariñado	+ sentirse	rebajado	+ verse
animado	+ encontrarse	encerrado	+ hallarse	reclinado	+ ir
aplastado	+ resultar	enclavado	+ ver	reducido	+ quedar
aprobado	+ tener	enfilado	+ tener	repartido	+ llevar
asegurado	+ tener	enfrascado	+ hallarse	repoblado	+ llevar
atendido	+ verse	enfundado	+ ir	reservado	+ tener
atraído	+ sentirse	engustado	+ quedarse	resuelto	+ quedar
balizado	+ quedar	ensimismado	+ quedar	revestido	+ ir
bordado	+ verse	envuelto	+ verse	rodeado	+ verse
buscado	+ tener	equilibrado	+ hallarse	servido	+ tener
callado	+ seguir	erguido	+ caminar	situado	+ hallarse
cazado	+ tener	escolarizado	+ quedar	sobrepasado	+ verse
cohibido	+ venir	escrito	+ hallarse	solucionado	+ tener
completado	+ quedar	estacionado	+ hallarse	subido	+ encontrarse
condenado	+ verse	exasperado	+ hallarse	sumergido	+ quedar
conmovido	+ sentirse	excitado	+ permanecer	terminado	+ quedar
convencido	+ quedar	explorado	+ quedar	tostado	+ venir
cortado	+ tener	extendido	+ quedar	transido	+ notarse
cubierto	+ quedar	forzado	+ encontrarse	ubicado	+ quedar
dado	+ venir	garantizado	+ quedar	vedado	+ tener
dedicado	+ tener	hecho	+ tener	velado	+ quedar
delimitado	+ quedar	hermanado	+ sentirse	vencido	+ sentirse
desarrollado	+ tener	instalado	+ hallarse		

Part III: Subsidiary corpus

	also in main corpus	concord: subject						object			aspect IMP		PERF		animacy	
		encontrarse	ir	quedar	resultar	venir	verse	llevar	tener	ver	present	other	preterite	other	animate	inanimate
abocado						1					1					1
acompañado	*			2									2		1	1
amenazado	*		1								1					1
aprisionado			1										1			1
asaltado						1							1		1	
conmocionado			1									1			1	
contusionado				2									2		2	
definido	*		1								1					1
demostrado			1										1			1
desperdigado	*									1	1					1
destinado		1										1				1
encarcelado		2									2				2·	
esparcido				1									1			1
excluído			1										1			1
hecho	*					1					1					1
herido			1	3							1		3		4	
impreso		1									1					1
instalado	*	1											1			1
invitado	*			1							1				1	
legitimado				1							1					1
limitado			1										1			h
muerto	*			2									1	1	2	
obligado	*				1						1					1
pedido										1	1				1	
privado	*				1							1			1	
reducido	*		1		1						1			1		2
rematado			1								1					1
roto				1									1			1
sometido	*				2						2				1	1
suspendido			1									1				1
transcurrido		1									1					1
troquelado									1		1					1

Part IV: Diachronic samples

	Crónica		Lucanor		Corbacho		Diálogo		Lazarillo		Persiles		Feijóo		Larra		Baroja	
	An	In	An	In	An	In	An	In	An	In	An	In	An	In	An	In	An	In
GS concord																		
andar	2	2						1	2			1		1	1			
caer					2													
considerarse														1				
fincar	1		1															
hallarse					1										2		3	1
ir	2		2		4		1		1							1	3	
manifestarse																1		
mostrarse											1							
parecer																	1	1
presentarse													1					
quedar							1	1	1		4			1	1	1	3	1
quedarse											1						1	
salir															2			
sentirse																	3	
venir	1						1								2			
verse	1				2				2	1			1					
GO concord																		
buscar									1									
dejar								1	1			1		1	1	1		
hallar			1						6		1							
llevar	1		1						1			1						
poner																		1
presentar															1			
tener	4		2		2		11		5	1	12	5	1	2	7			
traer			1						2									
ver	1				4		6				2		1	1				
	13	2	8	0	15	0	19	4	22	2	21	8	4	7	17	4	14	4

Chapter 6

ESSERE/STARE AS A ROMANCE PHENOMENON

Christopher Pountain

The contrast between the reflexes of *ESSERE-SEDERE
and STARE in Castilian has received a great deal of
attention from scholars, chiefly because of the
elusiveness of any general principle which will
satisfactorily describe their distribution.[1]
Latterly, interest in the Catalan development (Falk
1979) has revealed discrepancies between different
varieties of the language which must betoken an
interestingly unstable state of affairs, and has
also called attention to the differences between
Castilian and Catalan usage. Yet comparative study
should not be limited to the Iberian Peninsula: the
Romance-wide importance of the *ESSERE/STARE contrast
to which Peral Ribeiro (1958) pointed is worthy of
closer scrutiny, as much for what it can suggest
about the nature of linguistic change as for illumin-
ation of the Ibero-Romance phenomena.
    It is nevertheless in Castilian that the
*ESSERE/STARE contrast has been developed most fully,
and it is as well briefly to survey the data in this
language before embarking on a wider study. In my
view, if we are to achieve a satisfactory description
of the usage of ser and estar in modern Castilian we
must roundly reject the seductive possibility of
seeing in the superficial lexical unity of these verbs
a deeper semantic unity. Each verb has several different usages, which are not (except, as we shall
see, in purely historical terms) easily reconcilable.

*   I would like to express my thanks to Stephen
Parkinson, Bill Rothwell and Max Wheeler for their
most helpful comments on an earlier version of this
paper.

We are therefore on safer ground if we begin by
looking simply at the various syntactic contexts in
which ser and estar can occur. Setting aside for
the moment the usages of the two verbs with prepositional phrases, many of which have purely idiomatic
status, the picture may be summarised as follows:

(a) Ser is the only possibility with noun
complements.[2]

(b) Estar is the only possibility (except for a
very small number of principled exceptions[3]) with
locative adverbial complements.

(c) With a past participle, ser forms what may
be termed the 'action passive' while estar forms
what may be termed the 'resultant state passive'.
Castilian is hence able to make overt a distinction
which in many languages, English included, is covert.
In Castilian we have both

(1) a. Las proposiciones fueron [Preterite of ser]
         clavadas a la puerta (por Lutero)

         'The propositions were nailed to the door
         (by Luther)'

     b. Las proposiciones estaban [Imperfect of
         estar] clavadas a la puerta (*por Lutero)

         'The propositions were nailed to the door
         (*by Luther)'

The English translation is ambiguous between the
'action passive' reading, which is cognitively
synonymous with the active sentence '(Luther) nailed
the propositions to the door', and the 'resultant
state passive' reading, which renders the stative
result of the propositions having been nailed to the
door, and for which, in English as in Castilian, no
agent can be expressed.

(d) With an adjective complement, we may claim
as a general principle that the adjective following
estar cannot be construed syntactically as a nominal
or semantically as a classificatory or inherent
property: a simple but clear example is the contrast
between Juan está [estar] enfermo ('John is ill')
and Juan es [ser] enfermo ('John is an invalid,
belongs to the class of ill people, is inherently
ill'). Many adjectives used with estar have a
semantic force akin to that of a resultant state

140

passive, e.g. estoy [estar] seguro ('I am sure; something has happened to make me sure'). Others represent a state through which a subject is passing, e.g. la pera está [estar] verde ('the pear is green, unripe'). Estar + adjective may also convey an impression made on the speaker: ¡qué joven estás! ('How young you are, seem!').

Characteristic of Castilian, then, is that it has (a) different copular verbs for noun complements and locative adverbial complements and (b) two systematically contrasting copulas with past participles and adjectival complements.

Portuguese ser and estar come tantalisingly close to their Castilian counterparts in distribution (which may explain the dearth of studies of the phenomenon in this language); but there are differences. Castilian uses estar invariably with locative adverbial complements, while in Portuguese estar is used with such complements only when the subject of the verb is animate, 'necessary' position of inanimate subjects (see Querido (1976: 355-6)) requiring most usually ser; thus:

(2)   a. Juan está [estar] en Lisboa
         O João está [estar] em Lisboa
         'John is in Lisbon'

      b. Lisboa está [estar] en Portugal
         Lisboa é [ser] em Portugal
         'Lisbon is in Portugal'

With adjectives the contrast between Castilian and Portuguese is rather more difficult to establish. Peral Ribeiro (175-6) discusses a number of examples, concluding that the difference between the two languages is one of 'tendência': Portuguese allows, for example, both Os seus olhos estão [estar]/são [ser] cheios de caridade e de doçura ('Her eyes are full of love and sweetness'), whereas Castilian only accepts Sus ojos están [estar] llenos de caridad y de dulzura. It is interesting that Portuguese can use ser in precisely those cases which have sometimes been considered to constitute 'illogical' uses of estar in Castilian, i.e. where the adjective or adjectival past participle, though representing a 'resultant state', also represents an inherent property. In Castilian it is the 'resultant state' idea which seems to take precedence; in Portuguese, it is the idea of inherentness.

Catalan must also be discussed at this stage, since here too it can be claimed that there is a systematic contrast between ésser and estar. However, the distinction appears to have a different basis from that encountered in Castilian and Portuguese. With locative adverbial complements estar occurs with, or implies, a durative adverbial of fixed-time duration, while ésser carries no such implication:

(3) a. Estarem [estar](dues hores) a Barcelona
        'We shall be, stay, (two hours) in Barcelona'

     b. Som [ésser] a Barcelona
        'We are in Barcelona'

For some commentators, notably Badia Margarit (1962: 145ff.) the same aspectual distinction holds with adjective complements too, although this has recently been disputed by Falk (112ff.), who proposes that a subcategory of stative adjectives normally require estar when they occur with an animate subject (e.g. content 'happy', tranquil 'quiet', alegre 'happy', malalt 'ill'). However, the implication of 'fixed time duration' and compatibility with 'fixed time' durative adverbials remains a feature of these adjectives when used with estar. With past participle complements, modern Catalan appears genuinely to be in a state of flux: Badia (156) perceives a tendency to prefer estar, thus creating a resultant state passive as in Castilian; the conservative Vallcorba (1978: 110) admits only ésser in sentences like el gerro és [ésser] trencat 'the jug is broken' - obligatorily el jarro está [estar] roto in Castilian) in line with older usage. But in one written text I examined[4] the Castilian-like usage was clearly dominant.

Moving now to the historical perspective, we may say that what has happened in the Ibero-Romance languages is as follows: (a) STARE has weakened to a point at which it is almost entirely copular in function (though still strongly marked for aspect in Catalan); (b) STARE has encroached on some of the functions originally fulfilled by *ESSERE. The process is in origin comparable to the history of verbs like stand and rest in English, which also show some movement towards copular status in fixed expressions like stand corrected and rest assured. Hints not only of the beginning of this process but of its becoming fairly entrenched in the linguistic systems of Romania are widely distributed:

*ESSERE/STARE

A. Examples of the semantic weakening of STARE:

(a) The notion 'stand', one of the meanings, if not the chief meaning, of CL STARE, is everywhere rendered by a strengthening paraphrase: Fr. <u>être debout</u>, <u>se tenir</u>, Cast. <u>estar de pie</u>, It. <u>stare in piedi</u>, Rum. <u>a sta în picioare</u>.

(b) The reflex of STARE can have a meaning inconsistent with 'stand' or can combine with past participles or adverbs which are inconsistent with the meaning 'stand': Cast. <u>estar sentado</u>, Cat. <u>estar assegut</u>, It. <u>stare seduto</u>, all with the meaning of 'be seated'; Rum. <u>a sta</u> in the sense of 'sit'.

B. Examples of the participation of STARE in verbal paraphrases and idioms:

(a) Continuous verb-forms: Cast. <u>estar cantando</u>, Ptg. <u>estar a cantar</u>, <u>estar cantando</u>, Cat. <u>estar cantant</u>, It. <u>stare cantando</u>, Rum. <u>a sta şi...</u>.

(b) Immediate future ('to be on the point of...'): Cast. <u>estar para cantar</u>, Ptg. <u>estar para cantar</u>, Cat. <u>estar per cantar</u>, It. <u>stare per cantare</u>, Rum. <u>a sta să</u> + subjunctive.

(c) With IN, meaning 'to consist of': Cast. <u>estar en</u>, Ptg. <u>estar em</u>, Cat. <u>estar en</u>, It. <u>stare in</u>.

(d) With BENE, meaning 'to suit': Cast. <u>estar bien</u>, Ptg. <u>estar bem</u>, Cat. <u>estar bé</u>, It. <u>stare bene</u>, Rum. <u>a sta bine</u>. STARE is used generally with BENE, MALE and their comparatives.

C. With adjective complements. It is interesting to note the 'favouring' of STARE with certain adjectives in Italian and Rumanian, creating in embryo the kind of situation that today obtains with adjective complements in Catalan. In Italian, the adjectives tend to represent mental states, the most common being <u>tranquillo</u> 'quiet', <u>comodo</u> 'comfortable', <u>zitto</u> 'quiet', <u>fresco</u> 'in trouble' and <u>attento</u> 'alert'; associated with the locative function of <u>stare</u> are <u>solo</u> 'alone' and <u>fermo</u> 'motionless'. The Rumanian list is semantically similar: <u>liniştit</u> 'quiet', <u>trist</u> 'sad', <u>posomorît</u> 'gloomy', <u>îngîndurat</u> 'pensive', and the locative <u>nemişcat</u> 'motionless' and <u>ţintuit</u> 'motionless' (literally, 'nailed'). Copceag and Escudero (1966: 347-8) call attention

to the use of <u>a sta</u> with negative past participles
formed with the prefix <u>ne-</u>, which are used adject-
ivally with much the same force as the Castilian
resultant state passive: <u>necitit</u> 'unread', <u>nelocuit</u>
'unlived in', <u>nemaritat</u> 'unmarried', etc.

However, the Castilian-Portuguese development
in which STARE is shorn of full lexical value in its
progress towards pure copular status is not the only
development of interest in the history of STARE.
In Classical Latin, the semantic range of STARE is
fairly circumscribed; three full meanings can be
established, which I shall refer to as 'stand'$_1$
(with animate subject, opposed to 'sit'), 'stand'$_2$
(with inanimate subject, in the general sense of
'be situated') and 'stay'. Examples are:

(4) a. Hi stant ambo, non sedent (Plautus, <u>Capt.</u>,
        prol. 1 sq.)
        'They both stand, they do not sit'

     b. ... quorum statuae steterunt in rostris
        (Cicero, <u>de Or.</u>, 2,86,353)
        '... whose images stood on the tribune'

     c. ... qui domi stare non poterant (Cicero,
        Fl., 6,13)
        '... who were unable to stay at home'
        (Examples from Lewis and Short (1879: 1762-3)

Although Peral Ribeiro (149-50) and Bourciez
(1967: 253) have been able to select suggestive
examples of the use of STARE from Latin texts, it
must be stressed that STARE is in comparison with
<u>estar</u> in the modern Ibero-Romance languages by no
means common in either Classical or Vulgar Latin
documents. Plautus' <u>Aulularia</u>, for instance, yields
only one (triple) example, with the clear meaning of
'stand'$_1$; at the other end of the Latin period,
Gregory of Tours' <u>Historia Francorum</u> has no examples
at all in a sample I took consisting of the first
two books. The Vulgate is more rewarding, where
STARE regularly renders Greek ἱστημι, but otherwise
appears not to have substantial motivation; and the
<u>Peregrinatio Aetheriae</u> has eleven examples in the
first book, all with the meaning of 'stand'$_1$ or
'stand'$_2$, and all with an overt locative adverbial
complement (see Ernout (1954: 214)). Generally in
Romance, we find a marked increase in the frequency
of STARE, even outside the Iberian Peninsula, and
an expansion of its range of full lexical meaning.

*ESSERE/STARE

In Italian we may identify the new meanings 'wait',
'live', 'stop', 'take time' and, with di, 'abstain
from' – meanings which interestingly are all paralleled in Catalan, where the process of copular-
isation, as we have seen, is not as advanced as in
Castilian and Portuguese:

(5) 'Wait': It. Dobbiamo andare o stare?
                'Should we wait or go?'

            Cat. Quantes hores hi van haver d'estar?
                'How long did you have to wait
                there?'

    'Live': It. Dove sta di casa, Lei?
                'Where do you live?'

            Cat. Ell ara s'està al carrer de Provença
                'He lives in the Carrer de Provença
                now'

    'Stop': It. Stette un po', poi scrisse la lettera
                'He stopped a little, then wrote
                the letter'

            Cat. Per nosaltres no estigueu: podeu
                continuar
                'Don't stop on our account: you
                may continue'

    'Take time': It. Starà poco a tornare
                'He'll be back soon'

            Cat. Per a fer això han estat
                quatres hores!
                'To do that they've taken
                four hours!'

    'Abstain from': It. Non ha voluto starsene di
                mangiare
                'He didn't want to give up
                eating'

            Cat. Jo m'estic d'anar-hi
                'I won't go there'

(Italian examples from Reynolds (1962); Catalan
examples from Fabra (1977))

In summary, STARE undergoes one of three different types of fate in Romance. Castilian and Portuguese illustrate the first type, where it is retained as a copula, obligatory in certain contexts, and with a reduction in full lexical meaning. Italian and Rumanian, in different measures, represent the second type, where a range of full lexical meanings is retained and enlarged upon, although there is some development of copular and auxiliary functions too. Catalan and some dialects of Provençal appear to fall somewhere between the two. The third fate of STARE, illustrated conspicuously by French, is total disappearance. I will now examine the histories of these individual developments and suggest reasons for the divergences encountered across Romania.

Old French offers a pattern strongly reminiscent at first glance of the Italian type of solution. Here ester is the reflex of STARE, surviving today only in the archaic expression ester en justice 'to go to court'. Old French texts yield the following range of meanings and usages:

(6)   'Stand'$_1$: Sur l'erbe verte estut devant sun
                  tref (Chanson de Roland, 671)
                  'He stood on the green grass in front
                  of his tent'

      'Stand'$_2$: +Desus un pui vit une vile ester
                  (Aymeri de Narbonne, 160)
                  'He saw a town standing below a hill'

      'Stay':   El camp estez, que ne seium vencuz
                  (Chanson de Roland, 1046)
                  'Stay in the field, let us not be
                  vanquished'

      'Stop':   +Dameisele, estez! fet li nains
                  (Chrétien de Troyes, Erec et Enide,
                  163)
                  'Stop, mistress! said the dwarf'

      'Live':   +Adam formas et puis Evain sa per;
                  En paradis les en menas ester.
                  (Le couronnement de Louis, 699)
                  'You created Adam and then Eve his
                  companion; you took them to live in
                  paradise'

Also, as a reflexive, 'stand still':

> Li emperere s'estut si l'escultat
> (<u>Chanson de Roland</u>, 2105)
> 'The emperor stood and listened'

(Examples marked [+] are taken from Tobler and Lommatzsch (1925-))

Also frequently attested is the widespread idiom <u>laissier ester</u> (cf. It. <u>lasciare stare</u>, Cat. <u>deixar estar</u>) 'let alone'; this expression survives in French for much longer than the simple verb.[5] But it is significant what <u>ester</u> has <u>not</u> achieved in Old French: there seem to be no examples of the widespread use of STARE with BENE, etc., and neither has a continuous verb-form with <u>ester</u> as an auxiliary developed (indeed, if Old French can be said to have a continuous form at all, it is constructed with <u>estre</u> - see Menard (1973: 131)). As one might expect, there are no examples of <u>ester</u> with past participle or adjectival complements. The failure of <u>ester</u> to achieve anything approaching auxiliary or copular status in Old French must surely be a major factor in its fall. Morphological factors may also contribute to its demise: <u>ester</u> clashed homophonically in the preterite with <u>estovoir</u> 'to be necessary' (<u>estut</u>, etc.) and in the first and second persons plural with the new analogical imperfect of <u>estre</u> (<u>estiiens</u>, <u>estiiez</u>). This latter clash prompted some scholars to see the new imperfect of <u>estre</u> as deriving from <u>ester</u>; but it is difficult to square the other person-number inflections of <u>ester</u> with this view (see discussion in Peral Ribeiro (156-7)).

The closeness of association between STARE and *ESSERE in the proto-Romance period is, however, revealed in morphological mergers elsewhere. In French, Catalan and Italian, STARE supplies the past participle of the *ESSERE paradigm, so that in Catalan and Italian the compound forms of <u>estar/stare</u> and <u>ésser/essere</u> are indistinguishable (e.g. Cat. <u>ha estat</u>, It. <u>è stato</u>). In Gascon, other replacements seem currently to be in progress: Ronjat (1937: 289) observes in Béarn, where <u>esta</u> already supplies the infinitive, the almost total eclipse of the <u>houi</u> (<FUI) preterite by <u>estèi</u> or <u>estoui</u> and the coexistence in the imperfect subjunctive of <u>hóussi</u>, <u>estèssi</u> and <u>estóussi</u>. The entry for <u>està</u> in Palay (1980: 465) further gives <u>estau</u> as a present form and <u>estaràm</u> as a future, together with <u>seràt</u>. Badia (1950) has interesting data from a neighbouring

Pyrenean dialect which shows an apparently more
thoroughgoing mingling of the two verbs: here *ESSERE
supplies the imperfect, imperfect subjunctive and
conditional of STARE while STARE supplies the past
participle and gerund of *ESSERE.[6]
   The history of Provençal is instructive insofar
as STARE appears to have[7] suffered eclipse in several
dialects in modern times without there being the
same possibilities for homonymic clash as were
observed in Old French. Estar is attested in Old
Provençal with a fair range of values, although
'stay' seems to be its principal meaning, and I have
not come across a convincing example of 'stand'$_2$:

(7)   'Stand'$_1$: [+]Amors o fai si cum lo bons austors
                 Qe per talan no.is mou ni no.is debat,
                 Anceis esta entro c'om l'a gitat.
                 (Richart de Berbesill)
                 'Love behaves like the good hawk
                 which is not disposed to move or flap
                 but rather stays still until it is
                 despatched'.

      'Stay': ... et ab el estet tro que.l coms mori
               (Vidas, 21)
               '... and stayed with him until the
               count died'

      'Stop': [=]Venen escridan: Estatz, baro (Roman
               de Gerard de Rossillon)
               'They come shouting: 'Stop, sir'.

      'Live': [=]Ieu am mais estar en Fransa (Rambaud
               de Vaqueiras)
               'I prefer to live in France'

      'Suit': [=]Conois que miels m'estai
               Que si trop altament ames (G. Amiels)

               'I know that it suits me better than if
               I loved too highly'

      'Abstain from': [=]Seigner Conrat, eu sai dui rei
                       qu'estan
                       D'ajudar vos; ara entendatz
                       qui. (Bertrand de Born)
                       'Lord Conrad, I know two kings
                       who do not assist you; now hear
                       who they are'.

Also, as a reflexive, 'stand still':
+L'aygua s'estay, que non si mou (La vida
de Sant Honorat, 55,33)
'The water is still, it does not move'

(Examples marked + are taken from Levy (1894-
1924); those marked = from Raynouard (1838-44))

As in Old French, STARE seems to have failed to
form a continuous verb-form. Estar must have survived very much longer than French ester, however:
Mistral (1885) gives the meanings 'stay', 'live',
'suit', 'abstain from' and a number of set phrases,
including the adjectival complements siau 'quiet'
and segur 'sure', together with the ubiquitous
laissa esta 'let alone'. Alibert (1935) gives a full
paradigm for esta.
   Old Italian offers a significantly different
picture from Old French and Old Provençal, despite
similarities in the 'full' meanings of stare that
are encountered here as in the modern language.
But stare, in addition to forming the continuous
verb-form, is also regularly found with male and
bene and their comparatives, and with other adverbs
and adjectives which represent a mental, physical or
moral state:

(8) a. Chi starebbe meglio di me se quegli denari
        fosser miei? (Decameron, 2,5)
        'Who would be better than me if that money
        were mine'?

     b. Deh, Rinaldo, perché state voi così pensoso?
        (ib., 2,2)
        'Come, Rinaldo, why are you so pensive?'

Some indication of the possible complements of stare
is shown in the Vocabolario degli Accademici della
Crusca (1738: 7.709ff.), which, illustrating from
Renaissance writers, gives a profile of many adjectives and past participles which combine with stare,
as well as adverbs and prepositions (avanti, dietro,
etc.; sopra, sotto, etc.) and even nouns (stare
boccone 'to be face down', stare carpone 'to be on
all fours', stare sicurtà 'to stand surety').
   Estar in Old Catalan has certainly not acquired
the virtuosity of Old Italian stare; at first sight
it is much more akin to its closer congener in Old
Provençal:

(9)   'Stand'$_1$:   ... e.ls bons a la part dreta estar
                     farā... (from Russell-Gebbett (1965),
                     Text 41 1.33)
                     '... and he will make the righteous
                     stand on the right...'

      'Stand'$_2$:   Mare, levat aqexa pedra que.us sta
                     devant, et auretz ayga. (ib., 48, 1.36)
                     'Mother, lift that stone that is in
                     front of you, and you will have water'.

      'Stay':   ... car yo.y steguí I mes per fetz
                     del Gran Cham. (ib., 53, 1.7)
                     '... for I stayed there a month on
                     business with the Great Khan'

      'Live':   Enaxi, un ladre estave en aquel
                     bosch... (ib., 54, 1.17)
                     'So, a robber dwelt in that wood...'

It must be pointed out that 'stay' is without doubt
the principal meaning of estar here, especially with
animate subjects; the meaning of 'stand'$_1$ is rare.
But already there are examples where a simple locative copula reading is not out of the question:

(10) ... lo corp stava alt en un arbre ab un form-
      atge en lo bech... (ib., 59, 1.38)
      '... the crow was high in a tree with a [piece
      of] cheese in its beak...'

Past participle complements are also found, usually
with estar in its 'full' meaning of 'stay':

(11) Tancats aqestes portes, estien tancades tro jo
      torn (ib., 48, 1.21)
      'Once these doors are shut, let them stay shut
      until I return'

although there does appear to be movement in later
texts towards the modern copular value (pace
Vallcorba (52-4)):

(12) L'adolorit Rei... estigué admirat del somni que
      fet havia (Tirant lo Blanch, ch.6)
      'The grieving king... was amazed by the dream
      he had had...'

     Simply on the evidence so far presented, it
seems to me that we may refute any suggestion that
the early Romance languages are fairly similar in

their adoption of the values of STARE. On the
contrary, there are already by the time of the first
texts slight but significant differences which will
be intensified as each language develops. In particular, the later disappearance of French ester and
Provençal esta(r) is not simply a morphological
accident but is foreshadowed in the failure of STARE
to gain anything like the same ground in these
languages as it had gained in Italian and Catalan.
The history of STARE in Vulgar Latin cannot be a
uniform one, but must be a series of extensions of,
restrictions on and preferences for the different
meanings of the verb, together with the establishing of certain privileges of occurrence which are
eventually to achieve syntactic significance.

It is in this frame of mind that we must turn
back now to the Peninsular developments of STARE.
We might suspect the nascent impact of STARE in
Castilian and Portuguese from a slight but significant morphological phenomenon: STARE is not drawn
into the suppletive *ESSERE paradigm at all here,
with the result that STARE and *ESSERE are to be
kept very distinct; instead SEDERE is the verb that
is drawn in to provide the infinitive ser and the
past participle sido of *ESSERE. It is interesting
to note the consequences for SEDERE, incidentally:
although seer continues itself as a copula for some
time, it is sentar (associated with the transitive
asentar<*ADSEDENTARE - see Corominas 1954: 188)
that by the end of the sixteenth century has in its
reflexive form taken over the meaning of 'sit (down)',
with estar sentado as 'sit, be seated'. In Catalan
and Italian, where there is no mingling of *ESSERE
and SEDERE, SEDERE remains intact as seure and
sedere respectively with its original meaning.
French seoir is superseded by s'asseoir, the motiv-
ating factor in disappearance here being possible
homonymic clash between the future of seoir and
estre in Old French (see Orr (1939: 262)).

Looking at early texts in Castilian and
Portuguese, it is clear that STARE has already
staked out for itself a preference for association
with locative adverbial complements to a much greater extent than in other Romance languages. Pace
Saussol (1978: 67), who claims that the use of ser
and estar with locative adverbial complements in the
Poema de mio Cid is arbitrary, I observed that in
this text estar almost never took an inanimate
subject - a clear favouring of the 'stand'$_1$ meaning;
it is true, however, that ser occurs with both animate and inanimate subjects, although with animate

151

subjects it often has the overtone of 'arrive':

(13) Antes sere con vusco que el sol quiera rayar.
     (231)
     'I will be with you before the sun begins to
     shine'

My interpretation of the use of ser and estar at
this period of Old Castilian is that while both are
possible with animate and inanimate subjects in the
context of a locative adverbial complement, estar
tends to have a 'marked' meaning with inanimate
subjects and ser a 'marked' meaning with animate
subjects. Such a value for estar resembles modern
Portuguese, where a 'marked' meaning similar to
English 'stand' obtains:

(14) a. O banco é [ser] naquela rua
        'The bank is in that street'

     b. O banco está [estar] naquela rua
        'The bank stands in that street'

The same might be said of Old Portuguese, where
apparently inconsistent examples can be similarly
elucidated, e.g.:

(15) E, quando Alamafom, seu rey delles, que estava
     [estar] em Silves, sobe como aquellas companhas
     alli erão [ser], sahio a elles do lugar com a
     mais companha que pode, porque lhe dicerão que
     estava [estar] alli o mestre com todo seu poder,
     e ho mestre, como sobe que era [ser] fora,
     alçou-se loguo de sobre Paderna e veio-çe
     lançar sobre Silves. (Nunes (1970: 29))
     'And when Alamafom, their king, who was
     [unmarked] at Silves, knew that those troops
     were [had arrived] there, he went out to them
     from the place with all the forces he was able,
     because he had been told that the master was
     [unmarked] there with all his power, and the
     master, when he knew that he was [had moved]
     outside, rose then from above Paderna and came
     and threw himself on Silves'.

However, a weakened value of 'stand'[1] is not the
only meaning of estar in these early Castilian and
Portuguese texts; the sense of 'stay' still seems
to be present in some instances, e.g.:

*ESSERE/STARE

(16) Firme estido Pero Vermuez, por esso nos
      encamo... (Poema de mio Cid, 3629)
      'Pedro Bermúdez stood [remained] firm, he was
      not upset on that account...'

But I cannot agree with Peral Ribeiro's implication
(172) that the values of Old Portuguese estar are
similar to those of Italian stare; neither Castilian
nor Portuguese estar offer anything like the same
range of 'full' meanings evidenced for Italian stare
in early texts.
      An interesting development in Portuguese part-
icularly, but visible to a certain extent in
Castilian and even Catalan, is the rise of alternative copulas which threaten to be rivals for estar.
The following table shows frequencies of Castilian
fincar, seer, yacer and quedar, Portuguese ficar,
seer and jazer and Catalan restar in 10,000 word
samples of selected texts.

Castilian:

Poema de Mio Cid (12th. Cent.)	SER 144	ESTAR 20	FINCAR 6 SEER 4 YAZER 4
El Conde Lucanor (early 14th Cent.)	SER 140	ESTAR 39	FINCAR 7 YAZER 1
La Celestina (late 15th. Cent.)	SER 129	ESTAR 37	QUEDAR(SE) 8

Portuguese:

Livro de Linhagens (mid 14th. Cent.?)	SER 257	ESTAR 19	FICAR 25 JAZER 9
Os Lusíadas (late 16th. Cent.)	SER 92	ESTAR 49	FICAR 12 JAZER 2

Catalan:

Libre de Contemplació (late 13th. Cent.)	ESSER 360	ESTAR 11	
Tirant lo Blanc (mid 15th. Cent.)	ESSER 245	ESTAR 39	RESTAR 7

(Instances of ser/ésser as a perfect auxiliary have not been
counted).

It can be seen that in the Portuguese <u>Livro de Linhagens</u> text <u>ficar</u> in fact overtakes <u>estar</u> in frequency; it appears with adjective complements at a time when <u>estar</u> generally does not, e.g.:

(17) ... todo o campo ficou cheo de samgue e pedras
que hi auia. (258)
'... all the field was full of blood and stones
that were there'

<u>Ficar</u> has of course survived fairly forcefully into modern Portuguese, unlike its Castilian congener. As a copula, it is an alternative for <u>estar</u> in contexts where <u>estar</u> genuinely contrasts with <u>ser</u> (with past participle and adjective complements), but it may in non-contrastive contexts also replace <u>ser</u> itself. Thus as early as the <u>Lusiads</u> we find <u>ficar</u> occurring with a noun complement:[8]

(18) ... fica herdeiro
Um filho seu, de todos estimado... (3,90)
'... a son of his, held in esteem by all,
was heir...'

<u>Ficar</u> thus achieves a remarkable versatility as a copula which Castilian <u>quedar</u>, the form which superseded <u>fincar</u>, by no means shares. <u>Seer</u> and <u>jazer/yacer</u> make nothing like the same bid for copula status: the former's demise, in its weak copular function as in its 'full' meaning of 'sit', is accounted for, as we have seen, by clash with <u>ser</u>; the latter, now obsolescent and functioning only with the 'full' meaning of 'lie', have lost their weak copular value almost entirely. The importance of <u>ficar</u> in the history of Portuguese once again, therefore, denies us a generalisation about copulas in the two most closely related Peninsular languages, and underlines the capability of languages to develop aleatory preferences.

The early Romance development of *ESSERE and STARE in the Iberian Peninsula can therefore be visualised as a particular evolution of the values of these verbs in Vulgar Latin, similar to, but not identical with, developments in other Romance languages. The general Romance development involves both extension and reduction of their values and functions: the Castilian and Portuguese characteristic is to weaken the 'full' values of STARE whilst tending to grammaticalise its remaining functions, whereas other Romance languages appear to have extended its 'full' values and tended to avoid grammaticalisation. The failure to grammaticalise at all, however, as in French, leads to disappearance.

It is important to pause at the early medieval stage of Romance, since subsequent developments in the Peninsular languages are going to complicate the general Romance picture and make these languages look much more different from their relatives than in fact they were at this time. The foundations of the modern developments are, however, laid. The crucial feature of medieval Castilian and Portuguese is that estar has achieved copular status and has become associated with locative adverbial complements and with animate subjects. Another tendency can also be faintly glimpsed in the earliest texts – the association of estar with metaphorical locative adverbial complements which represent moral position or state. Saussol (29-30) points to examples in the Poema de mio Cid, and in Portuguese instances can even be found in the early cantigas, which have nowhere near as high an incidence of estar as do the chronicles:

(19) e meteron-m'en seu poder
     en que estou [estar] ...   (J Soares Somesso)
     '... and placed me in her power in which I
     [now] am...'

In Castilian, such usage is very common by the time of El Conde Lucanor (early fourteenth century). Here, there is a tendency for ser to be associated with prepositional phrase complements consisting of de + Noun and estar with those consisting of en + Noun; but ser still seems to be an alternative to estar in the latter context; compare:

(20) a. ... et dixol que fuese çierto que era [ser]
        en muy grant peligro del cuerpo et de toda
        su fazienda...(58)
        '... and said to him that it was certain
        that he was in great danger of body and of
        all his estate...'

     b. ... consejól que tomase una manera commo
        podría escusar de aquel peligro en que
        estava [estar] ...   (59)
        '... advised him that he should find a way
        of getting out of the danger he was in'

We may note that while Italian texts of the medieval
period show no such predilection on the part of
stare for metaphorical locatives, Catalan texts show
estar as following in this regard its Peninsular
congeners. I cite an interestingly inconsistent
example from the Libre de Contemplació of Ramon
Llull:

(21) So per que, Sènyer, molt home veg que està
     [estar] en peccat e nol pot hom alterar ni
     mudar de vicis en vertuts,... e per assò, ab
     poca de diligencia e ab poca de devocio no pot
     hom alterar lome qui es [ésser] en grans
     peccats e en greus culpes. (17)
     'And this, Lord, so that many a man should see
     that he is in a state of sin and he cannot be
     be changed, nor can vices be changed into
     virtues... and so, with little diligence and
     little devotion a man who is in a state of
     great sin and grave guilt cannot be changed'.

It is a short semantic step from a prepositional
phrase which expresses a state to a past participle
or adjective of similar value. These latter complement types take much longer to establish themselves,
however. In the texts I have sampled, the Poema de
mio Cid has no examples of past participle complements with estar; El Conde Lucanor has the sole
instance

(22) ... estó agora mucho afincado de mengua de
     dineros (85)
     '... I am at the moment very pressed through
     lack of money'

and although by the time of the Celestina examples
are more frequent, there are many cases in which a
past participle with apparently 'resultant state'
value is accompanied by ser, e.g.:

(23) En Dios y en mi ánima, que en ver agora lo que
     has porfiado y como a la verdad eres reducido,
     no parece sino que vivo le tengo delante. (72)
     'By God and my soul, seeing now how you have
     argued and how you have come round to the truth,
     it seems that he is standing alive in front of
     me'.

Keniston (1937: 472) traces the demise of ser in
this context through the sixteenth century. Only
the most marginal examples of adjective complements

with <u>estar</u> occur until fairly late on in the medieval
period: thus in <u>El Conde Lucanor</u> I noted

(24) Quando el philósopho que estava cativo... (58)
     'When the philosopher who was captive...'

where the choice of <u>estar</u> is most likely to be determined by an understood locative adverbial (see
Saussol (39-40) on similar examples in the <u>Poema de
mio Cid</u>). Even in the <u>Celestina</u>, adjectives with
<u>estar</u> are in a significant minority, and are clearly
linked with the idea of 'resultant state' - <u>espantado</u>
'frightened', <u>ensañada</u> 'annoyed' (themselves past
participles), <u>perplejo</u> 'perplexed', <u>discorde</u> 'out of
tune', <u>loco</u> 'gone mad' and <u>lleno</u> 'full'. The
Castilian chronology seems to be paralleled by
Portuguese. But Catalan quite noticeably lags behind its neighbours. No examples of <u>estar</u> with past
participle complements emerged from the Llull sample
I examined, although there were clear instances in
the fifteenth century <u>Tirant lo Blanc</u>, e.g.:

(25) ... hages bona confiança que lo Fill e la Mare
     t'ajudaran en aquesta gran tribulació en què
     posat estàs. (127)
     '... have confidence that the Son and the
     Mother will assist you in this great tribulation
     in which you are now placed'.

Genuine adjective complements with <u>estar</u> were not
even to be found in <u>Tirant</u>.
     The extension of <u>estar</u> to past participle comp-
lements in Castilian, Portuguese and Catalan makes
possible the development of a systematic opposition
between *ESSERE and STARE in the form of the action
passive and the resultant state passive. It seems
that Catalan is slower to achieve this, no doubt
because of the continuing importance of <u>estar</u> in its
'full' meaning of 'stay'. But achieve it it eventually does, and thereby takes the critical step that
sets it on the same path as Castilian and Portuguese.
The further development that we have noted in modern
Catalan towards <u>estar</u> becoming associated with
adjective complements is not necessarily attributable
solely to Castilian interference (although of course
it <u>may</u> be, as Falk contends); it may simply represent the later 'drift' of Catalan towards a Castilian-
like situation.[9] The remarkable similarity of
Castilian and Portuguese (and there is no reason
here to assume mutual interference - there are,
after all, a number of dissimilarities in the

development of copular patterns in the two languages)
may be accounted for by the early achievement by
STARE of copular status in both languages, and by
subsequent simultaneous expansion by 'drift' to more
contexts. Once the systematic opposition between
*ESSERE and STARE is reached, it is natural that
these languages should capitalise on it. It is
interesting to observe that as the domain of estar
is being marked out in the three Peninsula languages
under review, so that of ser/ésser is undergoing
restriction. In particular, the use of ser/ésser as
perfect auxiliaries is on the wane, (cf. Vincent,
this volume) so that in all the modern languages the
only perfect auxiliary is for Castilian haber, for
Portuguese ter (archaically haver) and for Catalan
haver. This means that there is a very clear formal
opposition in these languages between ser/ésser +
past participle, which functions only as an action
passive, estar + past participle, the resultant
state passive, and ter/haber/haver + past participle,
the perfect. Overall, estar is therefore able to
compete, so to speak, very forcefully with ser/ésser.
This contrasts with the Italian situation, where the
frequency of essere is extremely high, due to its
use not only as a copula and action passive auxiliary, but also as the perfect auxiliary for all
intransitive and reflexive verbs (and, in combination with ci, as the existential verb). Significantly, the generalisation of Catalan haver as the
perfect auxiliary is rather later than in Castilian
and Portuguese. While in the Celestina sample I
examined there were only three examples of ser still
being used as a perfect auxiliary[10] and many examples of haber being used as the auxiliary for
intransitive verbs, in Tirant the rule still seems
to be that intransitives and reflexives take ésser.
Obviously this hypothesised dependency between the
expansion of estar and the falling of ser/ésser as a
perfect auxiliary should not be taken too far - it
is well to remember that Rumanian has generalised
the auxiliary too, yet here a sta has not progressed
as far as in Ibero-Romance (though Copceag and
Escudero (349) optimistically suggest that Rumanian
may be on the way to a Castilian-like situation).
But it is a factor which may well play a rôle in the
encouragement of the development of STARE.

In conclusion, it is clear that the histories
of *ESSERE and STARE should be thought of as a
Romance, rather than as simply an Ibero-Romance,
phenomenon. All the Romance languages present at
the early medieval stage individual and interesting

distributions of the two verbs which suggest the
development of much earlier preferences during the
Vulgar Latin period. The motivation for these early
choices seems scarcely to run deeper than general
semantics, extension and restriction of fields of
reference operating more or less haphazardly, but
with a general drift towards the proliferation of
copular verbs. The crucial association of STARE
with locative adverbials, which takes place in varying degrees in the three main Peninsular languages,
ensures the strength of <u>estar</u> there and paves the
way for association with other contexts. Morphological developments, such as the obsolescence of <u>seer</u>,
and syntactic developments, such as the generalisation of a perfect auxiliary, conspire to create the
opposition between <u>ser/ésser</u> and <u>estar</u> that we know
today. And it is precisely this interplay of semantic and morphosyntactic factors that has produced
the complex synchronic situation in the Peninsular
languages and the intriguing similarities and dissimilarities in their development.

NOTES

     1. A convenient annotated bibliography of the
chief contributions to the topic appears in Navas
Ruiz (1977: 97-114).
     2. Counterexamples to this very general rule
have been proposed. They fall into two categories:
(a) usages which appear to be elliptical and are not
spontaneously accepted by all native speakers, e.g.
<u>El mar está espejo</u> ('the sea is [like] a mirror')
= <u>el mar está [hecho un] espejo</u> ('the sea is [has
been] made a mirror'), (b) one or two idioms, e.g.,
<u>estar pez de</u> ('to be ignorant of').
     3. These are: (a) sentences in which the subject
of the copula represents an 'event', e.g., <u>la
reunión es en el Aula Magna</u> ('the meeting is in the
Great Hall'), (b) cleft structures, e.g., <u>donde se
reúnen los ministros es en el Palacio Real</u> ('where
the ministers are meeting is in the Palacio Real'),
where the collocation of copula and locative adverbial is merely a surface phenomenon.
     4. In a sample consisting of the first four
chapters of Mercè Rodoreda's <u>La plaça del Diamant</u>
(Club Editor, Barcelona, 1962), I found 11 clear
examples of the resultant state passive usage with
<u>estar</u> as against one with <u>ésser</u>.
     5. Huguet (1946) gives the phrases <u>ester sur
les piedz</u>, <u>ester à droict</u> and <u>laisser ester</u> as surviving in sixteenth century French; <u>ester</u> is not

attested, however, in Rickard (1968).

6. Unfortunately, the data Badía presents is too restricted to admit of principled description. Although he speaks (135) of 'confusión de usos entre ser y estar', his examples of estar being used for ser all involve the infinitive, which may only indicate that, as in the Béarnais dialects I have referred to, estar supplies this form for the *ESSERE paradigm too.

7. Two well-known course books in modern Provençal, Bayle (1980) and Bazalgues (1975), make no mention of esta. I found no instance of the verb in a sample of Mistral's prose I examined.

8. Castilian estar also progressed in this direction: Bouzet (1953: 42-3) and Keniston (475) locate sporadic examples of noun complements.

9. Cf. Badia (1964: 66): '... no hem de veure, en aquesta extensió desmesurada d'estar, un castellanisme sistemàtic, sinó que molt sovint es tracta de les darreres etapes d'una evolució que el castellà realitzà en poc de temps, però que en català ha estat lenta i laboriosa'.

10. With pasar, caer and venir; two of these examples are undoubtedly the result of 'balancing' against passives:

> Deshecho es, vencido es, caído es... (65)
> 'He is undone, conquered, [has] fallen...'

Chapter 7

PRONOMINAL VOICE IN FRENCH*

Christopher Lyons

1. INTRODUCTION

In the evolution of the modern Romance languages
from Latin the most striking development affecting
the pronominal system is the appearance of a set of
clitic object forms, forms, that is, which are unstressed, occupy a fixed position in relation to the
verb, and cannot be modified or conjoined. Among
these object clitics is a set of forms derived directly from the Latin reflexive pronouns, which were
identical to the non-reflexive object pronouns except in the third person, where the form was se in
both singular and plural. But as well as becoming
clitics, these forms derived from the Latin reflexive pronoun have evolved a range of uses quite
distinct from the expression of reflexivity. Some
of these uses can be said to express voice, and their
appearance is no doubt to be linked with the decline
of the Latin inflectional system.
    The past few years have seen the production of
a considerable literature on pronominal verbs (that
is, verbs constructed with se), particularly in relation to French. This literature has been concerned
primarily with the syntactic structure of the se
clitics, and with trying to establish whether the
different uses of the construction should be handled
in a uniform manner or whether there is more than
one synchronic origin for the surface appearances of
se. I too shall confine myself to French in this

* This paper is based on ideas which grew out of
discussion with Rose Maclaran who also made extensive comments on an earlier draft, and I would like
to express my gratitude to her.

chapter, and will examine the relationship between
two of these uses. Traditional and generative grammarians (such as Grevisse (1980), Stéfanini (1962),
Kayne (1975), Ruwet (1972)) have identified the following uses of the se construction in French:

(i) Reflexive and reciprocal: The (direct or
indirect) object clitic is coreferential with the
subject. The reciprocal (each other) reading is,
for obvious semantic reasons, only available in the plural. These two uses are generally taken to have the
same synchronic origin syntactically (for example by
Kayne (1975), who argues for a semantic account of
differences between them), and I shall assume that
this is the case. Examples are:

(1)   Le prisonnier s'est tué
       The prisoner killed himself

(2)   Les prisonniers se sont tués
       The prisoners killed themselves/The prisoners
       killed each other

(ii) Middle: Very similar in meaning to an
agentless passive:

(3)   Ces lunettes se nettoient facilement
       These glasses clean easily/These glasses are
       easily cleaned

(iii) Neutral: Similar to (ii) but there is no
implication of the presence of an agent:

(4)   La branche s'est cassée hier
       The branch broke yesterday

(iv) Inherent: Some intransitive verbs (such as
s'évanouir 'to faint') always take se, which does
not seem to make any contribution to the interpretation of the sentence.

The obvious questions are, of course, whether
these uses are different interpretations of a single
syntactic construction, and whether some of these
interpretations should be taken to be identical semantically. Recent treatments in fact identify four
distinct constructions, some being more closely related than others, as will be shown below. My concern
is with uses (ii) and (iii), the two classes of pronominal verbs which clearly express voice. I will
argue that they are not syntactically or semantically

distinct constructions, and that their differences
can be given a functional explanation, as consequences of the lexical meanings of the verbs involved.
    Before comparing middle and neutral pronominal
verbs I propose to consider the syntax of se, so as
to establish how these verbs relate to the other
uses of se and to non-pronominal verbs taking
'ordinary' clitics.

2. THE SYNTAX OF PRONOMINAL VERBS

2.1 Reflexives

Recent discussions of the syntax of clitics in
general, and se in particular, show two general
approaches, the transformational and the lexical.
The difference, roughly speaking, is that the former
approach treats clitics as originating in NP
position and as being cliticised, moved, that is,
into their surface positions and deprived of NP
status, while the latter approach generates clitics
as clitics in the phrase-structure component. The
issue of which of the two accounts is to be preferred is not important to the present study. My
purpose in comparing them is to show that although
they generate the forms in different ways, they are
led to make essentially the same distinctions among
clitics, and for more or less the same reasons.
I begin by examining the analysis of reflexive se,
and how the two models distinguish reflexives from
other clitics; this is because reflexive se is the
least problematic use semantically, and the one
which can be most easily related to 'ordinary'
clitics as representing an argument of the verb -
it is not implied that the reflexive is in any sense
a more basic or central use than the others.
    The transformational treatment is associated
primarily with Kayne (1975). He has a rule of
Clitic Placement (Cl-Pl), which takes a pronoun,
initially generated in post-verbal NP (accusative or
dative) position, and moves it to its surface clitic
position. A pronoun so placed is spelled out as one
of the clitic forms le, la, les etc.; a pronoun not
operated on by the rule will appear in a 'strong'
form, lui, elle, eux etc. Kayne begins his discussion of reflexive clitics by entertaining the hypothesis that these are also a result of Cl-Pl; se is
the form taken by a cliticised pronoun when it is
coreferential with the subject. The appropriate
conditions of coreference would cause such a pronoun
(initially in postverbal object NP position) to be
marked with a feature [+ R], which would ensure the

spelling <u>se</u> in clitic position;[1] if this pronoun
were not operated on by Cl-Pl it would take one of
the strong forms mentioned above, since there is no
strong specifically reflexive pronoun form.[2]
    Kayne rejects this hypothesis in favour of the
view that reflexive clitics are the result of a separate, though similar, rule of <u>Se</u> Placement (<u>Se</u>-Pl).
<u>Se</u>-Pl is a cyclic transformation (which will itself
introduce the feature [+ R], rather than this feature being assigned by a separate rule prior to
cliticisation), and Cl-Pl is post-cyclic. This separation of the two cliticisation rules is necessary
because of their interaction with three other syntactic processes - passivisation, NP extraposition
and the causative <u>faire</u> construction.
    Non-reflexive dative clitics occur quite freely
in passive sentences:

(5)   Elle te sera décrite par ta femme
       She will be described to you by your wife

(6)   Ils vous seront présentés par Paul
       They will be introduced to you by Paul

Dative <u>se</u>, on the other hand, is no more possible in
passives like (7) and (8) than in actives like (9)
and (10) where it is coreferential with an accusative.
This is in spite of the fact that in (7) and (8) the
antecedent of <u>se</u> is the subject.

(7)   *Jean se sera décrit par sa femme
       Jean will be described to himself by his wife

(8)   *Ces filles se seront présentées par Paul
       Those girls will be introduced to one another
       by Paul

(9)   *Je se décrirai Jean
       I will describe Jean to himself

(10)   *Je se présenterai ces filles
       I will introduce those girls to one another

Kayne explains the impossibility of <u>se</u> in these
passives on the basis of the fact that its antecedent is not a subject in deep structure. The surface
subjects in (7) and (8) cannot serve as antecedents
for <u>se</u> because they were not subjects at the point
of application of <u>Se</u>-Pl; in other words, <u>Se</u>-Pl is
ordered before the Passive transformation. But non-
reflexive clitics must be placed after Passive, as

is shown by the behaviour of en, which can have an
object but not a subject as its source:

(11)   Paul en lira trois
        Paul will read three

(12)   *Trois en sont ici
        Three are here

Nor can the surface subject of a passive sentence
serve as the source of en:

(13)   *Trois en ont été lus par Paul
        Three were read by Paul

This follows from the ordering of Cl-Pl after
Passive.
        The rule of NP Extraposition is responsible for
the postverbal position of underlying subjects in
sentences like (14). It cannot apply to structures
containing a direct object NP, or a direct object
clitic ((15) to (17)):

(14)   Il est arrivé trois enfants
        Three children arrived

(15)   *Il a dénoncé la décision trois mille hommes
        Three thousand men denounced the decision

(16)   *Il a dénoncé trois mille hommes la décision

(17)   *Il l'a dénoncée trois mille hommes
        Three thousand men denounced it

It can apply, however, to structures containing a
dative clitic:

(18)   Il lui est venu une idée
        An idea came to him

Kayne's explanation is that NP Extraposition moves
a subject NP to direct object position, and is
blocked whenever this position is already filled.
This accounts readily for (15) and (16), and also
for (17) if it is assumed that the pronoun underlying the clitic is still in object NP position at
the point when NP Extraposition applies. In other
words, Cl-Pl must be ordered after NP Extraposition.
However, this transformation is compatible with
structures containing se derived from a direct object:

(19)   Il s'est dénoncé trois mille hommes
       Three thousand men denounced themselves

So it appears that se is moved to clitic position
before the application of NP Extraposition.
       Kayne's third argument is based on the Faire-
Infinitive rule (FI), which causes the subject of an
embedded infinitive to appear to the right of that
infinitive in causative constructions with faire
(and, optionally, laisser). The behaviour of se in
this construction is different from that of the non-
reflexive clitics, which must be attached to faire,
not to the infinitive, whether they correspond to
the underlying subject or to the object of the infinitive:

(20)   Elle fera partir ses amis
       She'll have her friends leave

(21)   Elle fera manger ce gâteau à Jean
       She'll have Jean eat that cake

(22)   Elles les fera partir
       She'll have them leave

(23)   Elle le fera manger à Jean
       She'll have Jean eat it

(24)   *Elle fera les partir

(25)   *Elle fera le manger à Jean

Se also can occur attached to faire, corresponding
either to the underlying object ((26)) or to the
underlying subject ((27)) of the infinitive:

(26)   Jean se fera connaître à Marie
       Jean will make Marie know him

(27)   Elles se font rire l'une l'autre
       They make each other laugh

But se can also be attached to the embedded infinitive, in which case it is understood as coreferential
with the underlying subject of that infinitive:[3]

(28)   La crainte du scandale a fait se tuer le frère
       du juge
       Fear of the scandal made the brother of the
       judge kill himself

Pronominal Voice in French

There is an additional difference. When FI applies,
à is inserted before the underlying subject of the
infinitive when that infinitive has an NP object,
even if this object NP is cliticised:

(29) Elle fera boire ce vin à son enfant
      She'll have her child drink that wine

(30) Elle le fera boire à son enfant
      She'll have her child drink it

The same is true of the clitic se when it is attached to faire, but not when it is attached to the
infinitive, in spite of the fact that it corresponds
to the underlying direct object of the infinitive:

(26) Jean se fera connaître à Marie

(28) La crainte du scandale a fait se tuer le frère
      du juge

(31) *La crainte du scandale a fait se tuer au
      frère du juge

      These three sets of facts make it clear that se
cliticisation is a different process from the placement of non-reflexive clitics.
      The lexical approach is to be found in the
account of Grimshaw (1980), who considers the same
range of syntactic data as Kayne (relying heavily,
in fact, on his discussion), but offers a different
kind of explanation. The two central characteristics of the lexical theory she applies to se are the
importance of grammatical functions (subject, object
etc) in syntactic rules (as argued in work by
Bresnan (e.g. 1978, 1980)), and the extension of lexical rules beyond derivational morphology to include
syntactic statements. Noting the fixed surface
order of French clitics when in combination, as
discussed by Perlmutter (1971) and Emonds (1975),
Grimshaw assumes a set of phrase-structure rules
which make available three clitic positions to the
left of the first auxiliary (if there is one) in the
expansion of $\bar{V}$, as shown in (32):

(32) $\bar{V} \rightarrow$ $(CL)_1$ $(CL)_2$ $(CL)_3$ (AUX) V

The clitic (CL) nodes are assigned grammatical
functions in the same way as NP nodes; direct object
clitics can occur in CL_1 and CL_2, indirect objects
in CL_1 and CL_3. The lexicon specifies a lexical

form for each verb, stating the verb's argument
structure - that is, the number of arguments the
verb takes, and the grammatical functions associated
with these arguments; thus, voir would have the lexical form voir ((SUBJ), (OBJ)), indicating that it
takes two arguments, a subject and a direct object.
Lexical entries for clitics give information about
their case, number, person and gender.

Grimshaw begins her discussion of the reflexive
clitics by considering, as does Kayne, whether they
should be treated in the same way as other clitics,
the only difference being their coreferentiality
with the subject. She too answers in the negative,
but the distinction she draws is very different from
that drawn by Kayne. She generates $\underline{se}$ in CL_1 position, along with other clitics, but $\underline{se}$ is not
assigned any grammatical function; it is not a pronoun and not an argument of the verb, but simply a
grammatical marker, a morpheme resulting from the
application of certain rules to the verb. In the
case of reflexive $\underline{se}$, a lexical rule of Reflexivisation operates on a representation of the semantic
composition of a verb, and binds one of the verb's
arguments to another; the effect is the formation of
a new, reflexive, derived verb. Thus an argument
structure $\underline{\text{Predicate}}$ (x, y, z) gives $\underline{\text{Predicate}}_{\text{refl}}$
(x, x, z) or $\underline{\text{Predicate}}_{\text{refl}}$ (x, y, x) (where
the change of y or z to x represents the binding of
this argument to the subject argument x). An indirect consequence of this change, by Grimshaw's rules,
is a change to the lexical form of the verb, whereby
the null symbol $\emptyset$ is assigned to an argument to indicate that that argument receives no syntactic expression and is unavailable for semantic interpretation.
Thus, the relevant lexical forms for a verb such as
voir would be voir ((SUBJ), (OBJ)) and the derived
$\underline{\text{voir}}_{\text{refl}}$ ((SUBJ), ($\emptyset$)). The rule of Reflexivisation
also includes a morphological statement which intro-
duces the clitic $\underline{se}$, which is not an argument and
has no case, but merely a morphological reflex of
binding in predicate argument structure.

Grimshaw justifies this analysis on the basis
of the same syntactic facts used by Kayne to motiv-
ate the separation of $\underline{\text{Se-Pl}}$ from Cl-Pl. NP Extraposition cannot apply to structures containing a
direct object; that is, it cannot apply where the
verb is transitive. This, in Grimshaw's account,
is because NP Extraposition is a rule which changes
a subject argument into a direct object; it cannot
apply to a transitive verb because the resultant
form would have the same function assigned to two

different arguments, and this is not permitted. But
verbs with reflexive clitics permit NP Extraposition
because these clitics are not objects, and the verbs
are not transitive (example, (19) above). The rules
which assign se to verbs make those verbs intransitive. Verbs with se also behave like intransitives
in the faire construction. As pointed out above
(examples (29) and (30)) the subject of the infinitive appears in a PP introduced by à if the infinitive has a direct object; but the postposed subject
NP cannot appear in a PP if the infinitive is intransitive. Verbs with se pattern like intransitives
in this respect.

2.2 Other pronominals

Grimshaw's initial justification for her position that se is not a pronoun but merely a morpheme
resulting from the operation of lexical rules on the
verb, is the fact that the inherent se of s'évanouir
clearly does not correspond to a logical argument of
the verb. The se of such verbs is not in complementary distribution with NPs or PPs; thus we have
s'évanouir, s'imaginer NP, but no *évanouir (à) NP,
*imaginer NP à NP. Moreover, non-reflexive accusa-
tive or dative clitics do not occur with these verbs
in the place of se:

(33) *Marie m'a évanoui

(34) *Jean leur imagine cela

Grimshaw's treatment of these intrinsic pronominals
is simple: the lexical entry of the verb marks it as
being intransitive and accompanied by a [+ reflexive]
clitic.

Kayne, on the other hand, proposes to derive
inherent se transformationally, by Se-Pl, in the
same way as reflexive se, in spite of the fact that
there is no obvious postverbal NP source for it.
He too notes that inherent se is not in complementary distribution with NPs, PPs or 'ordinary' clitics,
but argues that despite these facts inherent se does
pattern like other object pronouns. Thus, the past
participle agreement with reflexive se in (35) is,
because optional (that is, it is not always made in
spoken French), the same type of agreement as that
involving a preceding non-reflexive direct object,
as in (36). The agreement of a past participle with
the subject in the presence of être, as in (37), is
not optional in the above sense, and is therefore
not the type of agreement occurring in (35).

(35)   Marie se serait pris(e) pour une folle
       Marie would have taken herself for a crazy
       woman

(36)   Paul l'a mis(e) à la porte
       Paul threw her out

(37)   Marie est morte voilà deux ans
       Marie died two years ago

Now, inherent se shows the same agreement pattern as reflexive se:

(38)   Elle s'est dédit(e) le lendemain
       She recanted the following day

An additional argument is that there does not seem to be any verb which allows both an accusative and a dative complement in addition to inherent se. This is what would be predicted if, as seems to be the case, verbs can be subcategorised for at most one accusative and one dative complement, and if inherent se is itself derived from an accusative or dative object.

Kayne does not discuss the neutral se construction beyond giving an example of it:

(39)   La question s'est posée à moi
       The question posed itself to me

He suggests that this type of se should probably be treated like inherent se and derived by Se-Pl. Grimshaw also links neutral pronominals with the inherent class. She labels them 'inchoatives' and regards them as a productive subset of verbs with inherent se. With these inchoative verbs, since there exists a corresponding transitive, causative verb (for example briser corresponding to the intransitive pronominal se briser 'to break', by contrast with the non-productive intrinsics like s'évanouir), the se can be said to be in complementary distribution with NP objects and to meet the subcategorisation of the transitive verb. But se is not semantically an argument of the verb, and is rather to be regarded as a marker of an intransitive, inchoative verb form; in other words, se is in complementary distribution with NP objects, not because it is itself an object, but because it is introduced by a rule which takes a transitive verb and makes it intransitive. The rule in this case is Inchoativisation, which intransitivises a causative verb and

adds a [+ reflexive] clitic. With <u>briser</u>, the
lexical form is changed from <u>briser</u> cause ((SUBJ),
(OBJ)) to <u>briser</u> inch ((SUBJ)).
     As for middle <u>se</u>, Kayne shows that it differs
from both reflexive-reciprocal <u>se</u> and inherent <u>se</u>
in that it cannot be embedded in the <u>faire</u> construction; compare (40) with (28) (repeated here) and
(41).

(40)   *Les moeurs actuelles font se dire cela sur-
        tout pour ennuyer les gens
        Present day mores make that be said especially
        to annoy people

(28)   La crainte du scandale a fait se tuer le frère
        du juge
        Fear of the scandal made the brother of the
        judge kill himself

(41)   Le choc a fait s'évanouir la jeune femme
        The shock made the young woman faint

Kayne suggests that middle <u>se</u> should be derived
from the <u>on</u> construction, by a rule moving the
object NP to subject position and deleting the subject <u>on</u>; thus (42) would be related to (43) transformationally:

(42)   Cela se dit surtout pour ennuyer les gens
        That is said especially to annoy people

(43)   On dit cela surtout pour ennuyer les gens

This is the derivation proposed by Ruwet (1972), in
a more detailed discussion of middle <u>se</u>. To account
for the impossibility of (40) the rule would have to
be ordered after FI. Kayne argues that the <u>se</u> appearing in the derived structure is inserted directly into clitic position by the rule that replaces <u>on</u>
by the object, rather than being inserted into the
vacated object position and then moved by <u>Se-Pl</u>.
This is because middle <u>se</u> does not appear to show
object behaviour. First, it differs from the other
types of <u>se</u> and from non-reflexive direct objects
with respect to past participle agreement; compare
(44) with (35), (36) and (38)

(44)   Une phrase comme ça ne se serait pas dite
        (*dit) pour plaisanter
        A sentence like that would not have been said
        in order to joke

Second, in sentences containing two pronominal objects, Cl-Pl need not apply to the dative if it would lead to an impossible clitic sequence;[4] this is equally the case if the direct object is cliticised as se, but it is of doubtful acceptability with middle se:

(45)   *Jean me lui a présenté
       Jean introduced me to her

(46)   Jean m'a présenté à elle

(47)   *Jean se m'est présenté
       Jean introduced himself to me

(48)   Jean s'est présenté à moi

(49)   *Ça, ça pourrait se me dire
       That could be said to me

(50)   ?Ça, ça pourrait se dire à moi

Kayne's explanation is that for Cl-Pl not to apply to the dative, the cliticised pronoun must be accusative; middle se is not accusative because it has been inserted directly into clitic position.

Grimshaw's account of middle se is as close to Kayne's as the difference in theory allows. Middle se, like the other types of se, marks the application of a lexical rule, in this case the Middle Rule (which is very similar to passivisation, the difference being that the latter rule does not add se). The Middle Rule assigns the function ∅ to the former subject (indicating that this argument receives no syntactic expression or semantic interpretation, as pointed out above in relation to reflexives), and promotes the former object to subject.

It is clear from this discussion that neither of the two approaches examined gives a fully unified account of pronominal verbs. Kayne derives all types of se except the middle from a pronoun generated in object position; middle se is given quite a different origin. Grimshaw claims to offer a unified account of all the uses of se, and this claim is valid in as much as all the uses have the same phrase-structure source. But lexical rules of the kind discussed above form the core of the model she is using, and she has a different rule underlying each of the uses of se I have identified, except in the case of the intrinsics, where it is the lexical entry of the verb which specifies that it is

pronominal. I do not wish to suggest that a single
origin for all types of se is a practical proposition. My concern is with where the field should be
divided, in particular as regards the two uses which
seem to convey voice as this term is generally
understood for Latin, namely the middle and the
neutral. Both Grimshaw and Kayne take these two to
be quite distinct (though Kayne makes little reference specifically to the neutrals), the latter being
closely aligned with intrinsic se. In this they are
following Ruwet (1972), who discusses in detail the
differences between neutral and middle se, and con-
cludes that neutral se is not to be distinguished
from inherent se while middle se is derived by a
rule very similar to the Passive rule. In the next
section I will consider middle and neutral pronominals more closely and argue that they can be given a
unified treatment.

3. THE NEUTRAL AND MIDDLE CONSTRUCTIONS

Ruwet (1972) gives a detailed account of the
behaviour of neutral and middle se with a view to
showing that they have distinct derivations, neutral
se being accounted for by lexical redundancy rules,
and middle se being derived transformationally.
What the two constructions have in common is that
the verb shows selectional restrictions with its
subject which are identical with those holding between the verb and the object in the corresponding
transitive, non-pronominal, construction. In the
one case this fact is expressed by a redundancy rule,
and in the other by a transformation (similar to
Kayne's) which moves the object NP to subject position, where it replaces a dummy subject, and inserts
se. Ruwet justifies this distinction by pointing
to what he takes to be significant differences in
behaviour between the two types, and I propose to
examine these differences and assess their significance.
    Traditional grammarians, such as Grevisse (1980)
and Stéfanini (1962), distinguish the two constructions in semantic terms; the middle construction
implies the existence of an unspecified agent,
distinct from the surface subject, while no agent is
implied in the case of the neutral construction.
Ruwet appears to accept this characterisation, but
himself concentrates on distributional differences.
He points out that the middle construction is fully
productive, though subject to certain very general
constraints, whereas the neutral construction is not

productive and its possibility is limited by varied, idiosyncratic constraints of a lexical nature.

The middle construction is largely restricted to habitual or generic sentences rather than sentences expressing individual events; it is not generally found, therefore, in punctual tenses, especially when a precise point in time is indicated. This restriction to generic statements accounts for the fact noted by traditional grammarians that the construction often occurs with adverbs like <u>facilement</u> 'easily' and <u>fréquemment</u> 'frequently', and for the frequent copying of the subject as <u>ça</u> (which is common in generic sentences). Ruwet gives (51) to (53) as examples:

(51)   Ces lunettes se nettoient facilement
       These glasses clean easily

(52)   *Ces lunettes se sont nettoyées hier à huit
       heures et quart
       These glasses cleaned yesterday at quarter
       past eight

(53)   Une erreur pareille, ça se paie
       A mistake like that has to be paid for

The neutral construction, on the other hand, readily occurs with punctual tenses:

(54)   Cette branche s'est cassée hier à huit heures
       et quart
       This branch broke yesterday at quarter past
       eight

There are problems with this distinction however. Ruwet does in fact give an example of the middle construction occuring non-generically:

(55)   Ce livre s'est bien vendu
       This book sold well

He also gives (56) as an example of a neutral, though an agent seems to be clearly implied; this example is much closer to (51) and (55) than to the neutral (54), where the action is understood to have taken place spontaneously. If (56), and similar examples like (57), are taken to be neutrals because of the punctual tense, then the argument becomes circular.

(56) Les vols vers la lune vont s'espacer
      Flights to the moon are going to get spaced
      out

(57) La question s'est vite décidée
      The matter was quickly decided

If the neutral construction can be used where there
is necessarily an agent, or the middle can sometimes
appear in a punctual tense, then the distinction
between the two begins to be less clear. Nevertheless, the restriction of the middle interpretation
(implying an agent) to tenses like the present and
imperfect does seem valid for the great majority of
cases.
     The question of the productivity of the two
constructions needs to be looked at, since this
seems to be the principal difference between them
and is Ruwet's chief justification for giving a lexical rather than a transformational account of the
neutrals. He points out that exceptions to the general possibility of having a middle construction are
themselves of a very general character. For example,
the understood argument of middle sentences is necessarily interpreted as agentive, and probably as
human; for this reason verbs which, when used transitively, take a non-agentive subject, such as adorer,
amuser, toucher, are strange or impossible in the
middle construction. Again, the facts are not
straightforward; some of Ruwet's examples are less
acceptable than others, and this fact should be
borne in mind as, again, it weakens the clear distinction he attempts to draw between middle and
neutral se.[5] His claim is that restrictions on the
neutral construction are, unlike those on the middle,
of an idiosyncratic nature; many verbs appear in
both the transitive and the middle construction but
do not permit the neutral construction (for instance,
manger, vendre, nettoyer). But he does not really
show that these restrictions are not reflections of
some regularity as general as the one governing
exceptions to the middle construction. Most of the
examples he gives to show the lack of a regular,
productive transitive-pronominal correspondence involve inherent pronominal or reflexive verbs rather
than neutrals. The major problem is, in fact, that
he takes to be neutrals many pronominal verbs, occurring also in the non-pronominal transitive construction, which are not obviously neutrals; examples
are se réunir, se disperser, s'asseoir, se promener,
and, apparently, se coucher and s'agenouiller.

But it is to be noticed that these verbs do not meet the semantic characterisation of neutrals as implying no agent; the agent of the action is the same as the surface subject. These verbs would appear, then, to have more in common with reflexives like se laver than with clearly neutral pronominals like se briser, s'endormir.

The argument against treating se réunir etc. as reflexives is that in the case of the 'true' reflexives, the pronoun lui(-même) can occur in syntactic environments where se is ruled out, for example in the ne...que construction; but this does not work with the verbs under consideration:

(58)   Pierre ne regarde que lui(-même)
        Pierre is only looking at himself

(59)   Pierre n'admire que lui(-même)
        Pierre only admires himself

(60)   *L'équipe n'a réuni qu'elle(-même)
        The team only assembled itself

(61)   *Les manifestants n'ont dispersé qu'eux(-mêmes)
        The demonstrators only dispersed themselves

But this restriction can be explained in semantic terms without the need to conclude that se réunir etc. are not reflexives. It is commonly the case that a verb used reflexively describes a somewhat different action from that described by the same verb used non-reflexively. Thus, to lift oneself up (after falling, for example) involves a quite different action from lifting someone or something else up. And in (62) and (63) the physical actions performed by the subjects are not the same as those performed by the subjects in (64) and (65):

(62)   L'équipe s'est réunie
        The team assembled

(63)   La foule s'est dispersée
        The crowd dispersed

(64)   Le chef a réuni l'équipe
        The leader assembled the team

(65)   Les policiers ont dispersé la foule
        The police dispersed the crowd

The action of a group of people performing some
operation on itself is clearly different from that
involved when that group is operated on by some
external force, and the former action (which is perhaps in some sense the less literal interpretation
of the verb) does not permit any freedom in the
choice of object; the verb must be used reflexively
to have this interpretation. But the ne...que construction appearing in (60) and (61) presupposes that a
choice of objects is available. It thus imposes on
the verb the more 'literal' interpretation, which is
not compatible with the reflexivity of the sentence,
which as a result is semantically anomalous. The
situation here is similar, I believe, to a case discussed by Kayne, involving a different kind of verb,
but one which is undoubtedly reflexive:

(66)   Elle s'est jetée par la fenêtre
       She threw herself out of the window

(67)   Elle n'a jeté par la fenêtre que lui
       She threw only him out of the window

(68)   ?Elle n'a jeté par la fenêtre qu'elle-même
       She threw only herself out of the window

The physical movement involved in throwing oneself
out of a window is different from that involved in
throwing someone, or something, else out; the latter
case represents a more literal interpretation. But
the ne...que construction, presupposing a choice of
objects, imposes the more literal reading, and the
result is that (68) is anomalous. But one would not
want to conclude that se jeter is a case of inherent
se rather than being simply the reflexive of jeter.
     I am suggesting, then, that if the term
'neutral' is restricted to those pronominal verbs
corresponding to the traditional semantic characterisation of not implying the existence of an agent,
all other non-middle pronominals being either reflexive or inherent, then the neutrals form a lexical
class which can be given a general semantic definition. My claim is that all transitive verbs whose
action is compatible with a zero agent, such as
briser, endormir, casser, dissiper, can be used pronominally with a neutral interpretation. A qualif-
ication that must be added to this is that where the
non-pronominal form of a verb can be used intransitively, this may prevent the transitive verb appearing in the neutral construction. Thus, cuire 'to
cook' and sécher 'to dry', which fall under our

semantic definition of the class of verbs which
should permit neutral se, are used intransitively as
well as transitively:

(69)   Marie cuit le ragoût
       Marie is cooking the stew

(70)   Je sèche ma chemise
       I'm drying my shirt

(71)   Le ragoût cuit
       The stew is cooking

(72)   Ma chemise sèche au soleil
       My shirt is drying in the sun

This possibility prevents the use of se cuire, se
sécher as the neutral construction, which would be
synonymous with the intransitive (though they can of
course appear as the middle construction). Casser,
on the other hand, appears both to be used intransitively in its non-pronominal form and to permit
se casser as a neutral. We have seen, however, that
the constraints on the middle construction too are
not fully general and some awkward data remain unexplained; my point is that the restrictions on
neutral se are as general and regular as those on
middle se.
       If this is so, then neutral and middle se can
be taken to be a single construction, the use of se
as an object-promotion device and thus as an expression of voice. Whether or not there is understood
to be an unexpressed agent depends on the semantics
of the verb concerned; some verbs permit an agentless interpretation while most do not.[6] The tense
restrictions affecting middle se (but not neutral
se) are presumably to be accounted for in terms of
the interaction of this construction with two others,
the on construction and the passive. French has
three distinct structures close in meaning, and it
is to be expected that there should be restrictions
on the distribution of each. In fact, the on construction, which is used when there is an unnamed
human agent and is therefore very close in meaning
to (if not completely synonymous with) middle se, is
subject to no limitations of tense. It is because
this construction is always available that the
middle construction, which can often be ambiguous
even in generic expressions in the present or imperfect,[7] is restricted, though it is not clear why the
restrictions should be as they are; there is no

obvious necessity for middle se to be excluded from punctual tenses rather than from habitual ones, and the constraint seems to be arbitrary. In fact, the on construction is often preferred to middle se in generic contexts as well as for describing specific events; thus, many native speakers would prefer (73) to (74):

(73) On mange du pain à tous les repas

(74) Le pain se mange à tous les repas
      Bread is eaten at all meals

The arbitrary nature of the tense restrictions on middle se in French is clear from the fact that in other Romance languages, such as Spanish, the middle pronominal construction is used more widely, in punctual as well as habitual tenses:

(75) Se vendieron tres casas ayer
      Three houses were sold yesterday

(76) *Trois maisons se sont vendues hier

The on construction can never be equivalent in meaning to neutral se, because there is no unexpressed agent in the case of the latter, and can not therefore be used in place of neutral se. It is for this reason that se with a neutral interpretation is not excluded from punctual tenses. In other words, the middle-neutral pronominal construction can occur in any tense, but in punctual tenses it must be given an agentless interpretation; where there is an agent the on construction occurs instead in such tenses. And therefore a verb not allowing an agentless interpretation will be unacceptable if occurring in the middle-neutral form in a punctual tense. The true passive also overlaps with middle se; it too implies (if it does not express) an agent, or underlying subject, which, however, need not be human. But it is significant that the passive rarely occurs in non-punctual tenses. Stéfanini (1962) points out that the être and past participle construction expresses completion rather than passive action in the present. Thus, (77) is closer in meaning to (79) than to (78):

(77) Les livres sont vendus
      The books are sold

(78) On vend les livres
      The books are (being) sold

(79) On a vendu les livres
      The books have been sold

It is, then, precisely in the tenses where the true
passive is not generally used that middle <u>se</u> can be
used.
     As we have seen above in discussion of the
syntax of <u>se</u>, a major feature of middle <u>se</u> is the
impossibility of embedding it under <u>faire</u>. It is
not easy to establish whether neutral <u>se</u> can be so
embedded; examples are judged by native speakers to
be very awkward, perhaps because of some near-
incompatibility between the agentless reading of the
verb and the causativity of the <u>faire</u> construction.
Nevertheless, examples such as (80) to (82) are
judged to be more acceptable than (40)(repeated
here):

(80) J'ai fait se briser le miroir
      I caused the mirror to break

(81) Le mauvais temps a fait se casser la branche
      The bad weather has caused the branch to break

(82) J'ai fait se faner les couleurs au soleil
      I made the colours fade in the sun

(40) *Les moeurs actuelles font se dire cela
      surtout pour ennuyer les gens
      Present day mores make that be said especially
      to annoy people

Ruwet says it is because of the generic or habitual
value of the middle that it cannot be embedded under
<u>faire</u>[8], but the <u>faire</u> construction is not, in fact,
incompatible with habitual sentences; (83) can be
interpreted as habitual:

(83) La peur fait se réunir les gens
      Fear makes people get together

Example (84) is also habitual, but unlike (83) it is
ungrammatical:

(84) *La technologie moderne fait se laver facile-
      ment les chemises
      Modern technology makes shirts easily washed

The difference is that in (83) the embedded pronominal infinitive is reflexive while in (84), as in
(40), it is middle. It is clearly the embedding of

middle se under faire that makes these examples
ungrammatical, not some incompatibility between the
faire construction and habitualness. A simpler
explanation is that, again, it is the availability
of another construction which is responsible. In
this case it is the embedding of the bare infinitive,
without se, under faire, with passive meaning.
Thus, while (85), with an embedded pronominal infinitive, must be interpreted as reflexive (or reciprocal) and not as middle, (86), without se, has
precisely the meaning that the middle construction
would have if it were possible with faire:

(85) J'ai fait se laver les enfants
      I had the children wash themselves/each other

(86) J'ai fait laver les enfants
      I had the children washed

Again, as with on and the passive, the faire-
infinitive construction of (86) implies the existence of an agent, and so it can never be synonymous
with a neutral se embedded under faire. For this
reason neutral se is not excluded after faire.

4. CONCLUSION

To summarise, I have tried to present the
principal features of the behaviour of pronominal
verbs in French, relying heavily on the discussions
of Kayne, Grimshaw and Ruwet. The discussion shows
that there are a number of uses of se which probably
require to be accounted for by different rules. But
I have questioned whether the boundaries usually
drawn between these uses are correct. I have argued
that neutral se must be defined in such a way as to
make the class of neutral pronominal verbs considerably smaller than assumed by Ruwet; other pronominal
verbs which he terms neutral are examples of either
inherent or reflexive se. With this more restrict-
ive definition it is possible to claim that neutral
se is the same as middle se; the only difference is
that some verbs when used pronominally allow an
agentless reading, and these verbs are definable
semantically as a class. Limitations on the distribution of middle se are accounted for in terms of
the interaction of this construction with others,
the on construction, the passive, and the faire-
infinitive construction. The middle-neutral se
construction is somewhat marginal in French usage,
and alternatives, particularly on, tend to be

preferred. This preference runs as far as the total
exclusion of the pronominal construction in certain
environments (punctual tenses, and after _faire_)
where there is an alternative available; since the
_on_ construction, the passive and the faire-infinitive
construction cannot have an agentless interpretation,
they are never alternatives to _se_ in its neutral
reading, which is therefore not excluded from these
environments.

  There is one important use of _se_ occurring in
the Romance languages which I have not mentioned,
because it does not appear in Modern French. This
is the impersonal _se_ (or _si_), found, for example,
in Spanish and Italian, and exemplified in (87) and
(88). The verb has no subject expressed (but see
below), and may be transitive or intransitive.

(87)   Se canta
       Si canta
       One sings/There is singing

(88)   Se mató a los soldados
       Si ha ucciso i soldati
       The soldiers were killed

In (88) the NP following the verb is clearly the
object, since the verb does not agree with it in
number as it would with a subject, and since the
Spanish example shows the personal _a_ accompanying
human objects. It is tempting to try to integrate
these impersonal pronominals into the account; this
would involve arguing that the _se_ construction is
not so much an object-promotion device as a subject-
demotion one, subject-demotion not necessarily
entailing object-promotion, as proposed by Harris
(1978) following an argument for Welsh by Comrie
(1977). On the other hand, it has been argued by
Rizzi (1976) that the impersonal _si_ of Italian
functions as a subject pronoun, participating in
subject raising, and the same arguments presumably
work for Spanish too. Nevertheless, it is a wide-
spead phenomenon in the languages of the world for
reflexive, passive and impersonal meaning to have
the same morphological realisation, and this fact
remains to be explained. Indeed the passive
paradigm of Latin covered most of the range of uses
expressed by pronominal verbs in modern Romance,
including the impersonal (_itur_ 'people go', equivalent to Spanish _se va_). I shall not pursue these
speculations here, not least because the present
analysis has been restricted to French and based on

French data which in important respects does not
correspond to the facts of the other Romance
languages. But the difficulties encountered in
setting the boundaries between the different uses
of se suggest that these uses may be less discrete
than is generally supposed.

NOTES

1. It is only in the third person that the
feature ⌈+ R⌉ would have any morphological effect.
In the first and second persons reflexive clitics
are indistinguishable morphologically from non-
reflexive clitics.
2. Historically, of course, soi is the strong
form of se, but no longer functions in this way.
Kayne gives several compelling arguments for not
considering soi to be the strong form of se. For
example, soi is limited in its antecedents to a few
NPs such as on and chacun:

    (i)   Quand on parle trop de soi, ...
          When one talks too much about oneself

    (ii) Chacun pense à soi
          Each one thinks of himself

    (iii) *Mes amis sont fiers de soi
          My friends are proud of themselves

Also, unlike se, soi can have an antecedent in a
higher clause:

    (iv) On ne doit pas dire aux gens de parler de
          soi
          One shouldn't tell people to speak about
          one

3. Note the essential difference between sentences in which se is attached to faire, as (26)
and (27), and those with se attached to the embedded
infinitive, as (28). In the former, se is coreferential with the subject of the main clause (that is,
the subject of faire); this is the case no matter
whether se corresponds to the underlying object or
to the underlying subject of the embedded infinitive.
But in the latter, se bears no such relation to the
subject of faire. Thus, se can only occur attached
to the infinitive when its antecedent is the subject
of that infinitive rather than of faire.

4. A sequence of two object clitics of which
the accusative is first or second person or reflexive is ungrammatical, and is presumably ruled out by
a surface filter.
5. For example, the verb amuser, when used
transitively, can take an agentive or a non-agentive
subject. Thus, in (i), the presence of the verb
réussir, implying effort, imposes an agentive inter-
presentation on the human subject, while in (ii) the
non-human subject is necessarily non-agentive:

(i) Marie a réussi a amuser les enfants
    Marie succeeded in amusing the children

(ii) Les bandes dessinées amusent les enfants
     Strip-cartoons amuse children

This means that amuser (and similarly adorer) can in
fact occur in the middle construction provided they
have the agentive sense.
6. In fact it seems that verbs not normally
permitting the neutral interpretation with se can
sometimes have such an interpretation imposed:

Je ne nettoie jamais ma voiture. Je la laisse
se nettoyer toute seule sous la pluie
I never clean my car. I leave it to get clean
by itself in the rain

This reinforces the claim that neutral se is more
productive than is generally supposed.
7. Ruwet gives the following sentences as
ambiguous between a reflexive and a middle reading
(and, of course, a reciprocal reading):

(i) Les femmes, ça se fouette
    Women get whipped/whip themselves/whip
    each other

(ii) Les enfants, ça se lave en dix minutes
     Children are washed/wash themselves/wash
     each other in ten minutes

8. According to Ruwet, the middle cannot be
embedded under faire or laisser, but my informants
find the construction much more acceptable with
laisser:

Je laisse le caviar se manger avec de la vodka
I allow caviar to be eaten with vodka

Chapter 8

THE SYNTAX OF VERBAL WH-EXCLAMATIVES IN ITALIAN*

Andrew Radford

Recent work in generative grammar within the paradigm of Chomsky's Extended Standard Theory (inspired,
perhaps, by Chomsky's 1977 paper 'On wh-movement')
has led to considerable research into the syntax of
wh-constructions (wh-questions, relative clauses,
cleft sentences, etc.) in a variety of languages.
But one construction type which seems to have been
largely ignored in these discussions is wh-exclamatives; there is a certain amount of literature on the
syntax of these in French (cf. e.g. Milner 1974,
1977, 1978), but nothing comparable that I know of
on the syntax of Italian. This paper is an attempt
to present an analysis of a subset of wh-exclamatives
(i.e. those which contain a finite or nonfinite
verb). For the sake of the general reader, I have
sacrificed technical accuracy and complexity for
intelligibility: hence, more abstract theoretical
questions out of keeping with the essentially descriptive goals of this paper are not broached here.
    Let me begin by drawing a few simple - but
useful - taxonomic distinctions. We might distinguish between exclamations on the one hand, and
exclamatives on the other. A wide variety of phrase
and sentence-types can function as exclamations,
given an appropriate intonation contour: for example,
a relative Noun Phrase like:

* I am grateful to Guilio Lepschy for discussing
with me the data in the text, and the analysis of
them.

(1)   Il vino che ha bevuto!
       'The wine that he drank!'

can be used as an exclamation: and yet, in its
exclamatory use it has no special syntactic characteristics which mark it out as being a distinct
construction-type from the corresponding non-
exclamatory Noun Phrase with the same structure but
a different intonation contour: i.e. in either
exclamatory or non-exclamatory use, (1) consists
simply of a head nominal modified by a relative
clause. It would seem that in calling phrases like
(1) exclamations, we are referring to their pragmatic properties (i.e. the illocutionary force of the
utterance), not to any idiosyncratic syntactic properties they may have. So, let us reserve the term
exclamative (parallel to declarative and interrogative) for construction types which have an idiosyncratic set of morpho-syntactic properties identifying them as a unique construction type - i.e. for
expressions like:

(2)   Quanta gente (che) abbiamo incontrato oggi!
       'What a lot of people (that) we met today!'

Here we find a special wh-exclamative quantifier
(quanta) used, together with a special wh-exclamative
'particle' (che)[1]- and it is the (optional) occurrence of this particle which marks exclamatives like
(2) as a distinct construction-type from the corresponding interrogative (3):

(3)   Quanta gente (*che) abbiamo incontrato?
       'How many people (*that) did we meet?'

    A second distinction which will prove invaluable
in that between clausal exclamatives like:

(4)   Come canta bene!
       'How well he sings' (Lit. How he-sings well)

and phrasal exclamatives like:

(5)   Che noioso!
       How boring!

There are some rather puzzling restrictions on the
phrase-types which can be used as phrasal exclamatives - these include Adjectival Phrases like (5)
above, Noun Phrases like (6) below:

(6)   Che bella macchina!
       'What a lovely car!'

and some types of Prepositional Phrase:

(7)   Che in gamba!
       'How on the ball!' (Lit. How in leg)

but exclude Adverbial Phrases:

(8)   *Che lentamente![2]
       How slowly!

and other types of Prepositional Phrase:

(9)   *Di quante ragazze!
       Of how many girls!

The contrast between (7) and (9) is especially puzzling: perhaps it has something to do with the fact
that che in (7) quantifies the whole Prepositional
Phrase in gamba, whereas quante in (9) quantifies
only the nominal expression ragazze? This seems,
however, implausible.
       One minor problem which arises with the distin-
ction between clausal and phrasal exclamatives is
how we are to classify constructions like:

(10) Che bella, questa casa!
      'How nice, this house!'

(10) seems to contain an Adjectival Phrase che bella,
followed by a dislocated topic, the Noun Phrase
questa casa. Should we treat (10) as a clausal, or
a phrasal (perhaps bi-phrasal) exclamative? I can't
pretend to be able to give a principled answer to
this kind of question; all I can say is that constructions like (10) will not be the focus of my attention in this paper. Instead I shall be concerned
with exclamatives like:

(11) Com'è bella, questa casa!
      'How nice it is, this house'

- i.e. exclamatives which contain a verb (in this
case, è) - like (11) - rather than those which do
not - like (10). Hence, we might draw a further
distinction, between verbal exclamatives like (11),
and verbless exclamatives like (10). This paper
will be concerned largely with the syntax of verbal
exclamatives.

Wh-Exclamatives in Italian

Within the class of verval wh-exclamatives, a further distinction which we shall make considerable use of here is that between exclamatives containing a <u>tensed</u> (or finite) verb, like:

(12)   Quanti libri ha letto!
       How many books he read!

and those containing an <u>untensed</u> (nonfinite, or infinitival) verb like:

(13)   Quanti libri da leggere!
       'What a lot of books to read!' (Lit. by read)

Much of this paper will be devoted to a discussion of the similarities and differences between the two constructions illustrated in (12) and (13).
       But first, a brief discussion of the nature and function of exclamative wh-words in Italian, to provide us with some useful descriptive terminology. In modern (spoken) Italian we find essentially three exclamative wh-words - <u>quanto</u>, <u>che</u>, and <u>come</u> (I shall ignore <u>quale</u> here, which is now largely archaic as an exclamative word, and certainly not used in the spoken language). These three words may fulfil either (or both) of two primary syntactic functions: <u>adverb</u>, or <u>quantifier</u>. In adverbial function, we find <u>come</u> and <u>quanto</u>, but not <u>che</u>: cf.

(14)   Come/quanto/*che ha lavorato!
       How/how much/*what he worked!

By contrast, <u>che</u> and <u>quanto</u> may function as quantifiers, but never <u>come</u>: they may serve to quantify a variety of different constituent types - nominals:

(15)   Che macchina/quante macchine ha comprato!
       What a car/how many cars he bought!

or adjectivals:

(16)   Che/quanto forte sei!
       How strong you are!

or adverbials:

(17)   Quanto lentamente corre!   Che lentamente
       che corre!
       How slowly he runs!

188

or prepositionals:

(18) Che/quanto in gamba sei!
      How on the ball you are!

Hence, in crude terms we can say that come and
quanto function as adverbs, whereas che and quanto
function as quantifiers.
     A number of comments should be made about this
rather oversimplistic distinction between adverb
and quantifier, however; one such is that we could
in principle regard come and quanto in their adverbial function as expressions which quantify verbal
constituents (e.g. Verb Phrases) - in which case,
the distinction between quantifier and adverb would
be replaced by a distinction between different types
of quantifier (those which can quantify verbal expressions, and those which cannot); this is an
essentially theoretical issue which I shall not
dwell on here.
     A second problem which arises is what precisely
we mean by 'nominal', or 'adjectival', etc.. We can
illustrate the problem in relation to nominal expressions by the following paradigm:

(19) (a) Che macchina/quante macchine ha comprato!
           'What a car/how many cars he bought!'

      (b) Che bella macchina/quante belle macchine ha
           comprato!
           'What a nice car/how many nice cars he
           bought!'

      (c) *Che sua bella macchina/*Quante sue belle
           macchine ha venduto!
           'What a nice car of his/how many nice cars
           of his he sold!'

      (d) *Che quella sua bella macchina/*Quante
           quelle sue belle macchine ha venduto!
           '*What a that nice car of his/how many
           those nice cars of his he sold!'

Within the framework of X-bar Syntax (for an elemen-
tary introduction to this, see chapter 3 of my 1981
book Transformational Syntax) we might argue a Noun
is an N, an Adjective+Noun sequence is an N-bar, a
Possessive+Adjective+Noun sequence is an N-double-
bar, and a Demonstrative+Possessive+Adjective+Noun
sequence is an N-treble-bar. In this framework
and assuming this particular analysis...(which I do

in fact have reservations about) we might be more
precise and say that when we talk about che and
quanto quantifying nominal expressions, what we mean
is that they can quantify an N-bar, but not an
N-double-bar, or N-treble-bar (I assume here that
the simple noun macchina in (19)(a) is also an N-bar,
on the grounds that it has the same distribution as
the N-bar Adjective+Noun sequence bella macchina in
(19)(b); for a defense of the assumption that single
nouns can function as N-bar constituents, see
chapter 3 of my 1981 book, cited above). If it is
the case that che and quanto do quantify an N-bar,
we might go on to enquire whether the type of adjectival expression they quantify in (16) is an A-bar,
whether the type of adverbial expression they
quantify in (17) is an ADV-bar, and whether the type
of prepositional expression they quantify in (18) is
a P-bar. If all these assumptions turned out to be
vindicated, then we could argue that che and quanto
have the function of quantifying single-bar projections of all major (lexical) categories...except
verbs. This would leave us with a 'gap' in our
paradigm - i.e. there would be no expression quantifying single-bar projections of verbs (i.e. Verb
Phrases); but this 'gap' could be filled if the
exclamative adverbs come and quanto were reanalysed
as quantifiers which have the function of quantifying a V-bar (i.e. a Verb Phrase). Since I am not
primarily concerned with this type of problem here,
I leave this as a speculative suggestion, to form
the subject of future research.

A third problem which arises out of the adverb-
quantifier distinction concerns how to analyse the
function of quanto and come in sentences like:

(20) (a) Come/quanto sei forte!
           How strong you are! (Lit. How you-are
           strong)

      (b) Come/quanto canta bene!
           How well he sings! (Lit. How he-sings well)

      (c) Come/quanto sei in gamba!
           How on the ball you are! (Lit. How you-are
           in leg)

(Note that the quanto-forms here are more idiomatic
than their counterparts in (16), (17) and (18)).
There are two points of view we might take here:
one would be that come and quanto are quantifiers,
and that they quantify the adjectival forte in

(20)(a), the adverbial <u>bene</u> in (20)(b) and the prepositional <u>in gamba</u> in (20)(c). An alternative viewpoint would be to claim that <u>come</u> and <u>quanto</u> here are not in any way <u>syntactically</u> linked to <u>forte/</u> <u>bene/in gamba</u>,but rather are independent adverbs. So: adverb or quantifier? Which analysis are we to prefer?

I think there are perhaps two reasons why I would prefer the adverb analysis for sentences like (20). The first is that in general quantifiers in Italian cannot be separated from the expressions they quantify - hence the ungrammaticality of:

(21)   *Quante ha mangiato caramelle!
        '*How many he ate sweets!'

where the quantifier <u>quante</u> is separated from the nominal it quantifies, <u>caramelle</u>. If we analyse <u>come</u> and <u>quanto</u> as quantifiers in (20) we shall be faced with the intractable problem of explaining why quantifiers in Italian can be separated from adject- ival, adverbial, or prepositional constituents that they quantify - but not from nominal constituents. A second reason for being sceptical about the quant- ifier analysis is that it provides no principled basis for handling contrasts between <u>che</u> and <u>come</u> such as:

(22)   (a) Che/*come brava sei!
             How good you are!

        (b) Come/*che sei brava!
             How good you are! (Lit. How/what you-are good)

If we are to treat the wh-words in both (15-18) and (20) as quantifiers, then both <u>che</u> and <u>come</u> in (22) will have to be analysed as quantifiers (more pre- cisely, as expressions quantifying adjectivals). But then how are we to account for the fact that <u>che</u> cannot be separated from the adjective <u>brava</u>, where- as by contrast <u>come</u> must be? If both words belong to the same category of quantifier, we should expect them to exhibit identical syntactic behaviour - but clearly they do not. On the other hand, if we say that <u>che</u> functions as a quantifier, but <u>come</u> as an adverb, then we should precisely expect the contrast in (22), since quantifiers in general form a single constituent with the expressions they quantify and hence cannot usually be separated from them, whereas adverbs are independent constituents which do not

generally combine with other constituents (e.g.
adjectivals) to form a single, larger constituent.
And we see from (23) below that this is indeed true
of come:

(23)   (a) *Come macchina (che) ha comprato!
             '*How car that he bought!'

        (b) *Come lentamente (che) corre!
             'How slowly that he runs'

        (c) *Come in gamba (che) sei!
             'How on the ball (that) you are!'

If come were a quantifier, we should expect all of
the above to be grammatical (since they are grammatical with the quantifiers che and quanto in place
of come); but if come is (as we suggest) an adverb,
then since adverbs don't combine with nominal,
adjectival, adverbial, or prepositional constituents,
we should precisely expect the ungrammaticality of
(23). (Notice that we assume a categorial distinction between adverb and quantifier in this discussion; but if - as we hinted at earlier - adverbs are
reanalysed as expressions quantifying verbal constituents, the same arguments could be adduced in
support of positing two distinct types of quantifier).
     One final puzzle which we might mention in
relation to the syntactic functions of exclamative
wh-words in Italian concerns the following contrast
between che and quanto when used in verbless
exclamatives:
(24)   (a) Che macchina/Quante macchine!
             What a car/How many cars!

        (b) Che/*quanto bello!
             How nice!

        (c) Che/*quanto in gamba!
             How on the ball!

We have already seen from (15-18) that both che and
quanto in verbal exclamatives can be used to quantify nominal, adjectival, adverbial or prepositional
constituents: and from (8) that wh-quantified adverbials are ungrammatical if used as verbless, phrasal
exclamatives. We would presumably therefore expect
that either che or quanto could be used to quantify
nominal, adjectival or prepositional constituents in
verbless exclamations. But (24) indicates that
while this is true of che, it is not true of quanto

which (for reasons I cannot explain) cannot be used
to quantify adjectivals or prepositionals in verbless exclamatives. This is a perplexing restriction.[3]

Having looked in some detail at the syntactic
function of the three wh-exclamative words quanto,
che, and come in Italian, let me now turn to the
topic of more immediate concern to me here - namely
the syntax of tensed exclamatives like (25)(a) on
the one hand, and untensed exclamatives like (25)(b)
on the other:

(25)   (a) Che strana macchina (che) ha comprato
            Giorgio!
            What a strange car (that) Giorgio bought!

       (b) Che strana macchina da comprare!
            What a strange car to (Lit. by) buy!

Let me begin by sketching out two alternative possibilities, which I shall refer to as (i) the relative
clause analysis, and (ii) the main clause analysis.
Under the relative clause analysis, we might argue
that (25) are structurally parallel to typical
relative Noun Phrases like:

(26)   La macchina che ha comprato!
       The car that he bought!

(26) clearly comprises a head nominal macchina modified by the relative clause che ha comprato; the
whole expression la macchina che ha comprato is thus
a (complex) Noun Phrase. We might analyse (25)(a)
in a similar way, arguing that the whole expression
Che strana macchina (che) ha comprato Giorgio! is a
Noun Phrase, comprising a head nominal macchina modified by a relative clause (che) ha comprato Giorgio.
We might also analyse (25)(b) in a parallel fashion:
i.e. we might claim that the whole expression Che
strana macchina da comprare! is a Noun Phrase, comprising a head nominal macchina modified by an infinitival relative clause da comprare. (25)(b) would
then be structurally parallel to infinitival relatives such as:

(27)   Cerco una ragazza da baciare
       'I'm looking for a girl to kiss' (Lit. by kiss)

(for some interesting discussion of the syntax of
Italian infinitival relatives, see Napoli 1976).

So, one possible analysis of the exclamatives
in (25) is as relative Noun Phrases - i.e. Noun
Phrases containing a nominal modified by a relative
clause. However, a second possibility referred to
earlier is the Main Clause analysis: under this alternative analysis, we might analyse (25)(a) in much
the same way as we would analyse the corresponding
direct question:

(28)   Che macchina ha comprato Giorgio?
       What car did Giorgio buy?

No-one would - I hope! - claim that (28) is a relative Noun Phrase comprising a head nominal modified
by a relative clause. Rather, the traditional (and
common sense) analysis of (28) is that (28) comprises
a single (main, or root) clause containing an initial
interrogative wh-phrase che macchina. In much the
same way, then, we might suppose that exclamatives
like (25)(a) are simply main clauses containing an
initial exclamative wh-phrase. One apparent problem
faced by the main clause analysis concerns the occurrence of che in (25)(a), and da in (25)(b) - how
can we account for this? We might argue here that
che and da are complementisers: i.e. clause-
introducing particles which serve to mark clause-
boundaries (they are positioned immediately before
an S in the framework of X-bar syntax), and the
nature of the following clause (che generally intro-
duces finite clauses, and da infinitive clauses).
Even if we accept the complementiser status of che
and da, however, we are still left with the problem
that generally speaking overt complementisers cannot
be used to introduce main clauses in Italian -
rather, they are typically used to introduce subordinate clauses, as in:

(29)   (a) Dice che piove
           He says that it is raining

       (b) Ho da farlo
           I have to (Lit. by) do it

To analyse che and da as main clause exclamative
complementisers would thus require us to posit a new,
essentially idiosyncratic class of complementisers
in Italian, which have the unique property that they
can occur in main clauses - and only in exclamatives.
While this is obviously an eminently undesirable
state of affairs, I should point out that main
clause complementisers are common enough in other

languages: indeed, they are found in interrogatives
like:

(30)   Où que tu vas?
        Where (that) are you going?

in français populaire: and note that (30) contains
precisely the same sequence of wh-phrase+complement-
iser that we have in (25). Thus, although the main
clause complementiser analysis for che and da in (25)
does not inspire immediate confidence, it is by no
means implausible or unparalleled in a wider context.
        All we have attempted to do so far is to sketch
out two alternative analyses of the sentences in (25)
- the relative clause analysis and the main clause
analysis - and to point out that both have some
prima facie plausibility. But we now turn to the
more tricky question of trying to decide which analysis is the right one - and what criteria we are
going to apply. For each of the two sentence-types
(a) and (b) in (25) we might envisage three possibilities - viz.

(31)   (i) a main clause analysis only
        (ii) a relative clause analysis only
        (iii) structural ambiguity: both a main clause
              analysis and a relative clause analysis
              are appropriate

Since there is no a priori reason to expect that an
analysis appropriate for tensed exclamatives should
be equally applicable to untensed exclamatives, we
shall deal with the two separately, beginning with
tensed exclamatives like (25)(a).
        In the case of tensed exclamatives, I shall
attempt to argue that we have a case of structural
ambiguity: i.e. that expressions like (25)(a) may
either represent main clauses, or may represent relative Noun Phrases. I shall first of all try and
establish that constructions like (25)(a) must have
at least one possible source as main clauses, irresp-
ective of whether or not they have a second, alternative source as relatives.
        One argument in favour of the main clause
analysis concerns the omissibility of the che following the wh-phrase in expressions such as (25)(a).
Consider che-less exclamatives such as:

(32)   Quante gente abbiamo incontrato!
        What a lot of people we met

It is a fact about relative clauses in Italian that
che can never be omitted in a relative clause: cf.

(33)   (a) la gente che abbiamo incontrato
           the people that we met

        (b) *la gente abbiamo incontrato
           the people we met

Hence, it seems implausible to propose a relative
analyis for che-less exclamatives; instead, it seems
more plausible to treat them as simple main clauses,
very much parallel to interrogatives like (28).
    But from the fact that che-less exclamatives
are main clauses it does not necessarily follow that
che-exclamatives are relative clauses: on the contrary, we shall argue that they are structurally
ambiguous, and hence have both a main clause, and a
relative clause analysis. One curious fact which
suggests that not all che-exclamatives in Italian
can have a relative source concerns the fact that
exclamative che occurs not only after nominal wh-
phrases like che strana macchina in (25)(a), but
also after adjectival, adverbial, and prepositional
exclamative wh-phrases, as in:

(34)   (a) Che bravo che sei!
           How good (that) you are!

        (b) Che bene che canti!
           How well (that) you sing!

        (c) Che in gamba che sei!
           How on the ball (that) you are!

And yet, in che-relative constructions in Italian,
the antecedent is always a nominal expression, never
a non-nominal expression - e.g. we don't find adverbial che-relatives like:

(35)   *Paolo corre (il) rapidamente che corre
        Sebastian Coe!
        *Paolo runs (the) quickly that Sebastian Coe
        runs

Hence - unless we are prepared to countenance postulating an entirely new type of relative clause only
found in exclamatives - it seems implausible to
analyse (34) as relatives; a main clause analysis
seems more appropriate here too.

Wh-Exclamatives in Italian

A third argument in support of the claim that all che-less exclamatives and at least some che-exclamatives must have a non-relative source concerns their occurrence in indirect (or embedded) exclamatives like:

(36) Pensa un po' quanta gente (che) abbiamo incontrato!
Just think how many people (that) we met!

Under the relative analysis, the phrase quanta gente (che) abbiamo incontrato would be a Noun Phrase; hence we should expect to be able to replace it by another Noun Phrase like la sua bella macchina (his lovely car): but this is not the case at all: cf.

(37) *Pensa un po' la sua bella macchina!
'*Just think his nice car!'

The reason should be obvious enough: pensare does not permit a Noun Phrase complement in Italian - hence it seems implausible to analyse the embedded exclamative phrase quanta gente (che) abbiamo incontrato as a (relative) Noun Phrase in (36). By contrast, pensare does indeed permit clausal complements: cf.

(38) (a) Penso che partirà
I think that he will leave

(b) Pensa up po' chi potrebbe venire
Just think who might come

Since pensare permits clausal but not nominal complements, it seems most likely that the exclamative phrase quanta gente (che) abbiamo incontrato should be analysed as a simple clause, rather than as a relative Noun Phrase.

A fourth, and final argument in support of our twin claims that all che-less and some che-relatives have a non-relative source comes from a phenomenon known in the literature (after Ross 1968) as the Pied Piping of prepositions. In English, a wh-phrase which is the object of a preposition can be separated from the preposition, as in:

(39) What did you talk about?

(where the wh-pronoun what has been separated from its governing preposition about). In Italian, how-ever, this is not (in general - i.e. ignoring certain constructions involving clitic (unstressed) pronouns) possible: if a wh-phrase is moved to (or, more neutrally, positioned at) the front of a clause, so too must the preposition be: cf.

(40)   Di che cosa avete parlato?
       About what did you talk?

Thus, prepositions in Italian go with their objects, just like the rats followed the pied piper of Hamlin (hence Ross's metaphor); or, in Ross's terminology, prepositions are obligatorily pied-piped in Italian.
    In the light of this observation, let's return to exclamatives. Because pied piping of prepositions in English is generally optional rather than obligatory, we find exclamatives in English with stranded prepositions: cf. e.g.

(41)   What a lot of girls he's been out with!

But (41) has no direct counterpart in Italian, because of the obligatoriness of the pied-piping of prepositions. Under the main clause analysis of Italian exclamatives, we'd expect the corresponding preposition con in Italian to be positioned at the front of the main clause as a whole, just as it would be in the corresponding direct question:

(42)   Con quante ragazze è uscito?
       With how many girls has he been out?

But under the relative clause analysis of Italian exclamatives, we'd expect the pied-piped preposition to be positioned at the beginning of the relative clause, after the head nominal, just as in a relative Noun Phrase like:

(43)   le ragazze con cui è uscito
       the girls with whom he has been out

Which prediction is correct? Both! Hence the grammaticality of:

(44)   (a) Con quante ragazze (che) è uscito!
           With how many girls he's been out!

       (b) Quante ragazze con cui è uscito![4]
           What a lot of girls who he's been out with!

(44)(a) clearly requires a main clause analysis, whereas (44)(b) equally clearly requires a relative clause analysis (the only function of cui in Italian is as a relative pronoun). This supports our earlier claim that che-exclamatives are structurally ambig- uous as between a relative or main clause analysis. Notice, incidentally that another reason why (44)(a) could not have a relative source is because che can- not be used to relativise prepositional phrases - cf.

(45)   *Non son mai uscito con le ragazze che sei
         uscito tu
         I've never been out with the girls that you
         went out

    So, to summarise a relatively complex situation: what we have attempted to argue is that che-less exclamatives always have a non-relative single- clause source, whereas some che-exclamatives require a relative source, and others a non-relative source. Let's now turn to see whether a similar situation obtains in the case of untensed da-exclamatives like (25)(b). Here, I would like to argue that it does not, and that in fact infinitival exclamatives have a uniquely relative source (i.e. they can never be main clauses). It is perhaps useful to recapitulate the superficial properties of infinitival relatives (as discussed in Napoli 1976) first of all: to relativise direct objects, the complementiser da is used, whereas to relativise prepositional objects, the relative pronouns cui or il quale must be used: hence the contrast:

(46)   (a) Cerco una ragazza da baciare
            I'm looking for a girl to (Lit. by) kiss

        (b) Cerco una ragazza con cui/con la quale
            ballare
            I'm looking for a girl with whom to dance

Interestingly, infinitival exclamatives seem to show a similar paradigm:

(47)   (a) Quante belle ragazze da baciare!
            What a lot of pretty girls to kiss!

        (b) Quante belle ragazze con cui/con le quali
            ballare!
            What a lot of pretty girls with whom to
            dance!

So, it seems clear that at least some infinitival exclamatives must have a relative source in Italian.

But could there be a second, non-relative (main clause) source for infinitival exclamatives as well? This seems ruled out by evidence from the pied-piping of prepositions: we have already seen in relation to (44)(a) that non-relative analysis of tensed exclamatives is required by the sentence-initial position of the preposition con. But no parallel evidence is available for untensed exclamatives, since the infinitival counterpart of (44)(a) is ungrammatical:

(48)   *Con quante ragazze (da) uscire!
         '*With how many girls to (Lit. by) go out'

Nor indeed is (47)(b) grammatical with a sentence-initial preposition:

(49)   *Con quante belle ragazze (da) ballare!
         '*With how many pretty girls to (Lit. by) dance!'

Moreover, whereas the possibility of having exclamative che after a non-nominal exclamative wh-phrase in cases like (34) lends support to a non-relative (main clause) analysis, no such evidence is available for infinitival exclamatives, since these cannot follow a non-nominal wh-phrase: cf.

(50)   *Che bene da cantare!
         How well to sing![5]

In short, all the evidence seems to point to an exclusively relative analysis of infinitival wh-exclamations.

However, although there is general symmetry between the syntax of infinitival relatives and that of infinitival exclamatives, there is one puzzling difference between the two. Infinitival relatives in Italian (unlike their English counterparts) are subject to the restriction that they cannot be used to relativise a subject: cf.

(51)   *Cerco una ragazza da ballare con me
         'I'm looking for a girl to dance with me'

And yet, it is possible to construct infinitival exclamatives involving a relativised subject:

(52) (a) Che cosa strana da succedere!
          'What a strange thing to happen!'

      (b) Che oggetti strani da arrivare dallo
          spazio!
          'What strange objects to come here from
          outer space!'

although this is not always possible: cf. the oddity
of:

(53) (a) *Che bella ragazza da venire qui!
          'What a pretty girl to come here'

      (b) ??Che foglie strane da cadere dagli alberi
          'What strange leaves to fall from the
          trees!'

      (c) ??Che strano tipo da ammazzarsi!
          'What a strange bloke to kill himself!'

I have no explanation for the apparent asymmetry
between infinitival relatives and exclamatives, or
for the contrast between (52) and (53). I doubt,
however, that when the true nature of these restrictions comes to light, it will be such as to undermine
the relative analysis of infinitival exclamatives.
    Let me summarise what I have tried to argue in
this paper. I have attempted to show that infinitival exclamatives are purely relative in character,
whereas tensed exclamatives have both a relative,
and a non-relative source; on the relative analysis
of tensed exclamatives che (or its pronominal
counterparts cui and il quale) is obligatory, whereas
on the non-relative (main clause) analysis, che is
merely an optional exclamative complementiser,
unusual to the extent that it can be used not only in
indirect exclamatives such as:

(54) Pensa un po' in che bella città che abita!
      Just imagine what a nice town he lives in!

but also in direct (main clause) exclamatives such
as:

(55) In che bella città che abita!
      'What a beautiful town he lives in!'

But although treating che in cases like (55) as an
(optional) main clause exclamative complementiser
has the drawback that it involves postulating a

one-membered class of main clause complementisers in Italian, such an analysis is by no means implausible when seen in a wider context (cf. e.g. French examples such as (30)). Unless, of course, I'm wrong...!

NOTES

1. There are complex socio-stylistic factors governing the use of this particle che in exclamatives. To oversimplify, we might say that generally speaking the che-forms are more colloquial, whereas the forms without che are more literary (hence felt to be more 'correct', though in fact less usual). There are also syntactic restrictions on the use of this particle, the exact nature of which is not entirely clear to me. In some cases, che appears to be required: so, for example, Guilio Lepschy tells me that he finds

> (i) Che lentamente che corre! (cf. (17) in the
>   text)
>   How slowly he runs!

unacceptable without the italicised che. I have not dealt with these complex restrictions here.

2. However, Guilio Lepschy points out to me that

> (i) Che piano!
>   How slowly!

would be more acceptable than (8) in the text, with piano perhaps functioning as an adverb here. If indeed piano is an adverbial in (i), then this does of course suggest that some adverbs can be quantified by exclamative che. But there are two complications. One is that the form piano exists also as an adjective; hence it is difficult to be sure whether piano is adverbial or adjectival in (i). If indeed it is adjectival, then (8) can be handled in the same way as (5), and is not a counterexample to our claim that exclamative che cannot quantify adverbials. The second complication is that where adjective-adverb pairs have distinct morphological forms, only the adjective, not the adverb can be quantified by che in phrasal exclamatives:

> (ii) Che buono!
>   How good!

     (iii) *Che bene!
         How well!

3. Another problem not dealt with here is the status of phrases such as:

     (i) Quanto spende per la sua macchina!
        What he spends on his car!

One possibility is that (i) is not an exclamative in our sense, but rather just a relative nominal used like (1) as an exclamation. Certainly, (i) is paraphraseable by an overtly relative construction:

     (ii) Quello che spende per le macchine!
        What (Lit. that which) he spends on cars!

However, there are reasons for thinking that (i) must have an exclamative source in addition to a possible relative source. One (rather weak) piece of evidence in support of this claim is stylistic: that is, while it is true that quanto can be used as a free relative pronoun, as in

     (iii) Quanto dici è vero
        What you say is true

constructions like (iii) are essentially literary and non-colloquial; whereas (i) by contrast is far more colloquial in tone (or, more precisely, may be used colloquially).

This of course leaves us with the question of how to analyse exclamative quanto in cases such as (i). The traditional answer is to analyse quanto in such cases as a pronominal quantifier. Unfortunately, the question of what exactly is meant by a term like 'pronominal quantifier' is far from clear: to get into this kind of abstract theoretical question here would take us too far afield, however.

4. One problem posed by these sentences is that (44)(a) is more 'usual' than (44)(b), the latter being in some sense much 'stranger'. However, Guilio Lepschy points out to me that (44)(b) would be acceptable in an appropriate discourse setting: for example, in a conversation where one of the participants has just been listing all the girls that the person being talked about has been out with, (44)(b) would be an appropriate rejoinder by another participant.

5. However, as Joe Cremona (appropriately!) points out to me, we do find phrases such as:

(i) Che buono da mangiare!
    How nice to eat!

But there are a number of reasons for thinking that this is a different construction, and cannot involve a main clause in which an adjectival complement che buono of mangiare has been positioned initially. For one thing, mangiare is not subcategorised as taking adjectival complements: cf.

(ii) *Mangi buono
     '*You eat good'

And if indeed (i) were a main clause exclamative, we should expect the corresponding tensed version to be grammatical - but it is not:

(iii) *Che buono che mangi!
      '*How good that you eat!'

So, it seems implausible to analyse (i) as a main clause exclamative.

It seems more likely to me that (i) should be analysed in much the same way as phrasal exclamatives like:

(iv) Che buono/che bello!
     How good/how nice!

save that whereas che in (iv) quantifies an adject- ival expression comprising an adjective alone, by contrast che in (i) quantifies an adjectival expres- sion comprising an adjective + infinitival complement (buono da mangiare). Such adjective + infinitive constructions can of course occur independently of exclamative quantifiers in Italian, e.g. in:

(v) E buono da mangiare/bello da guardare
    It's good to eat/nice to look at

BIBLIOGRAPHY

Ahlqvist, A. (ed.) (forthcoming) *Papers from the 5th International Congress on Historical Linguistics*, Amsterdam: John Benjamins B.V.
Alarcos Llorach, E. (1947) 'Perfecto simple y compuesto en español', *Revista de Filologia Español*, 31: 108-39.
Alarcos Llorach, E. (1949) 'Sobre la estructura del verbo español', in Alarcos Llorach (1972) pp. 50-89.
Alarcos Llorach, E. (1959) '"Cantaría": modo, tiempo y aspecto', in Alarcos Llorach (1972) pp. 95-108.
Alarcos Llorach, E. (1972) *Estudios de gramática funcional del español*, Madrid: Gredos.
Alcina Franch, J. & Blecua, J.M. (1975) *Gramática española*, Barcelona: Ariel.
Alibert, L. (1935) *Gramatica occitana segón los parlars lengadocians*, Toulouse: Societat d'estudis occitans.
Allen, W.S. (1964) 'Transitivity and possession', *Language*, 40: 337-43.
Alonso, A. (1939) 'Sobre métodos: Construcciones con verbos de movimiento en español', *Revista de Filología Hispánica*, 1: 105-38. Reprinted in *Estudios lingüísticos I: Temas españoles*, Madrid: Gredos, 2nd ed., 1961, pp. 190-236.
Alvar, M. (1965) 'Notas sobre el español hablado en la isla de La Graciosa (Canarias Orientales)', *Revista de Filología Española*, 48: 293-319.
Ambrosini, R. (1969) 'Usi e funzioni dei tempi storici nel siciliano antico', *Bollettino del Centro di Studi Filologici e Linguistici Siciliani*, 10: 141-78.
Anderson, J.M. (1971) *The Grammar of Case*, Cambridge: Cambridge University Press.
Anderson, J.M. (1977) *On Case Grammar*, London: Croom Helm.
Ashby, W.S. (1977) *Clitic Inflection in French: An Historical Perspective*, Amsterdam: Rodopi.
Azevedo, M.M. (1975) 'On passive-like sentences in Brazilian Portuguese', *Language Sciences*, 38: 13-16.
Bach, E. (1967) '*Have* and *Be* in English syntax', *Language*, 43: 462-85.
Badía Margarit, A.M. (1950) *El habla del valle de Bielsa*, Barcelona: CSIC.

Bibliography

Badía Margarit, A.M. (1962) *Gramática catalana*, Madrid: Gredos

Badía Margarit, A.M. (1964) *Llengua^i cultura als països catalans*, Barcelona: Edicions 62.

Barbosa, J.M. (1965) *Études de Phonologie Portugaise*, Lisbon: Junta de Investigação Ultramarina.

Barrera-Vidal, A. (1972) *Parfait simple et parfait composé en castillan moderne*, Munich: Max Hueber.

Bartholomew, K.M. (1979) *Problems in Italian Morphophonology*, unpublished Ph.D. dissertation, University of Washington.

Bayle, L. (1980) *Grammaire provençale*, Toulon: L'Astrado (5th ed.).

Bazalgues, G. (1975) *L'occitan lèu-lèu e plan*, Paris: Omnivox.

Bello, A. & Cuervo, R.V. (1970) *Gramática de la lengua castellana*, 8th ed., Buenos Aires: Ed. Sopena Argentina.

Benveniste, E. (1960) '"Être" et "avoir" dans leur fonctions linguistiques', *Bulletin de la Société linguistique de Paris*, 55: 113-34. Reprinted in E. Benveniste *Problèmes de linguistique générale I*, Paris: Gallimard 1966 pp. 187-207.

Benveniste, E. (1968) 'Mutations of linguistic categories', in W.P. Lehmann & Y. Malkiel (eds.) *Directions for Historical Linguistics*, Austin, Texas: Texas U.P. pp. 83-94.

Benzing, J. (1931) 'Zur Geschichte von *ser* als Hilfszeitwort bei den intransitiven Verben in Spanischen', *Zeitschrift für Romanische Philologie*, 51: 385-460.

Berschin, H. (1976) *Präteritum- und Perfektgebrauch im heutigen Spanisch*, Tübingen: Niemeyer.

Blinkenberg, A. (1939) *Le patois d'Entraunes: I. Matériaux phonétiques, morphologiques et syntactiques*, Aarhus: Universitetsforlaget.

Blinkenberg, A. (1948) *Le patois de Benil: documents et notes*, Copenhagen: E. Munksgaard.

Blücher, K. (1973) 'Considerazioni sui costrutti del tipo *stare cantando*, *andare cantando* e *venire cantando*', *Revue romane*, 8: 13-20.

Blücher, K. (1974) *Studio sulle forme: ho cantato, cantai, cantavo, stavo cantando*, Bergen: Universitetsforlaget.

Bourciez, E. (1967) *Éléments de linguistique romane*, 5th ed., Paris: Klincksieck.

Bouzet, J. (1953) 'Orígenes del empleo de "estar"', *Estudios dedicados a Menéndez Pidal*, Vol. 4, pp. 37-58, Madrid: CSIC.

Brakel, C.A. (1974) 'Portuguese // r ≃ ř //: Lusitanean and Brazilian allophones', *Studies in Linguistics*, 24: 1-16.

Brakel, C.A. (1976-9) 'A gramática generativa e a pluralização em português', *Boletim de Filologia*, 25: 55-96.

Brasington, R. (1971) 'Noun pluralization in Brazilian Portuguese', *Journal of Linguistics*, 7: 151-77.

Bresnan, J.W. (1978) 'A realistic transformational grammar', in M. Halle, J.W. Bresnan, & G. Miller (eds.) *Linguistic Theory and Psychological Reality*, Cambridge, Mass.: MIT Press, pp. 1-59.

Bresnan, J.W. (1980) 'Polyadicity: Part I of a theory of lexical rules and representations', in T. Hoekstra, H. van der Hulst & M. Moortgat (eds.) *Lexical Grammar*, Dordrecht, Foris, pp. 97-123.

Bull, W.E. (1950) '*Quedar* and *quedarse*: a study of contrastive ranges', *Language*, 26: 467-80.

Bull, W.E. (1952) 'The intransitive reflexive: *ir* and *irse*', *Modern Language Journal*, 36: 382-86.

Bull, W.E. (1960) *Time, Tense, and the Verb*, Berkeley and Los Angeles: University of California Press.

Camproux, C. (1958) *Étude syntaxique des parlers gévaudanais*, Paris: Presses Universitaires de France.

Canale, M., Mougeon, R. & Belanger, M. (1978) 'Analogical levelling of the auxiliary *être* in French', in M. Suñer (ed.) pp. 41-61.

Castilho, A.T. de (1966) 'A sintaxe do verbo e os tempos do pasado em português', *Alfa*, 9: 105-53.

Chomsky, N. (1977) 'On *Wh*-movement', in P.W. Culicover, T. Wasow, & A. Akmajian (eds.) *Formal Syntax*, New York: Academic Press pp. 71-132.

Chomsky, N. & Halle, M. (1968) *The Sound Pattern of English*, New York: Harper & Row.

Christmann, H.H. (1959) 'Zum "Aspekten" im romanischen: Bemerkungen zu einigen neueren Arbeiten', *Romanische Forschungen*, 71: 1-16.

Clédat, L. (1903) 'Le participe passé, le passé composé et les deux auxiliaires', *Revue de Philologie Française et de Litterature*, 17: 19-62.

Cohen, M. (1960) 'Quelques considérations sur le phénomène des verbes auxiliaires (avec bibliographie) pour le français', *Studi şi Cercetări Linguistice*, 11: 433-42.

Cole, P. & Sadock, J.M. (eds.) (1977) *Grammatical Relations: Syntax and Semantics 8*, New York: Academic Press.

Colón, G. (1961) 'Le parfait périphrastique catalan
"va + infinitif"', in *Actas do IX Congreso Inter-
nacional de Linguistica Romanica*, Vol. I, Lisbon:
Centro de Estudos Filologicos, pp. 165-76.

Comrie, B. (1976) *Aspect*, Cambridge: Cambridge University Press.

Comrie, B. (1977) 'In defence of spontaneous demotion: the impersonal passive', in P. Cole & J.M.
Sadock (eds.), pp. 47-58.

Copceag, D. & Escudero, G. (1966) '"Ser" y "estar"
en español y en rumeno', *Revue Roumaine de Linguistique*, 11: 339-49.

Corominas, J. (1954) *Diccionario crítico etimológico
de la lengua castellana*, Vol. I, Madrid: Gredos.

Cotarelo Valledor, A. (1927) 'El castellano en
Galicia', *Boletín de la Real Academia Española*,
14: 82-136.

Cornu, M. (1953) *Les formes surcomposées en français*,
Berne: Francke.

Costabile, N. (1969) 'La flessione verbale italiana',
in W. D'Addio & R. Simone (eds.) *La sintassi: atti
del III congresso internazionale di studi*, Rome:
Bulzoni, pp. 219-60.

Costabile, N. (1973) *La flessione in italiano*, Rome:
Bulzoni.

Craddock, J.R. (1973) Review of J.W. Harris, (1969)
Linguistics, 109: 83-109.

Cressey, W.W. (1978) *Spanish Phonology and Morphology: a Generative View*, Washington D.C.: Georgetown University Press.

Criado de Val, M. (1958) *Gramática española*, (2nd
ed.) Madrid: SAETA.

Dauzat, A. (1937) 'Le fléchissement du passé simple
et de l'imparfait du subjonctif', *Français moderne*,
5: 97-112.

De Felice, E. & Duro, A. (1975) *Dizionario della
lingua e della civiltà italiana contemporanea*,
Palermo: Palumbo.

Dell, F. (1980) *Generative Phonology and French
Phonology*, Cambridge: Cambridge University Press.

Dias Da Costa, A. (1976) 'Periphrastic verbal expressions in Portuguese', in Schmidt-Radefeld, J.
(ed.) *Readings in Portuguese Linguistics*, Amsterdam: North Holland, pp. 187-243.

Diez, F. (1860) *Grammatik der romanischen Sprachen
III: syntax*, Bonn: Weber.

Diez, F. (1876) *Grammaire des langues romanes*, Paris:
A. Franck.

Duchaček, O. (1966) 'Sur le problème de l'aspect et
du caractère de l'action verbale en français', *Le
Français Moderne*, 34: 161-84.

Emonds, J.E. (1975) 'A transformational analysis of French clitics without positive output constraints', *Linguistic Analysis*, 1: 3-24.

Ernout, A. (1945) *Morphologie historique du latin*, Paris: Klincksieck.

Ernout, A. (1954) *Aspects du vocabulaire latin*, Paris: Klincksieck.

Ernout, A. & Thomas, F. (1951) *Syntaxe latine*, Paris: Klincksieck.

Ettmayer, K.V. (1921) 'Das westladinische Passivum', *Zeitschrift für Romanische Philologie*, 41: 34-56.

Fabra, P. (1977) *Diccionari general de la llengua catalana*, Barcelona: EDHASA.

Falk, J. (1979) *Ser y estar con atributos adjectivales*, Uppsala: Almqvist & Wiksell.

Fillmore, C.J. (1968) 'The case for case', in Bach, E. & Harms, R. (eds.) *Universals in Linguistic Theory*, New York: Holt, Rinehart & Winston, pp. 1-88.

Fillmore, C.J. (1971) 'Some problems for case grammar', in O"Brien, R.V. (ed.) *Report of the 22nd Annual Round Table Meeting on Linguistics and Language Studies*, Washington D.C.: Georgetown University Press, pp. 35-56.

Fillmore, C.J. (1972) 'Subjects, speakers and roles', in Davidson, D.A. & Harman, G.H. (eds.) *Semantics of Natural Language*, Dordrecht: D. Reidel, pp. 1-24.

Fillmore, C.J. (1977) 'The case for case reopened', in Cole, P. & Sadock, J.M. (eds.) pp. 59-81.

Fish, G.T. (1964) 'Two notes on *estar*: 1 *Estar* vs. *venir, ir, andar*, 2. *Estar* vs. E. progressive', *Hispania*, 47: 132-135.

Fleischman, S. (1982) *The Future in Thought and Language: Diachronic Evidence from Romance*, Cambridge: Cambridge University Press.

Florez, L. (1963) 'El español hablado en Columbia y su Atlas lingüístico', *Thesaurus*, 18: 268-356.

Foulet, L. (1920) 'La disparition du prétérit', *Romania*, 46: 271-313.

Foulet, L. (1925) 'Le développement des formes surcomposées', *Romania*, 51: 203-52.

Garde, P. (1968) *L'accent*, Paris: Presses Universitaires de France.

Garey, H.B. (1955) *The Historical Development of Tenses from Late Latin to Old French*, Language Dissertation 51 (Supplement to *Language* 31) Baltimore: Waverley Press.

Gili y Gaya, S. (1961) *Curso superior de sintaxis española*, (9th ed.), Barcelona: Bibliograf.

Givón, T. (1979) *On Understanding Grammar*, New York: Academic Press.

Gougenheim, G. (1951) *Grammaire de la langue française du seizième siècle*, Lyons-Paris: IAC.

Gramatica Limbii Romane, (1966) (2nd ed., revised and enlarged), Bucharest: Editura Academici Republicii Socialiste Romania.

Green, J.N. (1975) 'On the frequency of passive constructions in modern Spanish', *Bulletin of Hispanic Studies*, 52: 345-62.

Green, J.N. (1976) 'How free is word order in Spanish?', in Harris, M.B., (ed.) *Romance Syntax: Synchronic and Diachronic Perspectives*, University of Salford, pp. 7-32.

Green, J.N. (1978) 'Spanish voice relations in historical perspective', to appear in *Semasia*, 6.

Green, J.N. (1979) 'Towards a statistical delimitation of register in Spanish', *IRAL*, 17: 233-44.

Grevisse, M. (1980) *Le bon usage*, (11th ed.) Gembloux: Duculot.

Grimshaw, J. (1980) 'On the lexical representation of Romance reflexive clitics', to appear in Bresnan, J. (ed.) *The Mental Representation of Grammatical Relations*, Cambridge, Mass.: MIT Press.

Gruber, J. (1976) *Lexical Structures in Syntax and Semantics*, Amsterdam: North Holland.

Guillermon, A. (1953) *Manuel de langue roumaine*, Paris: Klincksieck.

Hahn, E.A. (1953) *Subjunctive and Optative. Their Origins as Futures*, New York: Lancaster Press.

Hall, R.A. (1948) *Descriptive Italian Grammar*, Ithaca: Cornell University Press and Linguistic Society of America.

Hall, R.A. (1971) *La struttura dell' italiano*, Rome: Armando.

Hanssen, F. (1910) *Spanische Grammatik auf historischer Grundlage*, Halle: Niemeyer.

Happ, H. (1967) 'Die lateinische Umgangssprache und die Kunstsprache des Plautus', *Glotta*, 45: 60-104.

Harmer, L.C. & Norton, F.J. (1957) *A Manual of Modern Spanish*, (2nd ed.) London: University Tutorial Press.

Harms, R.A. (1968) *Introduction to Phonological Theory*, Englewood Cliffs, N.J.: Prentice-Hall.

Harris, J.W. (1969) *Spanish Phonology*, Cambridge, Mass.: MIT Press.

Harris, J.W. (1974) 'Evidence from Portuguese for the Elsewhere Condition', *Linguistic Inquiry*, 5: 61-80.

Bibliography

Harris, M.B. (1970) 'The verbal systems of Latin
and French', *Transactions of the Philological
Society*, 1970: 62-90.
Harris, M.B. (1977) '"Demonstratives", "articles"
and "third person pronouns" in French: changes in
progress', *Zeitschrift für Romanische Philologie*,
93: 249-61.
Harris, M.B. (1978) *The Evolution of French Syntax:
a Comparative Approach*, London: Longman.
Harris, M.B. (1978a) 'Alternatives to the morpholo-
gical passive in Romance', *Semasia*, 5: 65-87.
Harris, M.B. (1980) 'Noun phrases and verb phrases
in Romance', *Transactions of the Philological
Society*, 1980: 62-80.
Harris, M.B. (1981) 'On the conditional as mood in
French', *Folia Linguistica Historica*, II/I, 55-69.
Harris, M.B. (forthcoming a) 'On the strengths and
weaknesses of a typological approach to historical
syntax', to appear in Fisiak, J. (ed.) *Historical
Syntax*, The Hague: Mouton.
Harris, M.B. (forthcoming b) 'On explaining language
change', to appear in Ahlqvist, A. (ed.).
Hauser-Suida, U. & Hoppe-Beugel, C. (1972) *Die
Vergangenheitstempora in der deutschen geschrie-
benen Sprache der Gegenwart*, Munich: Hueber &
Dusseldorf: Schwann.
Heger, K. (1963) *Die Bezeichnung temporaldeiktischer
Begriffskategorien im französischen und Spanischen
Konjugationssystem*, Tübingen: Max Niemeyer Verlag.
Herczeg, C. (1966) 'La locuzione perifrastica *and-
are* + participio passato', *Lingua Nostra*, 27: 58-
64.
Herzog, E. (1910) 'Das *to*-Partizip im Altromani-
schen', *Beihefte zur Zeitschrift für Romanische
Philologie*, 26: 78-186.
Hockett, C.F. (1954) 'Two models of grammatical
description', *Word*, 10: 210-34.
Hooper, J.B. (1976) *Introduction to Natural Genera-
tive Phonology*, New York: Academic Press.
Huguet, E. (1946) *Dictionnaire de la langue fran-
çaise du seizième siècle*, Paris: Champion.
Imbs, P. (1960) *L'emploi des temps verbaux en fran-
çais moderne*, Paris: Klincksieck.
Iordan, I. & Orr, J. (1970) *An Introduction to
Romance Linguistics*, Oxford: Blackwell.
Irmen, F. (1966) 'O pretérito composto em português',
Revista de Portugal, Serie A, 31: 222-238.
Kahane, H.R. & Hutter, H.S. (1953) 'The verbal cate-
gories of colloquial Brazilian Portuguese', *Word*,
9: 16-44.

Kany, C.E. (1951) *American Spanish Syntax*, Chicago: Chicago University Press.

Kayne, R.S. (1975) *French Syntax*, Cambridge, Mass.: MIT Press.

Keniston, H. (1937) *The Syntax of Castilian Prose*, Chicago: Chicago University Press.

Kiparsky, P. (1982) *Explanation in Phonology*, Dordrecht: Foris.

Klein, P.W. (1968) *Modal Auxiliaries in Spanish*, Seattle: Washington University Press.

Klum, A. (1961) *Verbe et adverbe*, Uppsala: Uppsala University Press.

Kock, J. de (1975) 'Pour une nouvelle définition de la notion d'auxiliarité', *La Linguistique*, 11: 81-92.

Kontzi, R. (1958) *Der Ausdruck der Passividee im älteren italienischen*, (Beiheft zur Zeitschrift für Romanische Philologie 99), Tübingen: Niemeyer.

Kuryłowicz, J. (1931) 'Les temps composés en roman', *Prace Filologiczne*, 15: 448-53. Reprinted in J. Kuryłowicz (1960) *Esquisses Linguistiques*, Wrocław-Krakow: Polish Academy, pp. 104-108.

Kuryłowicz, J. (1937) 'A propos des temps composés en roman: réponse à une critique de M.M. Nicolau', *Bulletin Linguistique*, 5: 195-199.

Lacerda, A. & Strevens, P. (1956) 'Some phonetic observations using a speech-stretcher', *Revista do Laboratorio de Fonética Experimental, Coimbra*, 3: 5-16.

Lamíquiz, V. (1972) *Morfosintaxis estructural del verbo español*, Seville: Facultad de Filosofía y Letras.

Langacker, R.W. (1976) 'Semantic representations and the linguistic relativity hypothesis', *Foundations of Language*, 14: 307-57.

Lapesa, R. (1980) *Historia de la lengua española*, (8th ed.), Madrid: Gredos.

Lass, R. (1980) *On Explaining Language Change*, Cambridge: Cambridge University Press.

Lausberg, H. (1966) *Lingüística románica*, Madrid: Gredos.

Lenz, R. (1920) *La oración y sus partes*, Madrid: Centro de Estudios Historicos.

Leone, A. (1954) 'A proposito degli ausiliari', *Lingua Nostra*, 15: 127-31.

Leone, A. (1966) 'Ancora su *andare* + participio passato', *Lingua Nostra*, 27: 117-121.

Leone, A. (1970) 'Una regola per gli ausiliari', *Lingua Nostra*, 31: 24-30.

Lepschy, A.L. & Lepschy, G. (1977) *The Italian Language Today*, London: Hutchinson.

Lepschy, A.L. & Lepschy, G. (1981) *La lingua italiana: storia, varietà dell 'uso, gramatica*, Milan: Bompiani.

Letelier, S. (1893) 'La voz pasiva en castellano', *Anales de la Universidad de Chile*, 84: 853-57.

Levy, E. (1894-1924) *Provenzalisches Supplement-Wörterbuch*, Leipzig: Reisland.

Lewis, C.T. & Short, C. (1879) *A Latin Dictionary*, Oxford: Oxford University Press.

Lightfoot, D. (1979) *Principles of Diachronic Syntax*, Cambridge: Cambridge University Press.

Lipski, J.M. (1973) 'Binarity and Portuguese vowel raising', *Zeitschrift für Dialektologie und Linguistik*, 40: 16-28.

Lo Cascio, V. (1968) 'Struttura, funzione, valore di *andare* + participio passato', *Lingua e stile*, 3: 271-93.

Löfstedt, E. (1938-9) 'Lateinisch-griechisches und lateinisch-romanisches', *Studia Neophilologica*, 11: 173-85.

Lorenzo, E. (1971) *El español de hoy, lengua en ebullición*, (2nd ed.), Madrid: Gredos.

Lucot, R. (1940) 'Remarque sur l'emploi de *habeo* avec le participe en *-to-*', in *Mélanges de Philologie, de Littérature et d'Histoire Anciennes offerts à Alfred Ernout*, Paris: Klincksieck, pp. 247-49.

Luján, M. (1981) 'The Spanish copulas as aspectual indicators, *Lingua*, 54: 165-209.

Luján, M. & Hensey, F. (eds.) (1976) *Current Studies in Romance Linguistics*, Washington D.C.: Georgetown University Press.

Lyons, J. (1977) *Semantics*, Cambridge: Cambridge University Press, 2 vols.

McClintock, D.R. (1978) 'Tense-groups and tense-metaphors', *Oxford German Studies*, 9: 19-43.

McCray, S. (1979) *Proto-Indo-European to Romance: Aspects of Verbal Morphosyntax*, unpublished Ph.D. dissertation, University of Michigan.

Manoliu, M. (1961) 'Remarks on the grammaticizing of verbs in the Romance languages', *Revue Roumaine de Linguistique*, 6: 217-38.

Marquèze-Pouey, L. (1955) 'L'auxiliaire ALLER dans l'expression du passé en gascon', *Via Domitia*, 2: 111-121.

Martins, M.R.D. (1973) 'Análise acústica das vogais tónicas em português', *Boletim de Filologia*, 22: 303-314.

Bibliography

Mason, I. (1977) *The Indicative Tenses and Past Time: Form and Usage in Two Varieties of the Norman Dialect: Jersey (C.I.) and Val de Saire (Manche)*, unpublished Ph.D. dissertation, Queen Mary College, University of London.

Mateus, M.H.M. (1975) *Aspectos da fonologia portuguesa*, Lisbon: Centro de Estudos Filológicos.

Matthews, P.H. (1972) *Inflectional Morphology*, Cambridge: Cambridge University Press.

Matthews, P.H. (1974) *Morphology: An Introduction to the Theory of Word Structure*, Cambridge: Cambridge University Press.

Matthews, P.H. (1981) 'Present stem alternations in Italian', in Geckeler, H. et.al. (eds.), *Logos semantikos: Studia Linguistica in Honorem Eugenio Coseriu, 1921-1981*, Vol. 4, pp. 57-65.

Matthews, P.H. (1981a) *Syntax*, Cambridge: Cambridge University Press.

Matthies, W. (1933) *Die aus den intransitiven Verben der Bewegung und dem Partizip des Perfektes gebildeten Umschreibungen im Spanischen*, (Berliner Beiträge zur Romanische Philologie 3), Jena-Leipzig: Gronau.

Mattoso Câmara, J. (1953) *Para o estudo da fonêmica portuguesa*, Rio de Janeiro: Organização Simões.

Mattoso Câmara, J. (1972) *The Portuguese Language*, Chicago: Chicago University Press.

Meillet, A. (1912) 'L'évolution des formes grammaticales', in Meillet, A. (1926), pp. 130-48.

Meillet, A. (1926) *Linguistique historique et linguistique générale*, Paris: Champion.

Menard, P. (1973) *Syntaxe de l'ancien français*, Bordeaux: SOBODI

Menéndez Pidal, R. (1952) *Manual de gramática histórica española*, (9th ed.), Madrid: Espasa-Calpe.

Meyer-Lübke, W. (1890-1906) *Grammaire des langues romanes*, Paris and Leipzig: Welter.

Meyer-Lübke, W. (1899) *Grammatik der romanischen Sprachen III: Syntax*, Leipzig: Reisland.

Millán Urdiales, J. (1966) *El habla de Villacidayo (Léon)*, Madrid: Bulletin de la Real Academia Española, 13.

Milner, J-C (1974) 'Les exclamatives et le Complementizer', in Rohrer, C. & Ruwet, N. (eds.) *Actes du colloque franco-allemand de grammaire transformationelle*, Vol. I, Tübingen: Niemeyer, pp. 78-121.

Milner, J-C (1977) 'De l'interprétation exclamative comme valeur sémantique résiduelle', in Ronat, M. (ed.) *Langue: Théorie générative étendue*, Paris: Hermann, pp. 109-122.

214

Bibliography

Milner, J-C (1978) *De la syntaxe à l'interprétation*, Paris: Éditions du Seuil.

Mistral, F. (1885) *Lou trésor dóu Felibrige*, Aix-en-Provence: Veuve Remondet-Aubin.

Molle-Marechal, P. van (1974) '*Andare* e *venire* ausiliari del passivo', in Medici, M. & Sangregorio, A. (eds.) *Fenomeni morfologici e sintattici nell' italiano contemporaneo*, Rome: Bulzoni, pp. 357-72.

Moreno De Alba, J.G. (1978) *Valores de las formas verbales en el español de México*, Mexico City: Universidad Nacional Centro de Lingüística Hispánica.

Napoli, D.J. (1976) 'Infinitival relatives in Italian', in Luján, M. & Hensey, F. (eds.), pp. 300-329.

Navas Ruiz, R. (1977) *Ser y estar: el sistema atributivo del español*, (2nd ed.) Salamanca: Almar.

Nicolau, M. (1936) 'Remarques sur les origines des formes périphrastiques passives et actives des langues romanes', *Bulletin Linguistique*, 4: 15-30.

Nunes, J. (1970) *Crestomatia arcaica*, (7th ed.) Lisbon: Livraria Clássica.

Nyrop, K. (1930) *Grammaire historique de la langue française*, Vol. VI, Copenhagen: Nordisk Forlag.

Orr, J. (1939) 'On homonymics', in *Studies in French Language and Mediaeval Literature presented to Professor Mildred K. Pope*, Manchester: Manchester University Press, pp. 253-97.

Paiva Boléo, M. de (1936) *O perfecto e o pretérito em português en confronto com as outras línguas românicas*, Coimbra: Biblioteca Geral da Universidade, 6.

Palay, S. (1980) *Dictionnaire du béarnais et du gascon modernes*, (2nd ed.) Montpellier: CNRS.

Palmer, L.R. (1954) *The Latin Language*, London: Faber & Faber.

Pardal, E. d'Andrade (1977) *Aspects de la Phonologie (Générative) du Portugais*, Lisbon: Centro de Linguística da Universidade de Lisboa.

Parkinson, S.R. (1979-80) *The Phonological Analysis of Nasal Vowels in Modern European Portuguese*, unpublished Ph.D. dissertation, University of Cambridge.

Penny, R.J. (1969) *El habla pasiega: ensayo de dialectología montañesa*, London: Tamesis Books.

Peral Ribeiro, J.A. (1958) '"Essere", "sedere", e "stare" nas linguas romanicas', *Boletim de Filologia*, 17: 147-76.

Perlmutter, D. (1971) *Deep and Surface Structure Constraints in Syntax*, New York: Holt, Rinehart & Winston.

Bibliography

Pichon, E. (1934) 'L'auxiliaire *être* dans le franç-
ais d'aujourd'hui', *Le Français Moderne*, 2: 317-
330.
Poirier, M. (1978) 'Le parfait de l'indicatif latin:
un passé accompli, ou un accompli pur et simple?',
Revue des Études Latines, 56: 369-78.
Pontes, E. (1972) *Estrutura do Verbo no Português
Coloquial*, Petrópolis: Vozes.
Porena, M. (1938) 'Sull'uso degli ausiliari "essere"
e "avere" in italiano', *L'Italia Dialettale*, 14:
1-22.
Posner, R. (1961) 'The imperfect endings in Romance',
Transactions of the Philological Society, 1961:
17-55.
Posner, R. (1970) 'Thirty years on', supplement to
Iordan, I. & Orr, J.
Posner, R. & Green, J.N. (eds.) (1980-82) *Trends in
Romance Linguistics and Philology*, 4 vols. The
Hague and Paris: Mouton.
Pottier, B. (1961) 'Sobre el concepto de *verbo aux-
iliar*', *Nueva Revista de Filología Hispánica*, 15:
325-31. Reprinted in *Lingüística moderna y filol-
ogía hispánica*, Madrid: Gredos, 1968, pp. 194-202.
Price, G. (1971) *The French Language: Present and
Past*, London: Edward Arnold.
Pulgram, E. (1978) 'Latin-Romance *habere*: double
function and lexical split', *Zeitschrift für Rom-
anische Philologie*, 94: 1-8.
Pullum, G.K. & Wilson, D. (1977) 'Autonomous syntax
and the analysis of auxiliaries', *Language*, 53:
741-88.
Querido, A.A.M. (1976) 'The semantics of copulative
constructions in Portuguese', in Luján, M. & Hen-
sey, F. (eds.) pp. 343-66.
Radford, A. (1981) *Transformational Syntax*, Cambri-
dge: Cambridge University Press.
Rallides, C. (1971) *The Tense-Aspect System of the
Spanish Verb*, The Hague: Mouton.
Ramat, P. (1981) 'Habere + PPP: Una Nota', in *Studi
in onore di G.B. Pellegrini*, Pisa: Pacini.
Ramsey, M.M. (1894) *A Textbook of Modern Spanish*,
(Rev. by R.K. Spaulding, 1956), New York: Holt,
Rinehart and Winston.
Raynouard, M. (1838-44), *Lexique roman*, Paris: Sil-
vestre.
Real Academia Española (1931) *Gramática de la lengua
española*, Madrid: Espasa-Calpe.
Real Academia Española (1973) *Esbozo de una nueva
gramática de la lengua española*, Madrid: Espasa-
Calpe.

Bibliography

Redenbarger, W:J: (1977) 'Lusitanean Portuguese [ɐ]
is [+ATR], [+CP]', in Hagiwara, M.P. (ed.) *Studies
in Romance Linguistics*, Rowley, Mass.: Newbury
House, pp. 26-36.

Redenbarger, W.J. (1978) 'Portuguese vowel harmony
and the Elsewhere Condition', in Suñer, M.(ed.)
pp. 258-78.

Reed, D. & Leite, Y. (1947) 'The segmental phonemes
of Brazilian Portuguese', in Pike, K.L. *Phonemics*,
Ann Arbor: University of Michigan Press, pp. 194-
202.

Reid, T.B.W. (1955) 'On the analysis of the tense
system of French', *Revue de Linguistique Romane*,
19: 23-38.

Reid, T.B.W. (1970) 'Verbal aspect in Modern French',
in Combe, T.G.S. & Rickard, P. (eds.) *The French
Language: Studies presented to L.C. Harmer*, London:
Harrap, pp. 146-71.

Remacle, L. (1956) *Syntaxe du parler Wallon de la
Gleize, Vol. II*, (Bibliothèque de la Faculté de
Philosophie et Lettres de l'Université de Liège 139)
Paris: Belles Lettres.

Reynolds, B. (1962) *The Cambridge Italian Dictionary*, Vol. 1, Cambridge, Cambridge University Press.

Rickard, P. (1968) *La langue française au seizième
siècle*, Cambridge: Cambridge University Press.

Rivarola, J.L. (1980) Review of Berschin, H. (1976)
Zeitschrift für Romanische Philologie, 96: 235-8.

Rizzi, L. (1976) 'La montée du sujet, le *si* imper-
sonnel et une règle de restructuration dans la
syntaxe italienne', *Recherches Linguistiques*, 4:
158-84.

Roca Pons, J. (1954) 'Sobre el valor auxiliar y
copulativo del verbo *andar*' *Archivum*, (Oviedo), 4:
166-82.

Roca Pons, J. (1955) '*Dejar* + participio', *Revista
de Filología Española*, 39: 151-185.

Roca Pons, J. (1958) *Estudios sobre perífrasis verbales del español*, (Anejo de la Revista de Filología Española 67), Madrid: CSIC.

Rohlfs, G. (1966-9) *Grammatica storica della lingua
italiana e dei suoi dialetti*, Turin: Einandi.

Rohlfs, G. (1975) *Rätoromanisch. Die Sonderstellung
des Ratoromanischen zwischen Italienisch und Fran-
zösisch*, Munich: Beck.

Rojo, G. (1974) *Perífrasis verbales en el gallejo
actual*, (Verba, Anejo 2), Universidad de Santiago
de Compostela.

Bibliography

Romaine, S. (1982) *Socio-historical Linguistics*, Cambridge: Cambridge University Press.

Romaine, S. (forthcoming) 'Syntactic change as category change and diffusion: some evidence from the history of English'. Paper given at the Second International Conference on English Historical Linguistics, Odense, Denmark, April 1981.

Ronjat, J. (1937) *Grammaire istorique des parlers provençaux modernes*, Vol. 3, Montpellier: Société des langues romanes.

Ross, J.R. (1968) *Constraints on Variables in Syntax*, Indiana University Linguistics Club.

Russell-Gebbett, P. (1965) *Medieval Catalan Linguistic Texts*, Oxford: Dolphin.

Ruwet, N. (1972) *Théorie syntaxique et syntaxe du français*, Paris: Editions du Seuil.

Saltarelli, M. (1970) *A Phonology of Italian in a Generative Grammar*, The Hague: Mouton.

Santamarina, A. (1974) *El verbo gallego: Estudio basado en el habla del Valle de Suarna*, (Verba, Anejo 4), Universidad de Santiago de Compostela.

Saussol, J-M (1978) *Ser y estar: orígenes de sus funciones en el Cantar de Mio Cid*, Seville: Seville University Press.

Schogt, H. (1964) 'L'aspect verbal en français et l'élimination du passé simple', *Word*, 20: 1-17.

Seço, R. (1953) *Manual de gramática española*, 10th ed., rev. by M. Seco, 1975, Madrid: Gredos.

Serbat, G. (1976) 'Le temps du verbe en latin, III: le parfait de l'indicatif actif', *Revue des Études Latines*, 54: 308-52.

Setterberg-Jörgensen, B. (1943) *ANDARE et VENIRE. Verbes copules en vieil italien aux XIIIe et XIVe siècles*, Uppsala: Lundeqvist. Revised and extended as: *Andare, venire et tornare, verbes copules et auxiliaires dans la langue italienne*, Aarhus, 1950.

Shepherd, S. (forthcoming) 'From deontic to epistemic: an analysis of modals in the history of English, Creoles and language acquisition', to appear in Ahlqvist, A. (ed.).

Siadbei, I. (1930) 'Le sort du prétérit roumain', *Romania*, 56: 331-60.

Skubic, M. (1964) 'Pretérito simple y compuesto en el español hablado', *Linguistica*, 6: 87-90.

Sneyders de Vogel, K. (1927) *Syntaxe historique du français*, (2nd ed.), Groningen: J-B Wolters.

Sommerstein, A.H. (1977) *Modern Phonology*, London: Edward Arnold.

Stéfanini, J. (1962) *La voix pronominale en ancien et en moyen français*, Aix-en-Provence: Ophrys.

218

Bibliography

Stockwell, R.P., Bowen, J.D. & Martin, J.W. (1965)
The Grammatical Structures of English and Spanish,
Chicago: Chicago University Press.

Stockwell, R.P., Schachter, P. & Partee, B.H. (1973)
The Major Syntactic Structures of English, New
York: Holt, Rinehart & Winston.

Strevens, P. (1954) 'Some observations on the phon-
etics and pronunciation of Modern Portuguese',
Revista do Laboratório de Fonética Experimental,
Coimbra, 2: 5-29.

Suñer, M. (ed.) (1978) *Contemporary Studies in
Romance Linguistics*, Washington D.C.: Georgetown
University Press.

Sutherland, D.R. (1959) 'Flexions and categories in
Old Provençal', *Transactions of the Philological
Society*, 1959: 25-70.

Tekavčić, P. (1970) 'Saggio di un'analisi del sistema verbale italiano', *Lingua e Stile*, 5: 1-23.

Tekavčić, P. (1972) *Grammatica storica dell'italiano, Vol. II: Morfosintassi*, Bologna: il Mulino.

Terrell, T.D. (1970) *The Tense-Aspect System of the
Spanish Verb: a Diachonic Study on the Generative
Transformational Model*, unpublished Ph.D. disser-
tation, University of Texas, Austin.

Thielmann, Ph. (1885) '*Habere* mit dem Part. Perf.
Pass.', *Archiv für Lateinische Lexicographie*,
2: 372-423, 505-49.

Thomas, E.W. (1969) *The Syntax of Spoken Brazilian
Portuguese*, Nashville: Vanderbilt University Press.

Tobler, A. & Lommatzsch, E. (1925-) *Altfranzösisches
Wörterbuch*, Berlin-Wiesbaden: Franz Steiner
Verlag.

Togeby, K. (1974) *Précis historique de grammaire
française*, Copenhagen: Akademisk Forlag.

Trager, G. (1943) 'Editorial Note', *Studies in
Linguistics*, 1 (15): 16.

Traugott, E. (forthcoming) 'From propositional to
textual and expressive meanings: some semantic-
pragmatic aspects of grammaticalisation', to appear
in Lehmann, W.P. and Malkiel, Y. (eds.) *Directions
for Historical Linguistics, II*, Amsterdam: John
Benjamins B.V.

Tumler, T. (1980) *Das Tempusgebrauch der Vergangen-
heit in der modernen italienischen Prosa*, Vienna:
Braumuller.

Vairel, H. (1978) 'Le valeur de l'opposition infec-
tum/perfectum en latin', *Revue des Études Latines*,
56: 380-412.

Vallcorba I Rocosa, J. (1978) *Els verbs 'ésser' i
'estar' en català*, Barcelona: Curial Edicions Cat-
alanes.

Viana, A. dos Gonçalves, R. (1883) 'Essai de phoné-
tique et de phonologie de la langue portugaise,
d'après le dialecte actuel de Lisbonne', *Romania*,
12: 29-98.

Viana, A. dos Gonçalves, R. (1903) *Portugais: Phoné-
tique, Phonologie, Morphologie, Textes*, Leipzig:
Teubner.

Vincent, N. (1980) 'Iconic and symbolic aspects of
syntax: prospects for reconstruction', in Ramat,
P. (ed.) *Linguistic Reconstruction and Indo-European Syntax*, Amsterdam: John Benjamins B.V., pp.
47-68.

Vincent, N. (1982) 'Il cambiamento sintattico e lo
sviluppo dei verbi ansiliari in italiano'. Paper
presented to the 16th International Congress of
the Società Linguistica Italiana, Florence, May
1982.

Vincent, N. (in prep.) 'A non-case of centre v.
periphery in Romance'.

Vocabolario degli Accademici della Crusca, 1738,
Florence: Manni.

Wheeler, M. (1972) 'Distinctive features and natural
classes in phonological theory', *Journal of Linguistics*, 8: 87-102.

Wheeler, M. (1979) *Phonology of Catalan*, (Publications of the Philological Society 28), Oxford:
Blackwell.

Wiegand, N. (forthcoming) 'From discourse to syntax:
For in early English causal clauses', to appear
in Ahlqvist, A. (ed.).

Wilhelm, A.E. (1979) *Pronomes de distância do
português actual em Portugal e no Brasil*, Lisbon:
Instituto Nacional de Investigação Científica.

Willis, R.C. (1971) *An Essential Course in Modern
Portuguese*, (2nd ed.), London: Harrap.

Wilmet, M. (1976) *Études de morpho-syntaxe verbale*,
Paris: Klincksieck.

NOTES ON CONTRIBUTORS

JOHN N GREEN is Senior Lecturer in the Department of Language in the University of York, and has published widely in the fields of General and Romance Linguistics. His publications include the revised version of Elcock's *Romance Languages* and he has edited (with R. Posner) *Trends in Romance Linguistics and Philology* (4 vols.). Much of his own work is centred on various exponents of voice in Spanish and related topics. He is currently preparing *The Evolution of Spanish*.

MARTIN HARRIS is Professor of Romance Linguistics in the University of Salford. His major work has been in the field of the Romance verb and on determiner systems in Romance and elsewhere. He edited *Synchronic and Diachronic Perspectives* (1976) and his own publications include *The Evolution of French Syntax: A Comparative Approach* (1978).

CHRISTOPHER LYONS is currently Lecturer in Linguistics in the University of Salford. After doctoral work in the area of deixis, he has published a number of articles on this topic and also in the field of the Romance verb. He is at present preparing *Definiteness: A descriptive, historical and comparative study*.

PETER MATTHEWS has recently returned to Cambridge, the university from which he graduated, as Professor of Linguistics after holding teaching posts at the Universities of Bangor and Reading. He has been a visiting researcher at the University of Indiana, King's College, Cambridge and the Netherlands Institute for Advanced Study in the Humanities and Social Sciences. Among his principal publications are *Inflectional Morphology* (CUP 1972), *Morphology* (CUP 1974), *Generative Grammar and Linguistic Competence* (George Allen & Unwin 1979), *Syntax* (CUP 1981), as well as numerous articles and reviews. He is a member of the Council of the Philological Society and from 1969 to 1979 was Joint Editor of the *Journal of Linguistics*.

Notes on the Contributors

STEPHEN PARKINSON is currently Lecturer in Linguistics at the University of Aberdeen. His doctoral work was concerned with the phonological analysis of nasal vowels in contemporary Portuguese, and his current interests include the morphophonology of the verb, both synchronic and diachronic, in the Hispanic languages. He has recently begun assembling a computer-readable archive of Old Portuguese texts for a chronological study of morphological and phonological changes.

CHRISTOPHER POUNTAIN, after seven years as Lecturer in Spanish and Linguistics in the University of Nottingham, is currently Assistant Lecturer in Romance Philology in the University of Cambridge and a Fellow of Queens' College. His doctoral work was in the field of tense and aspect in the Romance verb, and he has publications in this and related areas.

ANDREW RADFORD has taught at the Universities of East Anglia, Essex and Oxford and is now Professor of Linguistics at the University College of North Wales, Bangor. He has published widely in the fields of syntax and semantics, Italian and both in Romance and more generally. His major works include *Italian Syntax* and *Transformational Grammar*.

NIGEL VINCENT is a member of the Department of Linguistics in the University of Cambridge. His principal research interests lie in the general theory of language change and the history of the Romance languages, particularly Italian, topics on which he has contributed several articles and reviews to periodicals and conferences. He is currently preparing a book entitled *The History of the Italian Language: A Linguistic Introduction*. Since 1979 he has been an Assistant Editor of the *Journal of Linguistics*, and he is a member of the Council of the Philological Society.

222